DEDICATION

The Junior Board of the Tri-City Symphony Orchestra
Association fondly dedicates this collection of fine recipes to our
music director and conductor, James Dixon. Through the years
he has encouraged us to strive for quality and excellence in all
our endeavors, yet has shown patience and understanding. Not
only are his musical accomplishments worthy of a "Standing
Ovation", but his culinary talents are also to be praised. And, so
m, to you - - Our Best ! !

STANDING OVATIONS

a collection of recipes compiled by the
junior board of the Tri-City Symphony

Cover design and illustrations
by Mary Phares

Caricatures
by Bill Hannan

The Junior Board of the Tri-City Symphony
Orchestra Association
Davenport, Iowa
1979

The proceeds from the sale of STANDING OVATIONS
will go toward furthering our varied educational projects.

Copyright © 1979

The Junior Board of the Tri-City Symphony
Orchestra Association

Printed by:
Bawden Printing Inc.

ISBN: 0-9606524-0-X

Copies may be obtained by using form in back of book, or by addressing:

STANDING OVATIONS
Jr. Bd. of Tri-City Symphony
P. O. Box 67
404 Main Street
Davenport, Iowa 52805

Include your name and full address and a check for $9.50 (plus $1.50 for postage).
The check should be made payable to: Junior Board of the Tri-City Symphony.

The purpose of the Junior Board of the Tri-City Symphony is to bring fine music to the young people of our community. Each year we sponsor a School Music Tour and a Family Concert Series. We also help support the Tri-City Symphony's Youth Orchestra and provide deserving members with scholarships.

ORIGINAL
COOKBOOK COMMITTEE

Co-Chairmen	Heather Gosma
	Rose Ann Hass
Cover and Illustrations	Mary Phares
Home Economist and Testing Chairman	Bonnie Moeller
Recipe Chairman	Karen Opheim
Artists' Chairman	Judy Knutson
Restaurant Chairman	Anne Mairet
Typists	Sue Cleaver
	Jan Crow
	Helen DeKalb
	Jan Illingsworth
	Jan McMillan
Luncheon Chairman	Vicki Patramanis

INTRODUCTION

The "Standing Ovation" has traditionally been the coveted reward for an outstanding performance. Through the 65 years of the Tri-City Symphony, there have been many outstanding performances by orchestra, conductor and guest artists. It seems fitting, therefore, that the Junior Board of the Tri-City Symphony undertake this project to show appreciation and admiration for the contributions this great symphony orchestra and its conductor have made to this community.

Recipes were submitted by symphony patrons, members of the Symphony Board of Directors, Auxiliary and Junior Board, as well as orchestra members. We are especially proud to include favorite recipes from many guest artists who have performed with the Tri-City Symphony. These recipes are easily found in the Artists Section of the Index, and along with the orchestra members recipes, are designated by the following symbol:

Restaurants in the area have added much to symphony occasions before and after performances and the Junior Board is proud to include specialities from many of these most popular establishments. These fine recipes are located in their own special section.

All recipes were tested and evaluated by a large committee of Junior Board members to help insure that you will be pleased with the results of your culinary efforts. You will find that the difficulty of recipes varies, so that some will be appropriate for a simple family meal, while others will be perfect for the most elegant dinner party. We feel that the praise of family and friends for a job "well-perfected" in the kitchen is not unlike the "Standing Ovation" for a performer.

Our pride in our great symphony has been the motivation for compiling this collection of recipes. It is our sincere hope that this cookbook will bring pride in your cooking and that you will experience "Standing Ovations".

JUNIOR BOARD

TABLE OF CONTENTS

BEVERAGES

HOT CRANBERRY DRINK

15-20 Servings

A favorite beverage served at Jr. Bd. fall-winter meetings.

2 qts apple cider
1 qt. cranberry or
   cranapple juice
2 cups orange juice
1 tsp. whole cloves
1 tsp. whole allspice
3 sticks cinnamon broken
1 cup sugar

Place cider, cranberry juice and orange juice in bottom of coffee maker. Place spices and sugar in percolater basket and perk. Serve hot.

Penny Lounsberry (Mrs. John)

CRANBERRY-WINE WARMUP

14 Servings

Favorite at holiday open house.

1 bottle (32 oz.) cranberry
   juice cocktail
2 cups water
1 cup sugar (or a bit less
   to taste)
4 inches stick cinnamon
12 whole cloves
Peel of ½ lemon, cut into
   strips
2 fifths dry red wine
¼ cup lemon juice

Combine cranberry juice, water, sugar, cinnamon, cloves and lemon peel in a saucepan. Bring to boil, stirring until sugar is dissolved. Simmer, uncovered for 15 minutes, then strain. When ready to serve, add wine and lemon juice. Heat thoroughly, but do not boil.

Harriet Harmelink (Mrs. Roger)

HOT GRAPE PUNCH

10-15 Servings

1 gallon grape juice
1 tsp. whole cloves
2 sticks cinnamon
1 tsp. nutmeg
⅔ cup sugar
¾ cup lemon juice
1 cup orange juice

Heat grape juice, spices, and sugar in pan. Cover and simmer 15 minutes. Strain and add lemon and orange juice. Reheat to serving temperature.

Ann Green (Mrs. Fred)

2

FRESH MINT PUNCH
4-6 Servings

Made the day before to enhance flavors.

⅔ cup boiling water
⅓ cup crushed mint leaves
Juice of 3 lemons
1 can (6 oz.) frozen
    lemonade
1 quart ginger ale
Mint leaves
Ice

Pour boiling water over crushed mint leaves. Add juice of lemons and let this stand overnight; then strain. Add can of lemonade and refrigerate. Just before serving, add ginger ale. Garnish with mint leaves and ice.

Janet Schwarz (Mrs. Eric)

ZIPPY LIME PUNCH
20-25 Servings

A great, refreshing punch for receptions.

2 pkg. (0.23 oz. each)
    lemon-lime drink mix
    (unsweetened)
2 cups sugar
23 ounces of canned
    pineapple juice
1 can (16 oz. frozen
    orange juice
1 can (6 oz.)
    frozen lemonade
3¼ quarts water
1 quart ginger ale

Mix first 6 ingredients until well dissolved. Allow three hours for chilling time. Add the ginger ale just before serving.

Carole Sissel (Mrs. Gary)

LIME SHERBET PUNCH
35 Servings

1 can (6 oz.)
    frozen lemonade
3 cups water
1 pkg. (3 oz.) lime
    flavored gelatin
2 cups hot water
1 can (46 oz.)
    pineapple juice
1 quart ginger ale
Vodka to desired strength
    (optional)
1 quart lime sherbet (or
    more according to taste)
Strawberries

Dilute lemonade with 3 cups of water. Dissolve gelatin thoroughly in hot water. Combine lemonade, gelatin, and pineapple juice. Chill. Just before serving add ginger ale and vodka. Float scoops of sherbet on top and garnish with fresh strawberries for added color.

Jan McMillan

3

MODHOUSE PUNCH

A real thirst quencher!

1 pkg. (6 oz.) lime
   flavored gelatin
2 cups hot water
2 cans (12 oz. each)
   frozen lime concentrate
1 cup bottled lime juice
1 tsp. almond extract
1½ qts. cracked ice
9 bottles (10 oz. each) 7-up
2 cups vodka (optional)

Dissolve gelatin in hot water. Stir in frozen lime concentrate. Add lime juice and almond extract. To serve: Pour mixture into punch bowl. Add cracked ice, 7-Up and vodka.

Peggy Pierce (Mrs. Charles)

CHUCK'S PUNCH

1 can (46 oz.) pineapple
   juice, chilled
3 cans (12 oz. each)
   frozen lemonade
   concentrate
2 boxes frozen raspberries
   (10 oz. each)
½ gallon sauterne, chilled
1 pt. brandy
1 qt. sparkling burgundy,
   chilled

Combine all ingredients except the sparkling burgundy. Blend. At the last minute, add sparkling burgundy and serve.

Mary Andrews (Mrs. Charles)

RUM PUNCH

This was concocted after many scuba diving jaunts at Grand Cayman, B.W.I.

1 oz. lime juice
¼ oz. grenadine syrup
2 oz. pineapple juice
1 oz. unsweetened orange
   juice
2 oz. rum

Mix together and chill.

Kath Wilson (Mrs. Charles)

FROZEN DAIQUIRI

4-6 Servings

1 can (6 oz.) limeade
1½ cups light Cuban rum
2¼ cups water

Mix and freeze (take out just what you need; it doesn't freeze solidly). Put into blender and let run until slushy. Serve with straws.

Sue Von Maur (Mrs. Richard, Jr.)

GOLDEN DRIAM

Single Serving

Deliciously smooth!

1 oz. Galliano
½ oz. Cointreau
½ oz. orange juice
½ oz. half & half cream

Combine all ingredients and shake with cracked ice. Strain into cocktail glass.

Judy Seefeldt (Mrs. Joe)

HORS D'OEUVRES

OYSTERS ROCKEFELLER

24 oysters in shell
Salt
Pepper
3 T. onion, chopped
6 T. parsley, chopped
3 T. butter, melted
Dash hot pepper sauce
1 cup cooked chopped
   spinach, well-drained
1 cup soft bread crumbs,
   fine
½ cup (1 stick) butter
Paprika
Rock Salt
Lemon wedges

Open oyster shells with knife, remove oysters. Wash shells, place each oyster in deep half of shell. Season with salt and pepper. Combine onion, parsley and 3 T. melted butter; spoon over oysters. Top each with 2 tsp. spinach, then bread crumbs. Dot each with butter. Sprinkle with paprika. Arrange shells on bed of rock salt in a shallow pan. I usually serve directly from the pan, with lemon wedges dipped in chopped parsley. (Buy shucked oysters and reuse clean sterilized shells). Bake at 450° for 10 minutes.

Bernadette Murphy (Mrs. Joseph)

PACIFIC CRAB PUFFS

36 Puffs

1½ cups biscuit mix
   (baking mix)
⅓ cup grated Parmesan
   cheese
¼ cup finely chopped
   green onion (including
   some green tops)
8 oz. crabmeat
1 egg, slightly beaten
⅓ cup water
1 tsp. Worcestershire
   sauce
¼ tsp. liquid hot pepper
   seasoning
Salad oil for frying

MUSTARD DIP:
½ cup sour cream
2 T. Dijon Mustard
1 tsp. lemon juice

Combine biscuit mix, cheese and green onion. Shred crab meat and add to cheese mixture. Combine egg, water, Worcestershire and hot pepper seasoning. Stir into crab mixture just until blended. Heat about 1½ inches of oil in a deep frying pan, electric frying pan or wok. Fry 3 or 4 puffs at a time by dropping batter from a teaspoon into hot oil and cook, turning as necessary until golden on all sides (1½-2 minutes). Lift out with slotted spoon; drain. Keep warm until all are fried, or cool, wrap in foil and freeze. Serve with mustard dip made by combining ingredients. (If frozen, reheat in 350° oven for 12-15 minutes to heat through).

Kay Kaleba (Mrs. Richard)

CRAB STRIPS

60 Fingers

½ lb. processed cheese
½ cup (1 stick) butter, plus
2 T. butter
1 can (6½ oz.) crab,
  drained and flaked
1 loaf thinly sliced
  white bread
½ tsp. worchestershire
  sauce

Melt together the cheese and butter in a saucepan. Stir to blend together as it heats. (It will look oily; the crabmeat thickens it). Add the crabmeat. Cool before spreading. Remove crusts from bread and cut each slice into three fingers. Lightly toast each side under broiler. Spread mixture over fingers and place on cookie sheet. (Here you may freeze. When hard remove from sheet and store in freezer in plastic bag.) Broil about 7 inches from heat for 2 minutes. Watch carefully; cheese burns fast. Serve immediately.

Sue VonMaur (Mrs. Richard, Jr.)

QUICHE LORRAINE APPETIZERS

36 Pieces

An elegant hors d'oeuvre.

2-3 sticks pie crust mix
6-8 slices bacon, crisply fried
  and crumbled
½ cup swiss cheese,
  shredded
3 T. minced onion
2 eggs
1 cup whipping cream or
  half and half
¼ tsp. salt
½ tsp. sugar
Dash cayenne pepper

Preheat oven to 375°. Prepare pastry as directed on package. Roll 1/16 inch thick on lightly floured board. Cut into 1½-2 inch rounds. Fit rounds into tiny muffin tins. (May need to adjust size to fit tin used). Combine bacon, cheese, and onion. Fill each cup with approximately 1 T. of mixture. Beat eggs slightly. Beat in remaining ingredients. Pour 1 T. of cream mixture into each cup over bacon mixture. Bake at 375° for 20-25 minutes, or until light brown. Let cool in pans for 5 minutes before removing. Can also make 1 or 2 days ahead. Wrap in foil and reheat at 350° for 10 minutes before serving.

Connie Regan (Mrs. John)

SAUERKRAUT BALLS   48 Balls

They are worth every bit of the trouble to make them.

8 oz. sausage meat,
   crumbled
¼ cup onion, finely
   chopped
1 can (14 oz.) sauerkraut,
   well drained and snipped
2 T. dry bread crumbs
1 pkg. (3 oz.) cream
   cheese, softened
2 T. parsley
1 tsp. prepared mustard
Garlic salt
¼ tsp. pepper
1 cup all-purpose flour
¼ cup milk
2 eggs, well beaten
1 cup bread crumbs

In a skillet, cook sausage and onion until meat is brown. Drain. Add sauerkraut and 2 T. of bread crumbs. Combine cream cheese, parsley, mustard, touch of garlic salt, and pepper; stir into sauerkraut-sausage mixture. Chill. Shape into small balls, coat with flour. Add milk to beaten eggs. Dip balls into egg-milk mixture and roll in bread crumbs. Fry in deep fat to brown. Bake in 375° oven for approximately 15-20 minutes.

Helen DeKalb (Mrs. James)

SPINACH BALLS   48 Balls

2 pkgs. (10 oz. each)
   chopped, frozen spinach
2 cups seasoned com-
   mercial stuffing mix
1 cup grated Parmesan
   cheese
6 eggs, well beaten
¾ cup butter, softened

Cook spinach and drain very well. Combine spinach with remaining ingredients. Form into balls the size of a walnut. Freeze. Place on a cookie sheet and bake at 350° for 10 minutes. Will keep frozen for 30 days .

Virginette O'Donnell (Mrs. John)

PARTY-TIME MEATBALLS AND SAUCE   36 Balls

MEATBALLS:
- 1 lb. ground beef
- 1 egg, beaten
- ½ cup bread crumbs
- 1 tsp. parsley, chopped
- ½ onion, chopped
- 1 tsp. salt
- 1 tsp. Worchestershire sauce
- ¼ tsp. pepper

SAUCE:
- 1 jar (12 oz.) chili sauce
- 1 jar (10 oz.) grape jelly
- 1 tsp. lemon juice
- 2 T. brown sugar
- 1 T. soy sauce

Combine meatball ingredients and shape into balls the size of walnuts. Set aside.

In a sauce pan, combine sauce ingredients. Bring to a boil, stirring constantly. Add meatballs to sauce, cover and simmer for 30 minutes. Serve warm from a chafing dish. (Can be cooked in oven at 325° for 30 minutes.)

Evelyn W. Linden (Mrs. Paul)

BARBECUED CHICKEN WINGS   24 Wings

- 2 lbs. chicken wings, tips cut off and other two pieces separated
- ½ cup (1 stick) butter, melted
- ⅓ cup chili sauce
- 3 T. lemon juice
- 1 tsp. Worchestershire sauce
- 1 tsp. kitchen bouquet
- 1 tsp. salt
- 1 tsp. curry powder

Wash and dry chicken; dip in butter. Arrange in oven-proof pan. Add all the other ingredients to remaining butter. Pour over chicken. Bake at 350°. Turn every 15 minutes. Cook til tender, approximately 1 hour. May be made ahead and reheated.

Ginny Neiley (Mrs. George F.)

ARTICHOKE APPETIZER

48 Pieces

This delicious recipe comes from Syria.

1 can (14 oz.) artichoke
hearts, water-packed
1 cup real mayonnaise
¾ cup grated Parmesan
cheese
¼ cup mozzarella cheese,
grated
2 tsp. garlic powder
Salt
Pepper
2 boxes (10 oz. each)
frozen patty shells

Cut artichoke hearts into bite-sized pieces. Mix remaining ingredients together (except patty shells), and add artichokes. Roll out each patty shell 1/8 to 1/4 inch thick. Cut each into 4 sections. Fill center of each piece with one spoonful of artichoke mixture. Fold over ends and pinch closed. Bake on ungreased cookie sheet at 375° for 15-20 minutes. You may also use egg roll skin, but then each piece must be deep fat fried. An alternative filling would be: brown 1 lb. ground beef, 2 small chopped onions, 3 T. cumin, dash of red pepper, salt and pepper. Proceed as above.

Nada Diab (Mrs. Hasson)

MARINATED MUSHROOMS AND ARTICHOKE HEARTS

2 pkgs. (10 oz. each)
frozen artichoke hearts
2 lbs. small fresh
mushrooms
1½ cups water
1 cup cider vinegar
½ cup salad oil
1 clove garlic, halved
1½ T. salt
½ tsp. peppercorns
½ tsp. dried thyme
½ tsp. oregano

16-20 Servings

Cook artichoke hearts until just tender and drain. Slice mushrooms in half through stems. Combine with artichoke hearts. Combine water, vinegar, oil, garlic, salt, pepper and herbs. Add artichokes and mushrooms and toss lightly. Refrigerate covered, stirring occasionally. Leave overnight. Drain before serving.

Louise McCarty (Mrs. Harvey)

BROILED MUSHROOM PUFFS

36 Puffs

1 lb. mushrooms
¼ cup butter
1 pkg. (8 oz.) cream
  cheese
2 T. onion, grated
Salt
Pepper
1 T. parsley, finely
  chopped
2 T. Worcestershire
  sauce
1 tsp. curry powder
2 egg yolks
36 slices of bread, cut into
  rounds
Mayonnaise

Chop mushrooms and saute in butter. Mash cream cheese until very soft and season with onion, salt, pepper, parsley, Worcestershire and curry. Add egg yolks and beat until smooth. Toast one side of bread rounds only. Spread untoasted side with mayonnaise to cover and heap mushrooms on top. Cover mushrooms with cream cheese mixture and place under hot broiler until cheese puffs up and browns lightly. Can be frozen.

Charlotte Williams (Mrs. Don E.)

CHEESED MUSHROOMS

10 Servings

1 lb. fresh mushrooms
10 strips bacon, fried crisp
  and crumbled
¾ cup mayonnaise
½ cup sharp cheddar
  cheese, grated
1 medium onion, chopped
Seasoned salt

Remove stems and wash mushrooms; soak caps in salt water. Combining remaining ingredients; then drain mushrooms on paper towels. Place in buttered 9×13" baking dish. Fill hollows with bacon and cheese mixture. Bake at 325° for 15 minutes. Serve while hot. These may be prepared ahead and baked at a later time.

Marjorie Magers (Mrs. Tom)

WATER CHESTNUT RUMAKI

36 Pieces

2 cans (7 oz. each) water
   chestnuts
1 lb. bacon strips, cut
   in thirds
⅓ cup ketchup
½ cup granulated sugar
Toothpicks

Wrap water chestnuts in bacon strips, skewering firmly with toothpick. Place in baking pan and place in oven at 300°. Drain off fat as it collects, until bacon appears as dry as possible, but not burned; about 1 hour. Combine ketchup and sugar. Pour this sauce over wrapped water chestnuts; sauce need not cover completely. Return pan to oven for another hour. Chestnuts are ready when thickly coated and when sauce clings and does not drip. Be sure to place toothpicks upward, so they aren't too sticky to handle. Replace in oven briefly and serve hot. For variety, you may substitute olives for water chestnuts.

Betty Hillbloom (Mrs. James S.)

RUMAKI

36 Pieces

A family favorite and a hit at every party.

½ lb. chicken livers,
   cut in half
1½ T. honey
1 T. soy sauce
2 T. oil
½ clove garlic, crushed
1 can (7 oz.) water
   chestnuts
18 slices bacon, cut in half

Thoroughly clean livers and pat dry. Marinate livers for 30 minutes in honey, soy sauce, oil and garlic. Slice water chestnuts. Wrap bacon around liver and water chestnut. Secure with toothpick. (Note: Keep bacon chilled for ease in wrapping). Bake at 350° until bacon is crisp. Before serving, may cover lightly with foil to keep warm.

Donna Strieder (Mrs. Henry)

CURRY DIP
2 Cups

2 cups real mayonnaise
3 T. chili sauce
¾ tsp. curry powder
1 tsp. Worchestershire sauce
½ tsp. onion salt
½ tsp. seasoned salt

Place all ingredients in blender in order given. Blend according to blender manufacturer's instructions (a very short time). Refrigerate before serving. Prepare raw vegetables for serving with dip: romaine lettuce, green onions, cauliflowerettes, red radishes, green pepper strips, celery, carrots, turnips, and zucchini strips, and crisp broccoli flowerettes.

Barbara A. Searle

CRABMEAT DIP
3 Cups

1 pkg. (8 oz.) cream cheese, softened
2 cans (6½ oz. each) crab, rinsed and drained
Garlic salt to taste
¼ cup mayonnaise
1 tsp. dry mustard
¼ cup white wine
2 T. powdered sugar
1 tsp. onion juice

Blend all ingredients. To serve warm, bake in 350° oven for 15 minutes or until bubbly. Serve with large crackers. Can be served cold.

Marcia Keppy

SHRIMP DIP
2 Cups

½ cup chopped celery
1 can (4½ oz.) shrimp, washed, drained and shredded
½ cup mayonnaise
1 pkg. (3 oz.) cream cheese
¼ cup onion, chopped
2½ T. lemon juice
½ tsp. Worchestershire sauce
½ tsp. garlic salt
¼ tsp Tabasco sauce (optional)

Mix all ingredients together. Can be doubled safely. Serve with crackers.

Kay Runge (Mrs. Peter)

SPINACH DIP

1½ Cups

1 pkg. (10 oz.) frozen,
  chopped spinach
¾ cup real mayonnaise
2 green onions, finely
  chopped
1 tsp. salt
⅓ tsp. pepper

Thaw frozen spinach and squeeze out all moisture. Mix spinach thoroughly with mayonnaise, chopped onions, salt and pepper. Chill and serve -- especially good with "corn" flavored chips.

Janet Schwarz (Mrs. Eric)

DILL VEGETABLE DIP

2 Cups

1 cup real mayonnaise
1 cup sour cream
1 T. parsley flakes
1 T. dill seed (or weed)
1 T. minced dried onion
½ T. BeauMonde seasoning
  OR: ½ tsp. each of:
  celery salt, onion salt
  and salt

Combine ingredients. For a different flavor you may grate a peeled and seeded cucumber and add to the dip.

Jane Lofgren (Mrs. Jack)

CHILI DIP

6-8 Cups

2 lbs. ground chuck
3 medium onions, chopped
1 green pepper, chopped
2 T. chili powder
1 can (10¾ oz.) tomato
  soup
1 can (8 oz.) tomato sauce
1 can (6 oz.) tomato paste
1 lb. processed cheese,
  shredded

Brown ground chuck. Add the onions and pepper and saute until tender. Add the chili powder, tomato soup, tomato sauce and tomato paste. Cook 5 minutes; then add cheese and cook over low heat until melted. Dip should be served hot, surrounded with corn chips or tortilla chips. Very popular and tasty appetizer for parties. May also add chili beans.

Cindee Schnekloth (Mrs. John)

RAW VEGETABLE DIP

1 Cup

Men's Favorite!

1 cup real mayonnaise
4 tsp. soy sauce
1 tsp. powdered ginger
2 T. chives, chopped
1 tsp. wine vinegar

Mix well a few hours before serving. Serve with sliced raw vegetables: cauliflower, mushrooms, zucchini and celery sticks.

Lois Leach (Mrs. James A.)

DRIED BEEF DIP

2 Cups

1 pkg. (8 oz.) cream
  cheese
2 T. milk
½ cup sour cream
¼ cup green pepper,
  finely chopped
1 pkg. (4 oz.) dried beef
¼ tsp. pepper
2 T. minced onion or
  onion flakes
1 tsp. onion salt
Chopped walnuts
  or pecans

Mix ingredients thoroughly. Put in 2-quart baking dish. Sprinkle chopped walnuts or pecans on top. Bake at 350° for 20 minutes. Serve with crackers or bread. May substitute corned beef for dried beef for a different flavor.

Karen Opheim (Mrs. George)

CAULIFLOWER DIP

1 Cup

¼ cup sugar
1 tsp. garlic powder
1 tsp. salad oil
2 tsp. prepared mustard
½ cup salad dressing

Mix first four ingredients well until sugar is dissolved. Then add salad dressing. Refrigerate. May make the day before using. Good with all fresh vegetables.

Mary Jo Abbott (Mrs. Mark)

GATEAU FROMAGE

Outstanding with cocktails or as a fruit and cheese course.

1 pkg. (8 oz.) cream cheese
2 pkgs. (8 oz.) cream cheese broken into pieces
4 oz. camembert (leave rind on) cut into pieces
4 oz. gruyere
4 oz. mild bleu cheese
½ cup fresh parsley, chopped
½ cup pecans (ground)
Apple slices
Wheat wafers

Soften cream cheese and spread into an 8" circle on platter. Process remaining cream cheese, camembert, gruyere and bleu cheese until well blended, then mound the cheese mixture on top of the cream cheese. Garnish with parsley and pecans. This must sit overnight in refrigerator (covered). Before serving, let it stand at room temperature for 30 minutes. Place apple slices and wheat wafers around mixture.

MARGHERITA ROBERTI NOBIS

Margherita Roberti

MARGHERITA ROBERTI NOBIS, Mrs. Thomas Nobis of Davenport in private life, has appeared with the Tri-City Symphony in concert versions of operas on six occasions, as well as appearing with the Tri-City Youth Orchestra for a Family Concert Series in 1974. In 1970, she was knighted by the Italian government "Commendatore della Republica Italiana Dame Margherita Roberti Nobis," for her great contribution to Italian art by singing more Verdi heroines than any soprano of all time. Mrs. Nobis is a very active member of the Board of Directors of the Tri-City Symphony Association. Gourmet cooking is another of her great accomplishments. Music, however, remains her prime interest and she devotes a part of each day to practice and study.

HOLIDAY CHEESE BALL

15-20 Servings

Pretty for the holidays with red pimento and green pepper.

2 pkgs. (8 oz. each) cream
   cheese
2 cups sharp cheddar
   cheese, shredded
1 T. pimento
1 T. green pepper, minced
2 tsp. Worchestershire
   sauce
1 tsp. lemon juice
Salt
Chopped nuts

Cream all ingredients together using blender or electric mixer. Then the cheese mixture may be rolled in nuts or served in a bowl. The mixture may be served in a log form or rolled into two balls.

Sandra Fritz (Mrs. Manfred)

ROYAL CHEESE BALL

10-15 Servings

1 pkg. (8 oz.) cream cheese,
   softened
1 jar (5 oz.) neufchatel and
   bleu cheese spread
2 T. onion, finely chopped
1 garlic clove, minced
   (optional)
Parsley, chopped
Pecans, crushed

Combine softened cream cheese and the cheese spread. Mix until blended. Add onion and garlic. Mix well. Chill in ball. Roll in nuts and parsley.

Muriel Butler (Mrs. Allen)

WALNUT CHEESE BALL

15-20 Servings

2 pkg. (8 oz. each) cream
   cheese
1 cup green pepper,
   chopped
1 can (8½ oz.) crushed
   pineapple, well drained
½ cup green onion,
   chopped
1 cup walnuts or pecans,
   chopped
1 T. seasoned salt

Cream together the ingredients except nuts. Form into ball and roll in nuts. Serve with crackers.

Diann Moore (Mrs. Robert)
Joyce Whitlow (Mrs. Ted)

BLACK OLIVE & CREAM CHEESE BALL   1½ Cups

1 pkg. (8 oz.) cream
   cheese
1/8 tsp. (slight) Tobasco
1 T. dry minced onion
⅓ cup stuffed green olives,
   chopped
¼ cup black olives,
   chopped
1 cup fresh parsley,
   chopped

Combine all ingredients except parsley.
Form into balls. May be frozen at this
point. Before serving, coat with parsley.

Penny Lounsberry (Mrs. John)

KORZOTT (HUNGARIAN SPREAD)   10 Servings

*Served at Ashcroft, Colorado, with chilled wine and/or beer before lunch.
Our very nice cross country ski instructor asked the gals in the kitchen for the
exact recipe when we wouldn't stop raving -- and gobbling!

12 oz. cream cheese
½ cup (1 stick) margarine
½ cup sour cream
½ cup small curd cottage
   cheese
1½ T. anchovy paste
1 T. paprika
½ T. caraway seeds
¼ cup chopped green
   onions (tops, too)
1½ T. capers
1 pkg. pumpernickel bread

Have cream cheese at room temperature;
melt margarine; put both into small mixer
bowl with all ingredients except chopped
onions and capers and blend well. Put
chopped onion and capers in and hand
mix. Chill for an hour or more. Serve in a
mound in the center of a plate, surrounded
by "fingers" of the thin pumpernickel bread
(usually found in dairy case of supermarket
as it must be kept chilled). The 12 oz.
package size will make up about 4 plates.

Fran Osmundson (Mrs. William)

BLEU CHEESE BUTTER AND BRANDY APPETIZER SPREAD

15-20 Servings

6 oz. bleu cheese (put in
  freezer 1-2 hours for
  better crumbling)
6 oz. butter (do not use
  margarine) softened
1 tsp. prepared mustard
Dash nutmeg
2 tsp. brandy

Cream together bleu cheese and butter. Add remaining ingredients. Serve as a spread with cocktail party bread rounds or crackers. (Does not need to be chilled; spreads better if slightly soft).

Lance O. Willett

HOT MUSHROOM SPREAD

8-10 Servings

Delicious on small rye bread or crackers.

1 lb. fresh mushrooms,
  sliced
3 T. butter
2 T. flour
1 cup sour cream
1 tsp. lemon juice
1½-2 cups grated cheddar
  cheese

Saute mushrooms in butter until heated through. Add flour and cook 5 minutes on low heat. Add sour cream and lemon juice. Put in shallow dish and cover with cheddar cheese. Bake at 350° for 30 minutes or until bubbly. You can combine ingredients ahead of time, but serve immediately after baking.

Jane Royster (Mrs. Robert)

HOT CRABMEAT SPREAD

8 Servings

1 pkg. (8 oz.) cream
  cheese, softened
1 T. milk
1 can (6½ oz.) crabmeat
2 T. onion, finely chopped
½ tsp. creamstyle
  horseradish
¼ tsp. salt
½ cup toasted sliced
  almonds
Dash pepper

Rinse crabmeat in colander and press dry with paper towel. Blend well the remaining ingredients except sliced almonds. Pull apart crabmeat and add to mixture. Place in 1 qt. casserole and bake at 375° for 15 minutes. Add toasted sliced almonds over top before serving. Serve with small slices of icebox rye bread. If using frozen crab, drain very well or mixture will be soggy.

Jeanne Schebler (Mrs. Tom)

SHRIMP MOLD

15-20 Servings

Add green pepper at Christmas for holiday appeal.

1 T. gelatin, unflavored
¼ cup water
1 can (10¾ oz.) tomato soup
2 pkgs. (8 oz. each) cream cheese, softened
¾ cup celery, finely chopped
¾ cup onion, finely chopped
1 cup mayonnaise
2 cans (4½ oz. each) shrimp, deveined and drained

Soak gelatin in water and stir until dissolved. Heat soup until it bubbles, stirring constantly. Add cream cheese and mash with fork. Add gelatin mixture and stir until smooth. Cool to room temperature. Add rest of ingredients, stirring to combine well. Pour into a 3-quart mold. Chill for 24 hours. Use parsley to garnish. Serve with crackers. Lobster, crab or salmon may be substituted for shrimp.

Janna Rice (Mrs. John)
Sandra Fritz (Mrs. Manfred)

✓

CRABMEAT MOLD

20-30 Servings

Can be used as a fish course served in individual molds.

1½ T. gelatin, unflavored
½ cup cold water
½ lemon, squeezed
12 oz. cream cheese
1 can (10¾ oz.) cream of mushroom soup
1 medium onion, finely chopped
¼ green pepper, finely chopped
2 cans (6½ oz. each) crabmeat, drained and flaked
1 cup celery, chopped
1 cup mayonnaise

Sprinkle gelatin over cold water and lemon juice. Dissolve over low heat. Set aside. Combine softened cream cheese, soup and onion. Cook over low heat until smooth. Add gelatin and remaining ingredients. Mix well. Spoon into greased 4-cup mold. Chill 4-6 hours until firm. Unmold, serve with wafers.

Bobbie Searles (Mrs. John)

LIZ'S PARTY FAVORS

¾ cup butter
1 T. onion salt
1 tsp. garlic salt
½ tsp. Tabasco sauce
1 pkg. (10 oz.) LIFE cereal
1 bag (7½ oz.) pretzel
sticks
1 can (7 oz.) peanuts
1 can (3½ oz.) french fried
onion rings
1 large can or bag of
chinese noodles
1 box square cheese
crackers

Melt butter and blend in seasonings. Cor
bine all other ingredients except frenc
fried onion rings in a roaster. Toss wit
seasoned butter. Heat at 250° for 1 hou
stirring occasionally. Add onion rings a
end to prevent excessive browning.

Elizabeth Gosma

23

SOUPS

GERMAN CHERRY SOUP WITH DUMPLINGS

8 Servings

An old family favorite, especially good for Sunday night supper.

1 quart tart cherries (fresh,
   frozen or canned)
Water
½ cup sugar
Cinnamon stick (optional)

DUMPLINGS:
  1 cup water
  ½ cup butter
  ¼ tsp. salt
  1 cup flour
  4 eggs

Drain juice from cherries into a 4 cup measure, and add enough water to equal 4 cups. Bring cherries, juice and water, sugar and cinnamon stick to a boil in a 5 quart pan.

For dumplings: Boil water and butter. Add salt and flour and stir until it cleans the pan. Let cool a few minutes, then add eggs, one at a time, beating well after each egg. Drop by soup spoonfuls into boiling soup. Cook 10 minutes with lid on pan; turn off heat and let stand 5 minutes before serving.

Bonnie Moeller (Mrs. Gerald)

FRUIT SOUP

10 Servings

1 pkg. (12 oz.) pitted prunes
1 pkg. (6 oz.) dried apricots
1 can (16 oz.) sliced peaches
  in syrup
1 pkg. (8 oz.) pearl tapioca
1 pkg. (15 oz.) seedless
  white raisins
6 apples, peeled, cored and
  sliced
Sugar

Soak pearl tapioca overnight in water to cover. Cook apples in water to cover until done, but still holding their shape. Heat other ingredients except tapioca, separately in water. Combine all ingredients (including liquid) in a large kettle. Add sugar to taste and heat to dissolve sugar and cook tapioca. Remove from heat, cool and serve chilled.

Charlotte Durkee

NEWFIE PEA SOUP

10 Servings

1 lb. dried split peas
2 quarts water
1 ham bone or ham hocks
⅓ cup chopped carrots
½ cup chopped onion
½ cup chopped turnip
Salt
Pepper

Combine peas and water in large pan over medium heat to boiling. Boil 2 minutes; remove from heat. Cover; let stand 1 hour. Add remaining ingredients. Heat to boiling; reduce heat. Simmer uncovered, stirring occasionally until mixture is thick, about 2 hours. Adjust seasoning. Cut some ham from bone or hock for a more meaty soup or add water for a thinner consistency.

Shan Corelis (Mrs. John)

BROCCOLI SOUP

6-8 Servings

Thick and rich - nutmeg adds interesting flavor.

1 pkg. (10 oz.) frozen
   chopped broccoli
1 small onion, chopped
1 cup rich chicken broth
1 can (10¾ oz.) cream of
   mushroom soup
1 carton (8 oz.) sour cream
Nutmeg

Cook broccoli and onion in chicken broth. Add soup and sour cream. Serve hot or cold. Sprinkle nutmeg on top.

Gloria Strieter (Mrs. John R.)

SHERRIED CREAM OF MUSHROOM SOUP

1 lb. fresh mushrooms,
   washed and sliced
⅓ cup onion, finely
   chopped
1 clove garlic, minced
¼ cup butter or margarine
1 T. lemon juice
3 T. flour
1¾ cups chicken bouillon
¼ cup cooking sherry
1 tsp. salt
¼ tsp. pepper
2 cups light cream or milk

8-10 Servings

Saute mushrooms, onion and garlic in butter in 3 quart saucepan. Stir in lemon juice and flour. Gradually stir in bouillon, sherry, and seasonings. Cook over low heat until slightly thickened, stirring constantly. Stir in cream; continue cooking until hot, being careful not to let soup boil.

Joan Ferguson (Mrs. Wendell)

CREAM OF PEANUT SOUP

10-12 Servings

1 medium onion, chopped
2 ribs celery, chopped
¼ cup butter
3 T. flour
2 quarts chicken stock
2 cups peanut butter
1¾ cups half and half cream
Chopped peanuts

Saute onion and celery in butter until soft. Stir in flour until well blended. Add chicken stock, stirring constantly, and bring to a boil. Remove from heat and rub through a sieve. Add peanut butter and cream, stirring to blend thoroughly. Return to low heat, but do not boil, and serve garnished with peanuts.

LEONARD PENNARIO

Leonard Pennario

Pianist LEONARD PENNARIO has appeared with every major orchestra in the United States, as well as abroad. He made his New York debut in 1943, playing the "Liszt E Flat Concerto" with the New York Philharmonic. He received praise from Toscanni and Arthur Rubinstein for his "beautiful playing". Mr. Pennario performed Prokofieff's "Concerto for Piano and Orchestra No. 3 in C Major, Op. 26" in 1963 with the Tri-City Symphony.

TOMATO-CELERY SOUP

6-8 Servings

So versatile - makes an elegant first course or
fills a thermos for a football tailgate picnic.

1 can (29 oz.) whole
  tomatoes
1 cup celery, finely chopped
1 small onion, finely
  chopped
Baking soda
2 T. butter
2 T. flour
1 cup milk

Cook celery and onion until tender in juice
drained from tomatoes. Cut tomatoes into
small pieces and remove seeds. Add
tomatoes to juice mixture. In a separate
pan melt butter, add flour, then add milk,
stirring constantly to make a white sauce.
Add a pinch of baking soda to tomato-
celery mixture. Then combine with cream
sauce. Heat thoroughly, but don't boil.

Rose Ann Hass (Mrs. James)

TOMATO MADRILENE

8-10 Servings

¼ cup butter
¼ cup onion, chopped
2 cans (18 oz. each)
  tomato juice
2 cans (10½ oz. each) beef
  broth or bouillon
1 bay leaf
Sugar
Grated parmesan cheese
Parsley
Croutons (optional)

Saute onion in butter. Add tomato juice,
broth, bay leaf, and pinch of sugar. Heat
just to boiling, then simmer 5 minutes. Garnish with cheese and parsley. Add
croutons if desired.

Sue Shawver (Mrs. Ward)

WINTER VEGETABLE SOUP   8 Servings

3 onions, chopped
2 T. butter
2 lb. ground chuck
1 garlic clove, minced
3 cups beef stock, or
  consomme'
2 cans (1 lb. 12 oz. each)
  tomatoes
1 cup potatoes, cubed
1 cup celery, chopped
1 cup green beans
1 cup carrots, chopped
1 cup dry red wine
2 T. parsley, chopped
½ tsp. basil
¼ tsp. thyme
Salt
Pepper

In a soup kettle, cook onions in butter until they are tender and golden. Stir in the ground beef and garlic and cook the mixture, separating the beef with a fork, until it is brown. Add the beef stock, tomatoes, potatoes, celery, green beans and carrots. Add wine, parsley, basil, thyme and salt and pepper. Bring the soup to a boil, reduce the heat, and simmer it for about 1-1¼ hours.

Jean Stringham (Mrs. Wally)
Cindee Schnekloth (Mrs. John)

PARMESAN VEGETABLE CHOWDER   8-10 Servings

1½ cups chicken bouillon
1 stalk celery, diced
2 cups potatoes, diced
1 carrot, thinly sliced
¼ cup onion, chopped
1 tsp. salt
¼ tsp. pepper
2 T. margarine
¼ cup flour
2 cups milk
½ cup grated parmesan
  cheese
1 can (17 oz.) creamed
  corn

In large saucepan over high heat, combine chicken bouillon, celery, potatoes, carrots, onion, salt and pepper and heat until boiling. Reduce heat to low, cover and simmer 10-15 minutes until vegetables are fork tender. In small saucepan over medium heat, melt margarine, stir in flour until smooth. Slowly stir in milk, cook, stirring until sauce is smooth and thickened. Add cheese and heat until cheese is melted. Add cheese sauce and corn to undrained vegetables. Heat thoroughly, but do not boil. Can be reheated.

Heather Gosma (Mrs. John)

ITALIAN VEGETABLE SOUP

8-10 Servings

1 cup green onions, thinly
  sliced
1 large garlic clove,
  crushed
2 T. butter or margarine
3 cans (13¾ oz. each)
  chicken broth or
  equivalent amount
  chicken stock
1 cup tomatoes, peeled
  and diced
1 cup small carrots
  thinly sliced
1 cup celery, sliced
1 cup cabbage, coarsely
  chopped
1 tsp. salt
½ tsp. thyme
½ tsp. basil
⅛ tsp. pepper
Optional Garnish:
Toasted Italian bread
Grated parmesan cheese

It's best to have all vegetables prepared in advance. In large saucepan, saute green onions and garlic in butter 5 minutes. Add chicken broth, vegetables, salt, thyme, basil, and pepper; simmer 15 minutes, or until vegetables are just crisp tender. Serve in bowls topped with bread and sprinkled with cheese.

Lance O. Willett

STEW SOUP

10-12 Servings

This is a MEAL for those nights when everyone's hurrying in different directions, including the cook!

2 lbs. lean boneless chuck,
  cubed
2 pkgs. onion soup mix
6 cups water
1 bay leaf
2 pkgs. (10 oz. each) mixed
  vegetables, frozen
¾ cup instant barley
1 cup celery, chopped
1 green pepper, chopped
2 cans (16 oz. each)
  stewed tomatoes
Salt, pepper, parsley, and
  thyme to taste

Combine meat (no need to brown), soup mix, water and bay leaf in 5 quart pan. Bring to boil, then simmer 2 hours covered. Remove bay leaf. Add mixed vegetables, barley, celery, green pepper, and bring to boil again; then simmer ½ hour or until vegetables and barley are cooked. Add stewed tomatoes and seasonings to taste. Reheat and serve, with cole slaw and hard rolls.

Connie Green (Mrs. George)

TEXAS CHILI

**Delicious served with guacamole salad, hot buttered
flour tortillas and lots of iced cold beer!**

¼ cup corn oil
2 lbs. beef, diced in ½"
  cubes
1 onion, chopped
1 tsp. salt
1 tsp. paprika
3 tsp. powdered cumin
6 T. chili powder
1 (8 oz.) can tomato sauce
2 cans water
2 T. flour and warm water,
  to form a thick mixture

Sear meat in hot corn oil until brown. Add onions and brown. Sprinkle all spices on the meat and stir quickly. Add tomato sauce plus 2 cans water. Cover and simmer 1 hour and 15 minutes, or until meat is tender, stirring occasionally. Skim off grease. Mix flour with warm water into a thick but flavorful mixture. Stir into chili to "tighten" or "thicken" it. Note: William Walker says, "Never, but never use ground meat for chili. Venison makes excellent chili, if you can get it." The flavor of this chili develops overnight, so it's better to cook it a day ahead. It also freezes very well. Measurements are approximate. correct to your own taste and texture the second time around.

WILLIAM WALKER

William Walker

WILLIAM WALKER, baritone of the Metropolitan Opera Association, is a native Texan and presently resides in San Antonio. Not only has he distinguished himself with the Metropolitan Opera, but also in Broadway musicals and on television, including the Bell Telephone Hour and Tonight Show. He is remembered by his portrayal of Escamillo with the Tri-City Symphony in the 1969 performance of "Carmen."

SIMPLE LIVER-DUMPLING SOUP   8 Servings

7 cups beef soup stock
½ cup uncooked rice

DUMPLINGS:
¾ lb. beef liver
2 eggs
2 slices white bread,
    crumbled medium fine
1 small onion, chopped
Butter
½ tsp. salt
3 T. flour
Nutmeg
Parsley

Cook rice in soup stock until almost tender.

For dumplings: Saute onion in small amount of butter until tender. Blot liver with paper towel. Grind liver twice and remove gristle. Combine ground liver, eggs, bread, onion, salt, flour and nutmeg and beat for several minutes until fluffy. Drop by tablespoons into simmering beef broth, (if dumplings break apart, add more flour). Cook, covered for 5-10 minutes. Garnish with parsley.

Gloria Strieter (Mrs. John)

TURKEY TROT SOUP   8 Servings

Quick and easy, great if your family gets tired of turkey sandwiches after the big day

Turkey carcass (left over)
1 large onion, chopped
1 stalk celery, chopped
2 carrots, sliced
1 tsp. basil leaves
4 chicken bouillon cubes
Salt
Pepper
2 cups fine egg noodles

In dutch oven, place turkey carcass and onion, cover with water and simmer 2 hours until meat falls off bones. Remove carcass, cool and remove meat. Strain broth. Add celery, carrots, basil leaves, bouillon cubes, salt and pepper to broth. Add meat and egg noodles; cook until tender.

Linda Clarke (Mrs. Wade)

"SEASIDE" SOUP

**Created at the beach by David Amram and
printed according to his "precise instructions"**

1 can (46 oz.) chicken
 broth
½ lb. scallops
1 lb. fresh fish filets
3 celery stalks
4 medium white onions,
 sliced in half
1 bottle (2 oz.) clam juice
6 "handshakes"
 Worchestershire sauce
4 "squirts" Open Pit
 barbeque sauce
6 "squirts" New Orleans
 Hot sauce
4 "handshakes" garlic salt
2 cans (12 oz. each) beer
2 hot dogs, sliced
½ pt. plain yogurt or
 sour cream

Turn on flame or electricity; place big ceramic soup-stew pot over heat and set at medium. Add chicken broth. Place scallops and filets at bottom in broth. Add celery stalks, onions, clam juice, Worchestershire sauce, barbeque sauce, hot sauce and garlic salt. Add 2 cans beer. Let sliced hot dogs float on top. Cover and simmer on low for 25 minutes. Put a spoonful of yogurt or sour cream in each bowl, then pour soup over it.

DAVID AMRAM

David Amram

DAVID AMRAM'S compositions are as varied as his instrumental background - anything from classical to contemporary jazz. He was Leonard Bernstein's choice as first composer-in-residence of the New York Philharmonic and has composed over one hundred orchestral and chamber music works as well as film scores including, "Splendor in the Grass" and "The Manchurian Candidate." A long-time friend of Tri-City Conductor James Dixon, David Amram made many new friends when he first performed his own Triple Concerto with the Tri-City Symphony Orchestra in 1977 for the Family Concert Series. The following year, the Junior Board of the Tri-City Symphony commissioned him to compose a work in honor of James Dixon and the 20th Anniversary of the Tri-City Youth Orchestra, a full symphony orchestal composition "En Memoria de Chano Pozo".

EASY BOUILLABAISSE

6 Servings

2 T. butter
1 large onion, chopped
2 cloves garlic, chopped
1 cup sliced celery
¼ cup parsley, chopped
2 cans (16 oz. each)
   stewed tomatoes,
   undrained
1½ cups Niagara Type wine
3 cans (10¾ oz. each)
   condensed chicken
   broth, undiluted
½ tsp. thyme
½ tsp. chervil
2 pkgs. (10 oz. each)
   frozen cod fillets
   (cut while frozen into
   1" cubes)
1 lb. shrimp, shelled, raw
   and deveined
Salt
Pepper

Heat butter in kettle. Saute' onions, garlic, celery, and parsley for 5 minutes. Stir in tomatoes, wine, chicken broth, thyme and chervil. Cover and simmer for 15 minutes, or until vegetables are tender. Add cod and shrimp. Simmer for 5-6 minutes, or until fish is cooked. Season to taste with salt and pepper.

Meg Burrows (Mrs. John)

QUICK CLAM CHOWDER

2-4 Servings

2 T. butter
1 carrot, thinly sliced
1 stalk of celery, chopped
2 T. onion, chopped
1 can (10¾ oz.) cream of
   potato soup
10¾ oz. half and half cream
Red pepper
1 can (6½ oz.) clams,
   minced; reserve ¼ cup
   juice

Saute carrot, celery, and onion in butter until tender. Add rest of ingredients including liquid from clams. Bring just to a boil.

Diann Moore (Mrs. Robert)

BOATMAN'S STEW

6 Servings

A favorite of our family. Good with Italian bread and salad.

2 lbs. cod cut in large
    chunks
½ tsp. salt
2 onions, sliced
¼ cup cooking oil
1 (6 oz.) can tomato paste
3 cups water
¼ tsp. red pepper
1½ tsp. salt
¼ tsp. black pepper
1 cup parsley, finely
    chopped
⅓ cup dry white wine

Sprinkle fish with ½ tsp. salt. Let stand 1 hour. Meanwhile, lightly brown onion in oil; pour off fat. Stir in tomato paste, water, red pepper, salt, pepper, parsley, and wine. Simmer 30 minutes. Add fish, simmer about 10 minutes more or just until fish flakes easily with a fork. Fast for quick dinner as the fish does not have to be thawed before you first salt it; it will thaw enough to be cut into chunks at the end of the hour.

Mary Andrews (Mrs. Charles)

CRABMEAT SOUP

4 Servings

This is such a tasty and very attractive soup!

¼ cup onion, coarsely
    chopped
¼ cup green pepper,
    coarsely chopped
¼ cup celery, diced
4 T. butter
2 cans (13¾ oz. each)
    chicken broth
¼ cup small macaroni
    shells
1 cup tomatoes, coarsely
    chopped
1 can king crab meat or
    1 pkg. frozen crab
    with juice
1 T. fresh parsley, chopped
¼ cup tomato juice
Herbs

Cook onion, pepper and celery in butter until tender. Add all except crab meat and simmer until macaroni shells are tender. Allow soup to "rest" in pan at this stage for 20 minutes or so. Then season to please your taste with salt, freshly ground pepper and any favorite herb. (i.e. oregano, basil, etc.) Add crab meat and heat just before serving.

Fran Osmundson (Mrs. William D.)

CHRISTMAS EVE BISQUE

6 Servings

A salad and a flaming plum pudding make a festive eve

4 T. butter
½ cup celery, chopped
¼ cup onion, chopped
2 T. flour
4 cups half and half cream
1 tsp. salt
1 lb. crabmeat
¼ cup pale dry sherry
Paprika

Melt butter and saute celery and onion until tender. Add flour and blend until smooth. Add cream slowly, stirring constantly until mixture thickens. Add salt and crabmeat and keep on low heat until ready to serve (watch carefully). Add sherry and garnish with paprika immediately before serving. (Fresh oysters may be used also.)

Myrth Schuette (Mrs. John)

BREADS

WHEAT BREAD   3 Loaves

Makes excellent toast.

3 pkgs. (¼ oz. each) dry
  yeast in ½ cup warm
  water
12 cups whole wheat flour
5 cups hot water
2 T. salt
1 cup honey
1 cup oil

Mix yeast in ½ cup warm water and set aside for 15-20 minutes. Mix 7 cups flour into 5 cups hot water until blended. Mix in salt, honey, and oil until blended. Mix in 1 cup flour. Add yeast. Add 3-4 more cups flour. Knead until even consistency, about 10 minutes. Divide dough into thirds and shape into loaves. Place in oiled 9×5×3" pans. Cover with damp cloth and let rise in warm place 35 minutes. Bake at 350° for 40-45 minutes.

Jan Crow (Mrs. David)

HONEY WHOLE WHEAT BREAD   3-4 Loaves

Your "honey" will love this homemade bread!

½ cup warm water
2 pkgs. (¼ oz. each) dry
  yeast
3 cups whole wheat flour
3 cups enriched white
  flour
¼ cup powdered milk
Handful of wheat germ
½ cup bran
1 T. salt
⅓ cup honey
1 egg
2½ T. corn oil
2 cups cold water

Sprinkle two packages of dry yeast in warm water. Do not stir. Combine all dry ingredients. Add honey, egg, corn oil, cold water, and dissolved yeast to dry ingredients. Stir into a moderately stiff dough, adding about ¼ cup more flour if needed. Knead about 10 minutes. Shape and place in greased bowl, turning dough in bowl once. Allow to rise 1 hour. Knead again 10 minutes. Shape into loaves. Let rest on counter 10 minutes. Roll with rolling pin to dissolve air bubbles. Reshape. Place in 4 greased metal pans 7×3" or 3 greased metal pans 8×4". Let rise 1 hour. Bake at 350° for 30-35 minutes.

Joan Ferguson (Mrs. Wendell)

ANADAMA BREAD

2 Loaves

This is delicious with ham.

3½ cups water
1 cup molasses
½ cup butter or margarine
1 cup cornmeal
2 pkgs. (¼ oz. each) active dry yeast
1 T. salt
10 cups all-purpose flour (approximate)

In 4 quart saucepan over medium heat, heat water, molasses and butter (or margarine) to boiling. With wire whisk, slowly stir in cornmeal; cook 2 minutes, stirring constantly. Cool cornmeal mixture to very warm (120°-130°F) about 1 hour, stirring occasionally.

In large bowl, combine yeast, salt, and 2 cups flour. With mixer at low speed, gradually pour cornmeal mixture into dry ingredients. Increase speed to medium; beat 2 minutes, occasionally scraping bowl with rubber spatula. Beat in 1½ cups flour or enough to make a thick batter; continue beating 2 minutes, occasionally scraping bowl. With spoon stir in enough additional flour (about 5 cups) to make a soft dough.

Turn dough onto well-floured surface and knead until smooth and elastic, about 10 minutes, adding more flour (about 1 cup) while kneading. (Dough will be soft.) Shape dough into a ball and place in large greased bowl, turning dough over so that top is greased. Cover with towel; let rise in warm place (80°-85°F), away from draft, until doubled, about 1½ hours.

Punch down dough, turn dough onto lightly floured surface; cover with towel and let dough rest 15 minutes.

Grease two 9×5" loaf pans. Cut dough in half. On lightly floured surface with lightly floured rolling pin, roll one dough half into 12×8" rectangle. Starting with 8" end, tightly roll dough, jelly roll fashion. Pinch seam to seal; press ends to seal and tuck under. Place roll, seam side down, in loaf pan. Repeat with remaining dough. Cover with towel; let rise in warm place until double, about 45 minutes.

Preheat oven to 400°F. Bake bread 45 minutes or until loaves sound hollow when tapped with fingers. Remove from pans immediately; cool on wire racks.

Anne V. Mairet (Mrs. Richard A.)

SWEDISH RYE BREAD   4 Loaves

4 cups water
1 cup sorghum
⅓ cup brown sugar
⅓ cup shortening
1 T. salt
½ tsp. yellow food coloring
1 pkg. (¼ oz.) dry yeast
   dissolved in ⅓ cup water
4 cups rye flour
9 - 10 cups white flour

Mix the first six ingredients and heat to lukewarm. Remove from stove. Add to this yeast mixture and rye flour. Beat this with electric mixer. Knead in the white flour. Place in a large bowl when finished kneading. Let stand in a warm place until double in bulk. Form into 4 loaves and place in greased 9×5×3" loaf pans. Let rise again until double in bulk. Bake at 350° for 45 minutes.

Vicki Reschly (Mrs. Chris)

DELIGHTFUL FRENCH BREAD   2 Large Loaves
                                  or 3 Medium Loaves

This is an easy, inexpensive bread to prepare and makes a beautiful gift.

2½ cups water, warm
2 T. sugar
1 T. salt
2 T. cooking oil
6 cups flour, sifted
2 pkgs. (¼ oz. each)
   dry yeast
1 egg
Sesame or poppy seed
Cornmeal

Pour warm water (105°-115°F) into a large mixing bowl and stir in sugar, salt, oil, half the flour, and yeast. Beat vigorously 2-3 minutes. Add remaining flour and stir until all dry ingredients are thoroughly mixed. Leave the spoon in the heavy batter and allow it to rest 10 minutes. Stir down. Allow dough to rest 10 minutes and stir down again. Repeat this process until dough has been stirred down 5 times. Turn dough onto floured surface, knead only enough to coat dough with flour (2 or 3 times) so it can be handled. Divide in half and roll each part into a 9×12" rectangle and roll up each from the long side like a jelly roll. Pinch seam to seal dough and arrange loaves on baking sheets that have been sprinkled with cornmeal. Cover lightly and let rise at room temperature until nearly double in bulk, about 30 minutes. With a very sharp knife, cut three gashes at an angle on top of each loaf; brush with slightly beaten egg, and if desired, sprinkle with sesame or poppy seed. Bake immediately 25-30 minutes at 400° or until nicely browned. Remove from baking sheets and cool on racks.

Bonnie Moeller (Mrs. Gerald)   **42**

PEPPER CHEESE BREAD

Excellent toasted and served with salads.

2 pkgs. (¼ oz. each) dry
yeast
½ cup lukewarm water
1 tsp. sugar
¼ tsp. powdered ginger
3 tsp. powdered chicken
stock
3 cups warm water
4 T. sugar
9-11 cups flour
¾ cup dried skim milk
4 T. soft shortening
2 tsp. salt
3 eggs
2 to 3 tsp. coarse ground
black pepper
2 cups dry sharp cheddar
cheese, grated
1 egg yolk
2 T. water

Dissolve yeast in warm water, add sugar and ginger and let stand untill bubbly. Dissolve powdered chicken stock in ½ cup warm water, then combine with remaining 2½ cups water, sugar, 3 cups flour and dried skim milk. Beat the yeast mixture into the above. Then add soft shortening, salt, eggs, coarse ground black pepper and 6 cups flour, gradually. Stir until dough comes away clean from the sides of bowl. (You may need additional flour if eggs are extra large.) Spread an additional cup of flour on a pastry board and turn dough out. Knead well and add additional flour if needed for a smooth, elastic dough. Flatten dough with hands and sprinkle ½ cup coarsely grated cheese over surface. Roll up dough, flatten again, and repeat process until all 2 cups of cheese are added. Knead lightly to distribute cheese through the dough. Return to bowl, butter top of dough, cover and allow to rise until light (approximately 1 hour). Knead and divide the dough into 6 equal parts, rolling these into even length strips, tapered at each end. Lay 3 strips on each of 2 cookie sheets. Start in middle and braid strips to each end. Cover with light, damp towel and allow to rise again until light. Brush top with egg yolk beaten with 2 tablespoons water. Bake at 350° for 20 minutes, then reduce temperature to 325° and continue baking for an additional 25 minutes, until loaves are golden brown. Brush again with egg-water mixture 5 minutes before end of baking time. Cool on wire rack.

Mary Greenberg (Mrs. Martin)

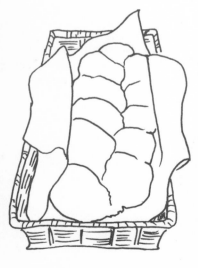

PICADILLY BREAD

5 "Flower Pots"
or 4 Small Loaves
or 2 Large Loaves

2 pkgs. (¼ oz. each) dry
  yeast
½ cup warm water
2 cups small curd cottage
  cheese, warmed
2 T. sugar
2 T. melted butter
2 T. dehydrated minced
  onions
4 tsp. dill seed
2 eggs
2 tsp. salt
4½ cups flour
5 new clay flower pots,
  approx. 4" high and
  4" in diameter

Soften yeast in warm water. Combine next
7 ingredients, add to yeast mixture. Add 2
cups flour and beat well (mix on low speed
with mixer). Add rest of flour and combine
well. Cover and let rise 1 hour. Meanwhile,
wash pots well and line with aluminum
foil, then grease foil generously. Punch
dough down and divide into five equal
parts. Place one part in each pot. Cover
and let rise again 30-40 minutes. Bake at
350° for 40 minutes or until done. Can also
be made in 4 small bread pans or 2 large
ones.

These little breads make deliciously attractive gifts in their flower pot containers!

Judy Dougherty (Mrs. William)

BREAD STICKS

20-22 Bread Sticks

¼ cup shortening
1½ T. sugar
1 tsp. salt
1 cup milk, scalded
1 pkg. (¼ oz.) active dry
  yeast
¼ cup warm water
2 cups sifted flour
1 egg white, stiffly beaten
1½ to 2 cups sifted flour
1 egg, beaten
1 T. milk
Coarse salt

Add shortening, sugar and salt to milk;
cool to lukewarm. Soften yeast in warm
water and stir into milk. Add 2 cups flour,
fold in egg white. Add remaining 1½-2 cups
flour to make a soft dough. Turn out on
lightly floured board and knead until
smooth and satiny. Place in greased bowl.
Grease surface of dough; cover and let rise
until double in bulk. Knead down; pinch off
pieces of dough about the size of a small
egg; roll about 8" long and ½" thick on
unfloured board. Keep uniform in size and
rounded at the ends. Place on lightly greased cookie sheet. Brush with egg and milk
mixture and sprinkle with coarse salt. Let
rise. Bake at 425° for 5 minutes. Reduce
heat to 350° and bake 10-12 minutes
longer so that sticks will be crisp.

Annabelle DeCock (Mrs. Dale)

CROISSANT DAINTIES   4 Dozen

Excellent fancy rolls to serve for luncheon or dinner.

1 cup butter or
  margarine, softened
2 cups flour
¼ tsp. salt
1 egg yolk, slightly beaten
¾ cup thick sour cream
½ tsp. vanilla
¾ cup sugar
1 tsp. cinnamon
¾ cup nuts, finely chopped

Cut butter into a mixture of flour and salt with pastry blender until mixture resembles small peas. Blend in a mixture of the slightly beaten egg yolk, sour cream and vanilla with a fork. Divide dough into thirds and chill in refrigerator several hours or overnight. Mix sugar, cinnamon and nuts together and divide into thirds. When dough is sufficiently chilled, take one of the thirds and roll it into a 12" round on a well floured surface. Sprinkle ⅓ of the sugar-nuts-cinnamon mixture evenly over the round. Cut round into 16 wedges. Roll each wedge firmly, starting at the outer edge. Place on ungreased baking sheets with points underneath. Curve rolls into crescent shape. Bake at 375° for about 17 minutes or until light brown. Remove and cool. Follow the same steps with the remaining dough and sugar-cinnamon-nut mixture.

Rolls freeze well.

Jeanne Schebler (Mrs. Tom)

YUMMY STICKY BUNS   2 Dozen

A quick and easy pecan roll.

1 pkg. (24 roll) of frozen
  yeast rolls
1 pkg. (3 5/8 oz.)
  butterscotch pudding
  mix (not instant)
½ cup chopped pecans
  or walnuts
1 tsp. cinnamon
¼ cup (½ stick) butter
  or margarine, melted

Thaw package of rolls. Combine pudding, nuts, and cinnamon. Dip each roll in melted butter, coat with butterscotch mixture. Arrange in pan and let rise until double in bulk. (To speed up this rising, heat oven to 150°, turn off and put rolls in to rise for 1-1½ hours.) Bake according to directions on roll package. Remove from pan immediately.

Impressive made in a bundt pan.

Pat Quill (Mrs. Hal)

DANISH KRINGLE

4 Coffee Cakes

These delicious coffee cakes require two days for preparation.

DOUGH:
- 6 T. sugar
- 1 pkg. (¼ oz.) yeast
- ½ cup lukewarm water
- 1 cup milk
- 4 cups flour
- 1 cup margarine
- 1 tsp. salt
- 3 egg yolks, beaten

Butter, softened
Sugar

ALMOND FILLING:
- ½ cup sugar
- 1½ T. cornstarch
- 1 tsp. salt
- 1 cup half and half cream
- 2 egg yolks, beaten
- ¼ cup butter or margarine
- ½ tsp. almond extract

ICING:
- 2 cups powdered sugar
- 3 T. butter
- ¼ tsp. salt
- 2 tsp. vanilla or almond extract
- Half and half cream or evaporated milk

For dough: Dissolve sugar and yeast in lukewarm water. Allow to stand about 5 minutes. Scald milk and cool. Blend flour, margarine and salt as for pie crust with pastry blender; add cooled milk, beaten egg yolks and yeast mixture. Stir only enough to blend ingredients. Refrigerate overnight in greased and covered bowl.

For filling: In the top of a double boiler, mix the sugar, cornstarch and salt. Gradually add the cream and stir constantly until mixture thickens. Cook a few minutes more. Stir some of this mixture into yolks and return to cream mixture. Cook 2 minutes longer. Remove from heat, add butter and almond. Filling should be thick enough to spread and hold its shape.

To assemble: Divide refrigerated dough into fourths and roll each fourth to about ¼" thickness (dough is quite soft so flour board generously). Fold circles in half and move gently to a baking sheet. Unfold, butter each circle lightly and sprinkle with small amount of sugar. Spread ¼ of filling on each round. Fold in outer edges, leaving some of the center uncovered. Let rise 2 hours or until double in bulk. Bake at 325° for 20-25 minutes.

For icing: Combine first 4 ingredients and beat until smooth. Thin to right consistency with cream. Frost coffee cakes while they are still warm. (If you plan to freeze coffee cakes, use evaporated milk to thin icing. It can be reheated without melting.)

Olivette Werling (Mrs. R.R.)

CHERRY STRUDEL FINGER BARS

4 Dozen

½ cup lukewarm water
1 pkg. (¼ oz.) dry yeast
¼ cup sugar
3 cups flour
1 cup soft margarine
3 egg yolks, beaten
1 tsp. vanilla
Melted butter
2 small jars cherry, apricot
   or apple preserves
Nuts
Sugar
Cinnamon

In tall glass mix yeast and water, adding a tsp. of the sugar. Set in warm place to rise. Sift flour and sugar and cut in margarine. Make a well in dry ingredients. When yeast mixture has come to glass top, add to beaten egg yolks and vanilla. Add to dry ingredients. Mix well, knead and divide into 4 parts. Let rest, covered, for 10 minutes. Roll out each quite thin in rectangle form. Spread with butter, preserves, nuts, cinnamon and sugar. Roll as a jelly roll. Sprinkle with sugar and cinnamon. Bake at 350° for 30-45 minutes on a cookie sheet. Slice desired width right out of the oven. Cool.

Jan D. Slivken

DANISH PUFF PASTRY

6-8 Servings

DOUGH:
½ cup (1 stick) butter or
   margarine
1 cup flour
1 - 2 T. water

TOPPING:
1 cup water
½ cup (1 stick) butter or
   margarine
1 tsp. almond extract
1 cup flour
3 eggs

ICING:
2 cups powdered sugar
3 T. butter
¼ tsp. salt
2 tsp. almond extract
Half and half cream

Maraschino cherries

For dough: Cut together, with pastry blender, the butter and flour. Add enough water to make pieces cling together in a ball. Divide dough in half. Pat balls into two strips, 3×12", on a cookie sheet.

For topping: Bring water and butter to a boil. Remove from heat and add almond and flour. Beat until smooth. Add eggs, one at a time, beating well after each addition. Spread half of mixture over each pastry strip and bake for 10 minutes at 400°: Reduce heat to 300° and bake about 45 minutes longer, or until tops are lightly browned.

For frosting: Combine first 4 ingredients, and beat until smooth. Thin to right consistency with cream. Garnish with maraschino cherries.

Jeanne Jackson (Mrs. Hal)

CARAMEL CINNAMON ROLLS

2 Dozen

1 pkg. (¼ oz.) active dry
   yeast
¼ cup warm tap water
½ cup milk, scalded
3 T. butter or margarine
3 T. sugar
¾ tsp. salt
2½ - 2¾ cups sifted all-
   purpose flour
1 egg, beaten
½ tsp. vanilla
Cinnamon
Sugar
Soft margarine (in a tub)
Brown sugar

Soften the yeast in warm water. Melt the 3 tablespoons of butter in the milk on the stove. Combine milk, butter, sugar and salt; cool to lukewarm; add 1 cup of the flour; beat well. Add the softened yeast, egg and vanilla. Mix in enough flour to make a soft dough. Knead lightly on floured surface. Place in a greased bowl; turn once to grease surface. Cover, let rise until double (1½-2 hours). Knead dough 100 times. Cut in half, shape into a flat round. Roll to 13×9" rectangle, about ¼" thick. Spread with soft margarine, then sprinkle sugar and cinnamon. Roll lengthwise, jelly roll fashion, seal edge. Slice twelve rolls out of dough. In muffin pan, sprinkle about ½ teaspoon brown sugar in each muffin cup, top with ¼ teaspoon soft margarine. Place one roll in each cup. Cover, allow to rise ½ hour. Bake at 325° for 9 minutes. (Some ovens are colder and rolls should be baked at a little higher temperature. When rolls are finished they look a yellowish-white. Don't overbake because the sugar/butter base will burn!) Serve warmed from oven.

These are small, so plan to make a double recipe for a party of eight.

Janet Peterson (Mrs. Fred)

BUTTERSCOTCH CRESCENT ROLLS   36 Rolls

This recipe may look long and complicated, but actually it is very simple and the product is quite special

DOUGH:
1 pkg. (¼ oz.) yeast
¼ cup lukewarm water
1 pkg. (3⁵/₈ oz.)
    butterscotch pudding
    mix (not instant)
1½ cups evaporated milk
    less 2 T. (reserve for
    glaze)
½ cup butter or margarine
2 eggs
2 tsp. salt
4½ - 5 cups flour

FILLING:
¼ cup butter or margarine,
    melted
⅔ cup coconut, grated or
    chopped
⅔ cup brown sugar, firmly
    packed
⅓ cup nuts, finely chopped
2 T. flour

GLAZE:
¼ cup brown sugar
2 T. evaporated milk
2 T. butter
1 cup powdered sugar,
    sifted

For dough: Soften yeast in lukewarm water; allow to stand at least 5 minutes. Cook pudding with evaporated milk. When thickened, add butter and cool to lukewarm. Blend in unbeaten eggs, salt, and softened yeast. Gradually add enough flour to make a stiff dough, beating well after each addition. Cover and let rise in a warm place (85°-90°F.) until light and double in bulk, about 1½ hours. Punch down and divide dough into thirds. Roll each third into a 15 inch circle. Cut into 12 pie shaped pieces.

For filling: Combine ingredients. Place rounded teaspoon of filling on each piece; roll up starting with wide end and rolling to point. Place point side down on greased cookie sheet, curving to a crescent shape. Let rise until light, about 1 hour. Bake at 375° for 12-15 minutes.

For glaze: Combine brown sugar, milk and butter. Blend in powdered sugar. Glaze while rolls are still warm.

Olivette Werling (Mrs. R.R.)

STARLIGHT SUGAR CRISPS

48 Rolls

1 pkg. (¼ oz.) dry yeast
¼ cup lukewarm water
3½ cups sifted flour
1½ tsp. salt
½ cup (1 stick) butter
½ cup shortening
2 eggs, beaten
½ cup sour cream
3 tsp. vanilla
1½ cups sugar

Dissolve yeast in water. Sift flour with salt; cut in butter and shortening. Blend in eggs, sour cream, 1 teaspoon vanilla and yeast. Mix well. Cover. Chill at least 2 hours. (dough may be stored in refrigerator up to 4 days and baked as needed.) Mix sugar and remaining vanilla (2 teaspoons) and sprinkle board with about ½ cup of this mixture. Roll out half of dough to a 16×8" rectangle; sprinkle with 1 tablespoon more vanilla-sugar. Fold one end of dough over center. Fold opposite end over to make 3 layers. Turn ¼ way around and repeat rolling and folding twice, sprinkling board with additional vanilla-sugar as needed. Roll out about ¼" thick. Cut into 4×1" strips, twist each strip 2 or 3 times. Place on ungreased baking sheets. Repeat entire process with remaining dough. Bake at 375° for 15-20 minutes or until golden brown.

Karin Pells (Mrs. Harry G.)

UNCLE STEVE'S POPOVERS

8-10 Popovers

Great brunch conversation piece!

Cooking oil
1 cup flour
½ tsp. salt
2 eggs
1 cup milk

Preheat oven for 20 minutes at 450°. Pour cooking oil in muffin tins. Fill them ¼ full. Let them heat with oil in oven for a good 10 minutes. Prepare batter: mix flour and salt. Beat eggs and milk. Combine liquid and dry mixtures and beat until well combined. The batter should have the consistency of heavy cream. Pull out the hot popover tins and fill just over ½ full (no more) with batter. Bake for 20 minutes. Reduce heat to 375° and bake for 20-30 minutes more.

Serve smothered in butter.

Nancy Thompson (Mrs. Robert)

CRISPY NUT ROLLS

20 Rolls

1 pkg. (¼ oz.) dry yeast
¼ cup warm water
¼ cup sugar
½ tsp. salt
½ cup milk
1 egg, beaten
2½ cups flour
½ cup (1 stick) margarine
¼ cup margarine, melted
1 cup pecans, finely
   chopped
1½ cups sugar

Dissolve yeast in warm water. Stir in sugar, salt, milk and beaten egg. Add 2 cups flour and beat until smooth. Turn onto floured board and sprinkle with remaining ½ cup flour. Roll to ¼" thickness. Divide ½ cup margarine into 8 parts. Put 4 parts down in middle of dough. Fold bottom over middle. Then place remaining 4 parts margarine on that and fold top third of dough over. Roll out. Fold in thirds again and roll. Repeat 4 or 5 times. Roll into 13×15" rectangle. Brush with melted (¼ cup) margarine. Mix pecans with sugar and sprinkle ¼ of it over pastry. Roll up like jelly roll and cut in 1½" slices. Place rolls on cookie sheet (cut side down with pecan-sugar mixture showing). Chill about 30 minutes. Remove from refrigerator and let stand 5 minutes. Place remaining pecan and sugar mixture on board. Roll each piece of dough in sugar mixture into rounds which are ¼" thick. Turn to coat each side. Rolls should be 4"-5" in diameter. Place on greased baking sheet. Let rise about 45 minutes. Bake in preheated 375° oven for 15 minutes.

Kathleen Butterworth (Mrs. Ben)

SOPAIPILLAS

24 Puffs

**These crisp, fried puffs are excellent
served in place of bread with Mexican food**

1 pkg. (¼ oz.) active dry
   yeast
¼ cup warm water
¾ cup milk, scalded
6 T. sugar
2 T. shortening
1 tsp. salt
1 egg, beaten
3 cups all-purpose
   flour (approximate)

Soften active dry yeast in warm water (110°F.). Combine milk, sugar, shortening, and salt; cool to lukewarm. Add softened yeast and egg. Gradually stir in flour; mix to a smooth dough. Let rise until double in bulk, about 1½ hours. Roll on floured surface to square 12×12"; cut in 24 strips, 2×3". Fry in hot deep fat (350°) about 3 minutes, turning once. Keep them warm in the oven until all are fried, then serve.

These are delicious served with honey.

Mary Glockhoff (Mrs. Roy H.)

REFRIGERATOR BRAN MUFFINS   7-8 Dozen

A bowl of prepared batter makes a nice gift.

6 cups bran
2 cups boiling water
1 cup butter, melted
3 cups sugar
4 eggs, beaten
1 quart buttermilk
5 cups flour
5 tsp. soda
2 tsp. salt

Pour boiling water over 2 cups of bran and let stand while assembling other ingredients. Add butter. Mix in remaining bran with sugar, eggs and buttermilk. Sift flour with soda and salt. Combine all ingredients and put in refrigerator. When needed, fill muffin tins ⅔ full and bake at 400° for 20 minutes. This mixture will keep six weeks in refrigerator. You can add variety by including dates, nuts, raisins or candied fruits at baking time.

Annabelle DeCock (Mrs. Dale)

DATE-PECAN MUFFINS   48 Miniature Muffins

Great for ladies' luncheon.

2 eggs, well beaten
1 cup light brown sugar
1 tsp. vanilla
⅔ cup flour
¼ tsp. baking powder
¼ tsp. salt
¾ cup dates, finely
   chopped
¾ cup pecans, finely
   chopped

FILLING:
1 pkg. (3 oz.) cream
   cheese
Orange marmalade

Cream eggs, sugar and vanilla. Sift flour, baking powder and salt together. Add to eggs and blend well. Add dates and nuts which have been very finely diced. Mix and spoon into miniature muffin pans which have been greased with spray cooking oil. Fill about ⅔ full. Bake at 400° for about 10 minutes or until lightly browned. Run a knife around the edge and turn onto rack to cool.

Filling: Prepare by mixing softened cream cheese with enough orange marmalade to make a spreading consistency. Split muffins and fill with cheese mixture just before serving. Let cheese ooze out a little.

Serve on footed cake plate for a fancy buffet.

Jackie Matthews (Mrs. Ben)

52

APPLE BREAD

1 Large Loaf
or 4 Mini - Loaves

½ cup shortening
1 cup sugar
2 eggs
3 T. sour milk or buttermilk
2 cups flour
½ tsp. salt
1 tsp. baking powder
1 cup apples, peeled
  and chopped
½ cup nuts, chopped
½ tsp. vanilla

Cream shortening and sugar. Add eggs and mix well. Sift dry ingredients and add alternately with milk. Stir in apple, nuts and vanilla. Pour into 1 large loaf pan or 4 mini - loaf pans, (well greased and floured). Bake at 350° for 1 hour (large loaf) or for 40 minutes (small loaves). You may add a mashed banana, a touch of orange peel or increase the chopped apple.

This is a moist fruit bread.

Bonnie Brotman (Mrs. Jerrel)

APPLESAUCE NUT BREAD

1 Large Loaf

1 cup granulated sugar
1 cup applesauce
⅓ cup oil
2 eggs
3 T. milk
2 cups sifted flour
1 tsp. baking soda
½ tsp. baking powder
½ tsp. cinnamon
¼ tsp. salt
¼ tsp. nutmeg
¾ cup chopped pecans

Combine sugar, applesauce, oil, eggs and milk. Add flour, baking soda, baking powder, cinnamon, salt and nutmeg and beat until well combined. Stir in pecan pieces. Pour into well greased and floured 9×5×3″ metal loaf pan. Combine ¼ cup brown sugar, ½ teaspoon cinnamon, and ¼ cup pecans and sprinkle over top of batter. Bake at 350° for 1 hour. After first 30 minutes, cap loosely with foil.

Mary Jo Jensen (Mrs. Henry)

ZUCCHINI BREAD

2 Loaves

3 eggs, beaten
1 cup oil
2 cups sugar
2 cups grated zucchini
2 tsp. vanilla
3 cups flour
½ tsp. baking powder
1 tsp. salt
1 tsp. soda
2 tsp. cinnamon
¾ cup chopped nuts

Add oil, sugar, zucchini and vanilla to the beaten eggs. Sift dry ingredients together and add to batter. Add nuts and place in 2 buttered 8×4×2" loaf pans. Bake at 350° for 1 hour.

Shan Corelis (Mrs. John)

PUMPKIN BREAD

2 Large Loaves

⅔ cup shortening
2⅔ cup sugar
4 eggs
1 can (16 oz.) pumpkin
⅔ cup water
3⅓ cup flour
2 tsp. soda
1½ tsp. salt
½ tsp. baking powder
1 tsp. cinnamon
1 tsp. ground cloves
⅔ cup chopped nuts
⅔ cup raisins

Cream shortening and sugar. Beat in eggs, one at a time. Add pumpkin, water and all sifted dry ingredients and blend well. Stir in nuts and raisins. Pour into greased 9×5×3" loaf pans. Bake at 350° for 60-75 minutes.

Jan Crow (Mrs. David)

EASY BOSTON BROWN BREAD

1 Loaf

1 cup raisins
2 cups water
1 T. shortening
1 cup sugar
Pinch of salt
1 tsp. baking powder
2 tsp. baking soda
2¾ cup flour
1 egg

Boil raisins, water and shortening for 10 minutes. Add sugar, salt, baking powder, baking soda, flour and egg. Mix well. Pour into greased 9×5" loaf pan. Bake at 350° for 1 hour.

Kathy Reimers (Mrs. John)

54

FANCIED FRUIT BREAD   2 Loaves

½ cup margarine, softened,
  or oil
1 cup sugar
2 eggs, beaten
3 bananas, mashed
2 cups flour
1 tsp. baking soda
½ tsp. salt
¼ cup chopped nuts,
  (walnuts or pecans)
¾ cup chocolate chips
¼ cup maraschino cherries,
  chopped

Cream shortening and sugar, stir in eggs
and mashed bananas and mix well. Add
the flour which has been sifted with the
soda and salt, stirring only until dry ingredients are well moistened. Stir in the nuts,
chips, and cherries, just to mix. Pour into
greased and floured 8×4″ loaf pans. Bake
at 350° for about 1 hour.

Harriet Harmelink (Mrs. Roger)

LEMON BREAD   1 Loaf

Delightful and refreshing change for morning coffees and brunches.

5 T. margarine
1 cup sugar
1 tsp. salt
2 eggs
Grated rind of 1 lemon
1½ cups flour
  3 tsp. baking powder
  ½ cup milk
  ½ cup chopped pecans

Juice of 1 lemon
  ½ cup sugar

Cream the margarine and 1 cup of sugar.
Add salt, eggs and grated lemon rind. Beat
well. Add flour, baking powder and milk.
Beat well again. Stir in pecans. Bake in
8×4×2″ greased loaf pan in preheated
350° oven for 35-40 minutes. Remove and
put on rack. Allow to cool slightly. Prick
top several places with a fork.

Heat the lemon juice and ½ cup sugar and
pour over the bread.

Jean Stringham (Mrs. Wally)

SWEDISH TEA LOG

2 Coffee Cakes

A most rich, delicious and elegant coffee cake!

DOUGH:
- 1 pkg. (¼ oz.) dry yeast
- ¼ cup warm water
- 2½ cups sifted all-purpose flour
- 2 T. sugar
- 1 tsp. salt
- ½ cup butter
- ¼ cup evaporated milk
- 1 unbeaten egg
- ¼ cup chopped raisins or currants

FILLING:
- ½ cup butter
- 1 cup brown sugar, firmly packed
- ½ cup chopped pecans

VANILLA GLAZE:
- 2 T. butter
- 1 cup sifted powdered sugar
- ½ tsp. vanilla
- 2 T. milk

For dough: Sift together flour, sugar and salt. Cut in butter until particles are fine. Add evaporated milk, egg, chopped raisins and softened yeast. Mix well. Chill 2 hours or overnight.

For filling: Cream the butter and brown sugar. Stir in pecans. Divide dough in half. Roll out one part on floured surface to an 18×6" rectangle. Spread with ½ of filling. Roll up, starting with 18" side; seal. Place in crescent shape on cookie sheet lined with aluminum foil. Make down-ward cuts through the dough. Each cut should be 1" apart and within ½" of center. Turn cut pieces on sides. Repeat with remaining dough. Let rise in warm place, about 45 minutes. Bake at 350° for 15-20 minutes.

For vanilla glaze: Brown the butter. Add powdered sugar and vanilla. Add milk. Pour over rolls when hot from oven.

Terry Longval (Mrs. Joe)

SIMPLE COFFEE CAKE

1 Coffee Cake

BATTER MIXTURE:
- 1 cup liquid shortening
- 1 cup sugar
- 2 eggs, beaten
- 1 tsp. vanilla
- ½ tsp. salt
- 3 tsp. baking powder
- 3 cups flour
- 1 cup milk

SUGAR MIXTURE:
- 1½ cups brown sugar
- 1 cup nuts
- 2 tsp. cinnamon

- ½ cup melted butter

For batter mixture: Blend sugar and shortening. Add eggs and dry ingredients, blend well. Add milk.

For sugar mixture: Combine brown sugar, nuts and cinnamon.

To assemble: Put half of the batter into a greased 9×12" cake pan, then sprinkle with half of the sugar mixture. Repeat this step. Drizzle the melted butter over the top. Bake at 375° for 25-30 minutes.

Jan Illingsworth (Mrs. R.N.)

SEED CAKE

1 Bundt Coffee Cake

Also makes a delicous dessert cake.

⅔ cup butter
2 cups sugar
4 eggs
2 T. grated orange rind
1 T. grated lemon rind
2½ tsp. baking powder
1 tsp. nutmeg
3 cups flour
1 tsp. salt
1 cup milk
1 tsp. cardamom seed
1 T. poppy seed
1 T. anise seed

GLAZE:
2 T. orange juice
1 tsp. lemon juice
1 cup sifted confectioners
  sugar

Cream butter and sugar until quite fluffy. Add unbeaten eggs one at a time and beat well after each addition. Then add grated rinds. Sift flour, salt, baking powder and nutmeg together. Add alternately with milk. Add about ¾ of the seeds with the last half of the flour. Reserve the rest of seeds. Pour into a large greased tube or bundt pan. Sprinkle remaining seeds on top of batter. Bake at 350° for 1 hour or until it recedes from edge of pan. Leave cake in pan to cool about 20 minutes. Remove from pan. While still warm, cover with glaze.

Joann Hanson (Mrs. James C.)

BOSTON BLUEBERRY COFFEE CAKE

1 Coffee Cake

½ cup (1 stick) margarine
1 cup sugar
1 egg, unbeaten
2½ cups sifted flour
2½ tsp. baking powder
½ tsp. salt
½ cup milk
2 cups (1 pint) blueberries

Beat shortening and sugar; add egg and beat again. Sift in dry ingredients and add milk. Beat again - - batter will be stiff. Fold in blueberries (which have been rinsed in cold water and dried well on paper towels). Gently spoon batter into greased 9×9″ pan or angel food tin. Sprinkle sugar over top and bake at 350° for 45 minutes, until golden brown.

Kay Kaleba (Mrs. Richard)

PANCAKES FROM SESAME STREET AND
BOB McGRATH
1 cup serves 4

Let the kids put these together for Sunday brunch!

SESAME SEED PANCAKES

Pancake batter
Sesame seeds
Syrup
Butter

Mix up pancake batter, pour large puddle on a griddle or pan. Sprinkle with sesame seeds on top. Turn when cooked. Serve.

BANANA PANCAKES

Pancake batter
Bananas, thinly sliced
Syrup
Butter

Mix up pancake batter, pour large puddle on a griddle or pan. Put slices of banana on top. Turn when cooked (don't undercook).

BOB McGRATH

Bob McGrath

In 1976, BOB McGRATH, who has "lived" on Sesame Street since its inception, provided a special Valentine treat for Family Concert Series goers. Appearing with his own family and the Tri-City Symphony, he sang his way into hearts of all with his rendition of favorite Sesame Street songs and ballads.

SOUR CREAM PANCAKES

6-8 Servings

¼ cup melted butter
2 T. sugar
4 eggs, separated and
  beaten
1 cup half and half cream
2 cups dairy sour cream
1 tsp. soda
1 cup sifted flour
½ tsp. salt

Mix all ingredients well. Fold in the stiffly beaten egg whites last. Bake on a hot griddle.

Will keep well refrigerated several days.

Darline Streed (Mrs. Warren)

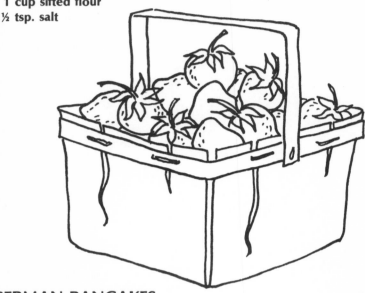

GERMAN PANCAKES

4-6 Pancakes

Great breakfast for guests!

¼ cup butter
½ cup flour
½ cup milk
2 eggs
Dash nutmeg (optional)

Preheat oven to 425°F. Put butter in 10" fry pan and set in oven. While heating, mix remaining ingredients to smooth batter, may add optional dash of nutmeg. Stir with fork to smooth consistency. Add to melted butter in pan, and bake in oven for 20 minutes. Serve cut into wedges with any toppings of your choice. (Will resemble large mixing bowl in shape when done.)

May be served with strawberries and whipped cream as a dessert, meat fillings as main dish - - use your imagination!

Jan McMillan

CHEESE PANCAKES

4 Servings

1 lb. cottage cheese or
   Farmer's cheese
3 large eggs
½ cup matzo meal
1 T. sour cream (heaping)
1 T. sugar
½ tsp. salt
Cinnamon and sugar
   to taste
Extra sour cream

Mix cheese, eggs, matzo meal, sour cream, sugar and salt together as for any pancake batter; then fry on oiled griddle like regular pancakes. Serve with cinnamon and sugar and sour cream. If preferred, the cinnamon can be mixed with other dry ingredients.

ROBERT MERRILL

Robert Merrill

ROBERT MERRILL, star baritone of the Metropolitan Opera, is one of the world's most celebrated artists. He is well known to millions through his countless performances on opera and concert stages as well as his frequent appearances on television and at major music festivals. One of the Tri-City's favorite artists, Robert Merrill last appeared with the Tri-City Symphony in February, 1976, thrilling the audiences with his operatic renditions from "Don Carlos", "Andrea Chenier", "La Traviata", "Don Giovanni" and "Othello", as well as "Medea's Meditation and Dance of Vengeance" by Barber.

EBLESKIVER (DANISH PANCAKES)   24 Pancakes

2 eggs
1 T. sugar
2 cups flour
1 tsp. baking powder
½ tsp. soda
½ tsp. salt
½ tsp. cardamom
½ tsp. grated lemon rind
1½ cups buttermilk

Beat eggs and sugar well. Sift dry ingredients and add to egg mixture. Add buttermilk and beat until batter is smooth. Fry in ebleskiverpan as follows: Heat pan over medium heat, melt 1 teaspoon butter in each hole. Fill holes completely, let bake over heated burner for a few minutes. Turn ebleskiver with a meat skewer. Fry until golden brown. Serve hot with jam and sugar.

Mary Greenberg (Mrs. Martin)

RAISED WAFFLES   6 Servings

Prepare the night before, for a fast breakfast.

½ cup lukewarm water
1 pkg. (¼ oz.) yeast
2 cups lukewarm milk
1 tsp. salt
1 tsp. sugar
½ cup butter, melted or salad oil
2 cups flour
2 eggs
Pinch of baking soda

Combine water and yeast in a large mixing bowl and let stand for five minutes. Then add milk, salt, sugar and butter. Beat in 2 cups flour until batter is smooth. Cover the bowl and let stand overnight or at least eight hours at room temperature. When it is time to cook waffles, add eggs and soda. beat well. The batter will be very thin. Cook on hot waffle iron.

Olivette Werling (Mrs. R.R.)

SALADS

SUNSHINE SALAD

12 Servings

1 pkg. (6 oz.) orange
  flavored gelatin
2 cups boiling water
1 cup apricot juice
½ cup pineapple juice
1 can (16 oz.) apricots,
  mashed and drained,
  reserve liquid
1 can (20 oz.) crushed
  pineapple, drained,
  reserve liquid

TOPPING:
½ cup sugar
3 T. flour
2 T. butter
1 egg, beaten
½ cup pineapple juice
½ cup apricot juice
1 cup heavy cream,
  whipped
Cheddar cheese, grated

Dissolve gelatin in hot water in glass 9×9″ pan. Add 1½ cups juice drained from cans. Stir well. Add mashed apricots and pineapple. Refrigerate until firm.

For topping: Combine sugar, flour, butter and egg and beat well. Stir in juices. Cook over medium heat until thickened. Let cool. Whip cream until stiff. Fold into above mixture. Spread over top of gelatin. Chill. Cheese may be grated over top if desired. This salad also may be molded in a 2 quart mold, then serve the topping in a separate dish.

Judy Knutson (Mrs. Eugene)
Lynn Goebel (Mrs. George)

CONSTANCE'S THANKSGIVING SALAD

12 Servings

This recipe originated in Honolulu, Hawaii.

1 pkg. (6 oz.) peach
  flavored gelatin
3⅓ cups peach nectar,
  heated
4 T. diced preserved
  ginger
1 cup Raffettos nut
  chutney
⅔ cup celery, diced
1 can (8 oz.) crushed
  pineapple with juice
Watercress
Mayonnaise
Light cream
Curry powder

Dissolve gelatin in hot nectar. Chill until it begins to set. Then add ginger, chutney, celery and pineapple. Place in 12 individual molds. Chill until firm. Garnish with watercress and serve with mayonnaise thinned with cream and a touch of curry powder.

Mollie Montgomery (Mrs. Thomas)

64

BANANA-PINEAPPLE SALAD

8-10 Servings

1 cup pineapple juice
1 pkg. (3 oz.) lemon
   flavored gelatin
1 pkg. (3 oz.) cream
   cheese
1 banana, diced
4 slices pineapple, diced
½ cup walnuts, chopped
1 cup heavy cream,
   whipped

Bring pineapple juice to a boil and dissolve lemon gelatin in hot juice. Add cream cheese which has been whipped until fluffy. Add pineapple, banana and nuts. Whip cream until stiff. Fold in whipping cream. Place in a 1 quart mold and refrigerate for at least 4 hours.

Karen Hanson

FRUITED NECTAR SALAD

6-8 Servings

1 can (12 oz.) apricot
   nectar
1 pkg. (3 oz.) lemon
   flavored gelatin
½ cup water
1 T. lemon juice
1 can (11 oz.) mandarin
   orange sections, drained
1 cup seedless grapes,
   halved

Heat nectar to boiling. Add gelatin; stir until dissolved. Add water and lemon juice. Chill until partially set; fold in oranges and grapes. Pour into 4½ cup mold. Chill until firm. Before serving, unmold salad on to lettuce lined plate. If desired, serve with mayonnaise.

Gail A. Diehl (Mrs. David)

Mayonnaise

BLUEBERRY SALAD

6-8 Servings

Deliciously different!

1 pkg. (3 oz.) red raspberry
  flavored gelatin
1 cup hot water
1 can (8 oz.) crushed
  pineapple, drained,
  reserve liquid
1 can (20 oz.) blueberries,
  drained, reserve liquid
1 cup mixture of pineapple
  and blueberry juice
½ cup chopped nuts
  (optional)
1 cup heavy cream,
  whipped
Cheddar cheese, shredded

Mix gelatin and hot water together, stir until gelatin is completely dissolved. Combine pineapple, blueberries, juice and nuts and add to gelatin. Pour into a 2 quart salad mold. Chill until firm. Top with cream whipped until stiff. Sprinkle shredded cheddar cheese over topping.

Chris Ahlstrand (Mrs. David)

MANDARIN ORANGE SOUFFLE

12 Servings

1 pkg. (6 oz.) orange
  flavored gelatin
1 cup hot water
1 cup orange juice
1 cup sour cream
2 cups orange sherbet
1 cup pineapple tidbits
2 cups mandarin oranges,
  well-drained
1 cup coconut
Lettuce leaves or mint

Add hot water to gelatin. Stir until dissolved, then add orange juice. Chill until mixture begins to thicken, about 10-15 minutes. Stir in sour cream and orange sherbet. Beat until thick and foamy. Fold in drained pineapple and oranges. Pour into a 2 quart greased mold. When set, turn onto lettuce leaves, or decorate with mint leaves. Sprinkle with coconut and garnish with orange sections.

Mary Anne Dailey (Mrs. William H.)

CRANBERRY SALAD

12 Servings

1 lb. raw cranberries
¾ cup water
1½ cup sugar
1 pkg. (6 oz.) cherry
  flavored gelatin
1 cup celery, chopped
1 cup apples, chopped
1 cup grapes, seeded
  and chopped
1 cup pineapple chunks
1 cup pecans, coarsely
  chopped

Cook cranberries, water and sugar together until cranberry skins pop. Stir in gelatin and let it cool. Add celery, apples, grapes, pineapple and nuts. Place in a 9×12" glass pan. Refrigerate overnight, or until firm. (An orange, with rind finely chopped, adds an interesting variation.)

Carole Sissel (Mrs. Gary)

24-HOUR FRUIT SALAD

10-12 Servings

"A special salad served for years at family Thanksgiving dinners"

3 egg yolks
2 T. sugar
2 T. cider vinegar
2 T. pineapple juice
2 cups pineapple chunks
2 cups White Royal Anne
  cherries
2 cups mandarin oranges
2 cups miniature
  marshmallows
1 cup heavy cream,
  whipped

Cook egg yolks, sugar, vinegar and pineapple juice over very low heat until thickend. Set aside to cool. Meanwhile, drain fruits very well and pit cherries. Whip the cream. Add the egg yolk mixture and blend until smooth. Add the marshmallows to the fruit and fold in the whipped cream-egg yolk mixture. Place in a serving bowl and chill 24 hours, or overnight.

Mary Hass (Mrs. Arthur)

GRAPEFRUIT SALAD

6-8 Servings

2 (¼ oz. each) envelopes
  unflavored gelatin
½ cup cold water
½ cup boiling water
Pulp and juice of three
  grapefruit
1 cup sugar
½ tsp. onion juice

Dissolve gelatin in ½ cup cold water; let stand 5 minutes (no more). Add ½ cup boiling water; stir until completely dissolved. Meanwhile, remove pulp and juice from grapefruit. Add sugar and onion juice to grapefruit and stir. Add gelatin and pour into ring mold. Chill and serve.

Heather Gosma (Mrs. John S.)

PINEAPPLE/RASPBERRY MOLD

6-8 Servings

1 pkg. (3 oz.) raspberry
  gelatin
1 pkg (3 oz.) lemon
  gelatin
1 cup boiling water
1 can (13 oz.) evaporated
  milk, chilled
1 can (8 oz.) crushed
  pineapple, undrained
½ cup pecans

In blender place gelatin and boiling water. Blend until dissolved. Add milk and pineapple. Blend 10 seconds. Add nuts and blend 5 seconds until nuts are coarsely chopped. Pour into mold and chill until set. Unmold and serve.

Rochelle Livingston (Mrs. Albert)

FROZEN FRUIT SQUARES

6-8 Servings

1 pkg. (8 oz.) cream
  cheese, softened
1 cup sour cream
¼ cup sugar
¼ tsp. salt
1 can (16 oz.) apricot
  halves, drained
1 can (16 oz.) crushed
  pineapple, drained
1 can (16 oz.) pitted
  dark sweet cherries,
  drained
1 cup miniature
  marshmallows

In large mixing bowl, beat cheese until smooth. Add sour cream, sugar and salt; blend on low speed; cut apricots in half. Stir fruits and marshmallows into cheese mixture. Pour into a 9×9" pan. Freeze overnight. Let stand 10-15 minutes before serving.

Kristyn Mahler (Mrs. Michael)

FROZEN FRUIT CUP   20 Servings

Also makes a delicous refreshing dessert.

Juice of 2 oranges
Juice of 2 lemons
Rind of 1 orange
3 bananas, diced
3 cups crushed pineapple
    (do not drain)
½ cup sugar
1 qt. ginger ale

Mix all of the ingredients together in a large container. If other fruit is in season (i.e.; blueberries, strawberries), they can also be added. Spoon mixture into foil cup-cake holders being sure to put solid fruit in each cup equally. Freeze. Ten minutes before serving remove from the freezer. To serve, arrange on a large platter.

Theona Fahl (Mrs. John W.)
Janet Schwarz (Mrs. Eric)

FROZEN CRANBERRY SUPREME   10 Servings

Needs to be prepared two days in advance - well worth the fuss!

1 cup raw cranberries,
    chopped
¾ cup sugar
1 cup heavy cream,
    whipped
1 pkg. (3 oz.) cream
    cheese at room temp.
2 bananas, diced
½ lb. Tokay grapes,
    halved and seeded

Combine cranberries and sugar and allow to stand overnight. Whip cream until stiff. Blend in cream cheese until smooth. Fold in bananas and grapes. Add to cranberries and sugar. Pour into 2 quart mold. Freeze overnight. Remove from freezer 1 hour before serving.

Helen DeKalb (Mrs. James)

MANDARIN ORANGE AND LETTUCE SALAD

DRESSING:
2 tsp. salt
1 tsp. paprika
1 tsp. pepper
¼ tsp. dry mustard
¼ tsp. powdered sugar
¼ cup vinegar
1 cup salad oil

SALAD:
6 pieces crisp bacon, crumbled
¼ cup toasted almonds
1 can (8 oz.) mandarin oranges, drained
2 large Bib or Boston lettuce heads

8 Servings

For dressing: Combine all ingredients and shake well. Chill until ready to use. (Use dressing sparingly as this recipe makes enough dressing for several salads and can be kept refrigerated for several weeks.)

For salad: Combine ingredients in large salad bowl. Toss with small amount of dressing. For variation: you may also add celery and green onions to the lettuce.

Anne Nagan (Mrs. Mark)
Pat Agnew (Mrs. Robert)

FRUIT SALAD WITH SWEET SOUR DRESSING

DRESSING:
¾ cup sugar
¼ cup vinegar
¼ tsp. salt
1 cup salad oil, chilled
1 - 2 tsp. onion, grated
1 T. poppy seed

SALAD:
2 cans (11 oz. each) chilled mandarin oranges
2 cans (16 oz. each) chilled grapefruit sections
2 avocados
1 pkg. (4 oz.) bleu cheese, crumbled
Lettuce

4-6 Servings

For dressing: Whip sugar, vinegar and salt until sugar is dissolved. Add cold oil, grated onion and poppy seed. Stir well with fork or whisk.

For salad: Place several lettuce leaves on a plate, arrange orange and grapefruit sections, place slices of avocado around them, sprinkle with crumbled bleu cheese. Pour dressing over all.

Jan Crow (Mrs. David)

SPINACH SALAD

DRESSING:
- ½ cup olive oil
- ¼ cup cider vinegar
- ¼ cup sugar
- ½ tsp. salt
- ¼ tsp. dry mustard
- ⅛ tsp. coarsely ground fresh pepper
- ¼ tsp. celery salt
- ½ small white onion, finely chopped

SALAD:
- 1½ lbs. fresh spinach, washed and trimmed
- 9 fresh mushrooms, sliced
- ½ lb. bacon, fried, drained and crumbled
- 1 can (11 oz.) mandarin oranges, drained
- 1 large ripe avocado

For dressing: Combine all ingredients in a jar with a lid. Shake thoroughly. Refrigerate until ready to use. Shake again before pouring over salad.

For salad: Chill all ingredients. Tear spinach into bite-size pieces. Mix spinach, mushrooms and half the bacon and oranges together in a large bowl. Just before serving, slice and add avocado. Toss with dressing. Top with remaining bacon and oranges. For variation: Add hard cooked eggs or grated cheese.

Sandy Hass (Mrs. John)
Joan Mills (Mrs. Judd)

CEASAR SALAD

- ⅔ cup salad oil
- 1 clove garlic, crushed
- 2 qts. Romaine lettuce, torn
- 1½ cups dry bread cubes
- ½ tsp. salt
- Freshly ground black pepper
- 2 eggs boiled - 1 minute
- ¼ cup lemon juice
- 4 - 6 anchovy fillets, chopped
- ½ cup grated parmesan cheese

Combine garlic and oil. Let stand at room temperature for three hours. Place washed and drained greens in a bowl lined with paper towels. Cover and chill. Brown bread cubes in 3 T. garlic oil. Remove towels from bowl. Salt and pepper greens. Pour remaining oil on and toss. Add eggs and lemon juice, toss well. Sprinkle with anchovies and cheese. Toss lightly. Add bread croutons. Toss just until mixed. Serve immediately on chilled plates.

Jean C. McHard

GREEN SALAD WITH SOUR CREAM DRESSING

DRESSING:

6-8 Servings

1 cup sour cream
1 small onion, finely
  chopped
1 tsp. sugar
½ tsp. salt
¼ tsp. pepper
3 T. white wine vinegar
2 T. bacon drippings

For dressing: Mix together all ingredients, thoroughly. Allow at least one hour for dressing to chill and blend.

For salad: Pile greens into large salad bowl, pour dressing over them. Mix lightly to coat completely. Sprinkle bacon bits over all.

SALAD:

2 qts. salad greens, chilled
  and torn
6 slices fried bacon,
  drained and crumbled

Heather Gosma (Mrs. John S.)

MARINATED MUSHROOM SALAD

12 Servings

1 lb. fresh mushrooms
2 medium onions, thinly
  sliced
⅔ cup salad oil
½ cup tarragon wine
  vinegar
2 - 4 drops Tabasco sauce
1 tsp. salt
4 tsp. parsley, minced
2 medium heads lettuce
2 large tomatoes, peeled

Rinse mushrooms, pat dry and slice lengthwise through stems. Combine mushrooms and onions. Over this, pour salad oil, vinegar and seasonings. Mix gently. Cover, let stand at least 4 hours. Wash lettuce, drain well, wrap in damp towel, refrigerate until chilled and crisp. Break lettuce. Add tomato wedges, then marinated onions and mushrooms and toss. Serve immediately.

Heather Gosma (Mrs. John S.)

MARINATED CARROT SALAD

10-12 Servings

"Everyone enjoys this unusual use of the carrot!"

5 cups carrots, sliced
  and cooked
1 onion, sliced
1 green pepper, chopped

DRESSING:
  1 tsp. salt
  ½ tsp. pepper
  1 can (10¾ oz.) tomato
    soup
  ½ cup salad oil
  ¾ cup white sugar
  ¼ cup brown sugar
  ½ cup vinegar
  1 tsp. dry mustard
  1 tsp. Worcestershire
    sauce

Cook carrots for 5 minutes only so they are still slightly firm. Pour blended dressing over carrots, onions and peppers. Let marinate in a 2 quart casserole with lid overnight in the refrigerator. This is a great dish for a potluck or picnic.

Mr. and Mrs. William A. Quiram

FRESH VEGETABLE MARINADE

4-6 Servings

2 cups fresh broccoli
2 cups cherry tomatoes
½ lb. fresh mushrooms
1 medium onion
1 medium green pepper
1 pkg. (6 oz.) Italian
  dressing mix
½ cup vinegar
2 T. water
⅔ cup salad oil
1 T. dill weed

Cut broccoli into chunks, slice the onion and cut green pepper into strips. Prepare dressing by combining dressing mix, vinegar, water, oil and dill weed. Mix well. Marinate fresh vegetables in dressing for a few hours or overnight. Cucumbers are also quite good in this salad.

Annabelle DeCock (Mrs. Dale)

SPROUT KRAUT

12-15 Servings

"Especially good for a summertime relish tray."

2 cups sugar
⅔ cup vinegar
½ tsp. salt
1 can (27 oz.) sauerkraut
1 can (16 oz.) bean
 sprouts, drained
1 jar (2 oz.) pimento,
 chopped
1 cup celery, chopped
2 cups green pepper,
 chopped

Mix first three ingredients and let stand while you prepare the vegetables. Mix remaining ingredients and add the dressing. Chill in tightly covered quart jars at least three hours. Can be stored in refrigerator up to a month.

Lynn Batcher (Mrs. Richard)

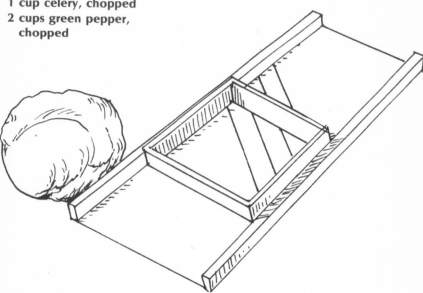

GERMAN COLESLAW

8 Servings

1 head cabbage, shredded
2 onions, sliced thinly
⁷/₈ cup sugar

DRESSING:

¾ cup vinegar
¾ cup salad oil
1 tsp. dry mustard
1 tsp. celery seed
2 T. sugar

Layer the cabbage and onions in glass or pottery bowl. Cover with 7/8 cup sugar. Boil dressing ingredients and pour over cabbage while still hot. Refrigerate covered, overnight.

Jan Crow (Mrs. David)

CELERY VICTOR SALAD   6 Servings

3 bunches celery, about 2
   inches in diameter
1½ cups chicken stock
   (fresh or canned)
4 sprigs parsley
1 bay leaf
Celery leaves (tied together)
Salt
Freshly ground pepper
3 T. white wine vinegar
½ cup olive oil
12 flat anchovy fillets
12 strips pimento
6 tomato slices
6 hard cooked eggs, sliced
1½ tsp. parsley, chopped

Remove outer stalks of celery, cut each celery heart into sections ending up about 1 inch wide and 6 inches long. Cut away all but small leaves and barely trim root ends (Do not cut too deep, as you want sections to hold together). Place in skillet side by side. Cover with chicken stock, herb bouquet; salt and pepper to taste. Bring to a boil; cover tightly; reduce heat and simmer about 15 minutes (until tender). Place on deep platter, single layer, with tongs or vegetable spoon. With a whisk, beat vinegar and oil together and pour over the celery while still warm. Refrigerate at least an hour, overnight won't hurt.

For serving: Place on chilled salad plate and criss-cross 2 anchovy fillets and 2 strips of pimento, sliced tomato and sliced hard boiled eggs. Moisten with spoonful or two of vinegar-oil sauce. Sprinkle with chopped parsley.

Mary Thoms (Mrs. Stuart W.)

TOMATOES VINAIGRETTE AUX HERBES   4 Servings

"An easy substitute for lettuce salad"

2 red, ripe, unblemished
   tomatoes
Salt
Freshly ground pepper
1 T. red wine vinegar
3 T. olive oil
1 T. chives, finely chopped
1 T. parsley, finely chopped

Refrigerate the tomatoes one day. At this time, prepare the sauce ahead. Blend the vinegar, olive oil, chives and parsley in a tightly covered small jar. Add some salt and pepper to taste. Shake vigorously and refrigerate. Before serving, cut away and discard the core from the tomatoes. Slice the tomatoes and arrange them in a serving dish. Sprinkle with salt and pepper. Pour sauce over tomatoes and serve.

Lance O. Willett

GREEN PEPPER SALAD   10 Servings

DRESSING:
 1 cup olive oil
 ⅓ cup red wine vinegar
 1 clove garlic, crushed
 1 tsp. salt
 1 tsp. tarragon
 ¼ tsp. pepper
 2 T. fresh parsley, chopped
 2 T. fresh chives, chopped

 8 medium green peppers
   (2½ lbs.)
 2 small onions, chilled
 4 large ripe tomatoes
   chilled
 2 cans (2 oz. each)
   anchovy fillets
   (optional)
10 ripe olives
Fresh ground pepper

For dressing: Make vinaigrette dressing in jar with a tight fitting lid. Shake vigorously. Refrigerate until ready to use. Shake again before using.

To prepare green peppers: Wash whole peppers and place on cookie sheet and broil about 6 inches from heat, turning frequently, until skin of peppers becomes blistered and slightly charred-about 15 minutes. Then place peppers in kettle and cover to keep warm for 15 minutes. Meanwhile prepare other vegetables. Then cut each pepper into fourths. Do not peel off charred skin. Remove rib and seeds, cut into julienne strips ½ inch wide. Toss with 1 cup vinaigrette dressing in glass bowl, refrigerate several hours.

To serve: Center a mound of green peppers on a platter. Arrange thinly sliced chilled onion around peppers. Next arrange thinly sliced, chilled tomatoes. Garnish tomatoes with anchovies and olives. Spoon rest of dressing over tomatoes. Grate with fresh pepper.

Carole Beeson (Mrs. Robert)

CUCUMBERS IN SOUR CREAM   8 Servings

DRESSING:
 1 cup sour cream
 2 tsp. salt
 ¼ tsp. Tabasco sauce
 1 T. lemon juice
 2 tsp. fresh dill, chopped
 1 T. chives, chopped

 3 cucumbers peeled,
   sliced and chilled

Combine dressing ingredients and add to the cucumbers. Chill at least ½ hour.

Mary Phares (Mrs. William)

SWEET AND SOUR ZUCCHINI   8 Servings

2 T. dehydrated onions
⅓ cup wine vinegar
5 - 7 zucchini squash
¾ cup sugar
1 tsp. salt
½ tsp. pepper
⅓ cup salad oil
⅔ cup cider vinegar
⅔ cup green pepper,
    chopped
½ cup celery, chopped
1 jar (2 oz.) pimento,
    diced

Soak onions in wine vinegar for 20-30 minutes. Meanwhile, slice zucchini paper thin. Then add sugar, salt, pepper, oil, and cider vinegar to onions. Pour this over zucchini, green pepper, celery and pimento. Marinate for 6 hours, or overnight before serving. This will keep for a week, if refrigerated.

Mary Greenberg (Mrs. Martin)

MOSTACCIOLI SALAD   12-15 Servings

1 lb. Mostaccioli
Oil
1 onion, chopped
1 cucumber, chopped
    (do not peel)

DRESSING:
½ cup sugar
½ cup vinegar
1 tsp. salt
1 tsp. pepper
1 tsp. MSG
1 tsp. garlic powder
2 T. parsley
1 jar (2 oz.) pimento

Cook Mostaccioli in salt water. Drain. Coat with oil until covered and drain again. Add onion and cucumbers. Combine remaining ingredients and pour over salad.

Kathy Reimers (Mrs. John)

HOT POTATO SALAD

6-8 Servings

6 - 8 slices bacon, diced
¼ cup onion, chopped
1 T. flour
1 T. sugar
1½ tsp. salt
Dash pepper
⅓ cup vinegar
¼ cup water
4 cups potatoes, cooked
   and sliced (keep warm)
3 hard cooked eggs, sliced
1 T. parsley, chopped
½ tsp. celery seed

Fry bacon until crisp. Remove bacon and save about 2 T. bacon fat. Add onion to bacon fat and cook 1 minute. Blend in flour, sugar, salt and pepper; add vinegar and water; cook and stir until thick. Pour vinegar mixture over hot potatoes. Layer in serving dish with sliced eggs. Sprinkle with parsley and celery seed. Serve warm.

Charlotte Griggs

SOUR CREAM POTATO TOSS

10-12 Servings

6 cups potatoes peeled,
   cooked and diced
¼ cup green onions with
   tops, chopped
1½ tsp. salt
1 tsp. celery seed
6 hard boiled eggs
1 cup sour cream
½ cup real mayonnaise
2 T. white wine vinegar
1 tsp. prepared mustard

Combine potatoes, chopped green onions, salt and celery seed. Separate whites of 4 hard boiled eggs from yolks; chop whites and add to potato mixture. Chill thoroughly. Mash the egg yolks, blend in sour cream, mayonnaise, vinegar and mustard. Pour this dressing over potato mixture. Toss lightly. Let stand for at least 30 minutes. Garnish with slices of remaining 2 eggs.

Mary Andrews (Mrs. Charles)

SPINACH MOLD

6 Servings

2 pkgs. (10 oz. each)
  frozen chopped spinach
1 envelope (¼ oz.)
  unflavored gelatin
½ cup water
½ cup onion, chopped
½ cup celery, chopped
1 cup Old English cheese
  (cubed or grated)
4 hard boiled eggs,
  chopped
1¼ cup mayonnaise
½ tsp. Tabasco sauce
½ tsp. salt
1½ tsp. vinegar
2 tsp. horseradish

Thaw and drain spinach well. Soften envelope of gelatin in ½ cup water. Stir in thoroughly all of the remaining ingredients. Spoon into greased 2 quart mold and chill 24 hours. Serve on a bed of lettuce.

Virginia Kirk (Mrs. George)

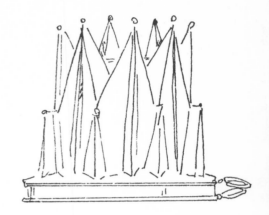

CHEESE-SALAD RING

8-10 Servings

1 envelope (¼ oz.)
  unflavored gelatin
1 cup cold water
1 can (10¾ oz.) tomato
  soup, undiluted
1 pkg. (8 oz.) cream cheese
Juice of ½ lemon
1 cup pecans, chopped
1 green pepper, minced
1 small onion, minced
1 cup celery, minced
Dash Tabasco
Dash salt
1 cup mayonnaise
Parsley

Dissolve gelatin in cup of cold water. Add this to hot soup, stir well. Add cream cheese and stir soup mixture until cheese is completely dissolved. Remove from heat and cool. Add lemon juice, pecans, green pepper, onion, celery, Tabasco, salt and mayonnaise and stir. Pour into a 9×9" pan or 1 quart mold and chill. Garnish with fresh parsley.

Janet Schwarz (Mrs. Eric)

BLEU CHEESE DRESSING   3 Cups

2 cups sour cream
¼ cup real mayonnaise
½ tsp. garlic salt
½ tsp. celery salt
½ tsp. paprika
½ tsp. black pepper
½ tsp. salt (coarse salt
  preferable)
2 T. tarragon vinegar
¼ (or ½) lb. crumbled
  bleu cheese

Place all ingredients in mixing bowl except for the bleu cheese. Whip them together with a wire whisk or a fork until fluffy and well blended. Add the crumbled bleu cheese, tossing with a fork until it is blended. Chill, or serve it immediately.

Barbara A. Searle

TANGY FRENCH DRESSING   4 Cups

1 cup sugar
2 tsp. salt
2 tsp. paprika
1 cup salad oil
½ cup vinegar
⅔ cup ketchup
1 small onion grated, or
  2 tsp. dehydrated onion
  flakes

Put all ingredients in a quart jar, and shake well. Chill thoroughly. The dressing is better as flavors blend after several hours.

Susan Jacobs (Mrs. Steven)

FRENCH DRESSING

3 cups

¾ cup vinegar, either
  red or white
1 cup salad oil
1 cup sugar
1 tsp. salt
1 tsp. dry mustard
2 tsp. paprika
1 clove garlic, whole

Put all ingredients into a small electric mixer bowl and beat well. (The garlic will not break apart, but will add flavor.) Put the dressing into a jar, including the garlic clove, and refrigerate. Shake well before serving.

Mary Hass (Mrs. Arthur)

GARLIC AND HERB DRESSING

3 Cups

5 cloves garlic (peeled)
½ cup vinegar
1 tsp. paprika
1 tsp. dry mustard
1 tsp. Worcestershire
  sauce
1 tsp. seasoned salt
1 tsp. parsley flakes
1½ tsp. rosemary
1½ tsp. ginger
1½ tsp. black pepper
1½ tsp. celery seed
1½ tsp. basil
1½ tsp. sesame seed
1 T. sugar
2 cups corn oil

Put all ingredients, except oil, in blender, turn to "chop" for 30 seconds. Then turn to "stir" and gradually dribble the oil into the mixture. Blend for two minutes. You may add or subtract the amount of vinegar to suit your own taste. Chill for at least two hours before serving. This dressing is delicious on all salads, also good when deviling eggs.

Betty Stevens (Mrs. Dale)

POPPY SEED DRESSING

4 Cups

1½ cups sugar
2 tsp. dry mustard
2 tsp. salt
⅔ cup vinegar
3 T. onion juice, or
   grated onion
2 cups salad oil
3 T. poppy seed

Mix first five ingredients in sauce pan. While ingredients are heating, add oil until mixture thickens. Add poppy seeds. Cool. Excellent on cabbage salad.

Kristyn Mahler (Mrs. Michael)

HONEY DRESSING

2 Cups

½ cup vinegar
¼ cup sugar
¼ cup honey
1 tsp. dry mustard
1 tsp. paprika
½ tsp. salt
½ tsp. celery salt
1 tsp. celery seed
1 tsp. onion juice
1 cup salad oil

Mix first five ingredients together and boil for 3 minutes. Cool. Place in a jar. Add the remaining ingredients and shake vigorously. Refrigerate. Shake well before using. Serve with fresh, or frozen fruit salad.

Joan Ferguson (Mrs. Wendell)

MAYFAIR DRESSING

4 Cups

1 clove garlic, or ⅛
    tsp. garlic powder
1 stalk celery
½ medium onion
1 can (2 oz.) flat anchovies-
    drained or paste
3 whole eggs
1 tsp. ground black pepper
1 tsp. (heaping) MSG
½ tsp. sugar
2 T. Dijon-style mustard
1 T. lemon juice
2 cups salad oil

Peel and slice the garlic, scrape and slice celery; peel and slice onions. Put these together with anchovies, black pepper, MSG, sugar, mustard, and lemon juice into a blender and whirl for about two seconds. Add eggs and blend again for a few seconds. Add the oil, ¼ cup at a time, blending well after each addition. Blend a few more seconds after all the oil has been added. Let season overnight. Keeps well. Refrigerate. Delicous on any crisp salad greens.

Jan Crow (Mrs. David)

GERMAN MAYONNAISE

3 Cups

5 eggs
1 cup sugar
3 T. flour
¼ tsp. dry mustard
¼ tsp. salt
½ cup vinegar
1 cup water

Beat eggs well. Mix all ingredients. Bring to a boil, stirring constantly. When thickened, remove from heat. Refrigerate.

Mary Jo Abbott (Mrs. Mark)

VEGETABLES

ASPARAGUS AU GRATIN   8 Servings

2 cans (15 oz. each)
  asparagus spears
4 T. butter
1 T. green pepper, minced
1 T. onion, minced
1 T. celery, thinly sliced
1 can (8 oz.) water
  chestnuts, sliced
2 T. flour
½ cup asparagus liquid
½ cup milk
Salt
Pepper
½ cup slivered almonds
½ cup sharp cheese,
  grated

Drain asparagus and reserve ½ cup liquid. Arrange asparagus spears in loaf pan. Saute' green pepper, onion and celery in butter. Add water chestnuts. Stir in flour, asparagus liquid and milk. Stir until smooth. Season to taste with salt and pepper and pour over asparagus. Sprinkle almonds and cheese on top. Bake uncovered at 350° for 20 minutes.

Linda Clarke (Mrs. Wade)

ASPARAGUS AU SAUTERNE   6 Servings

2 lbs. fresh, or 2 pkgs.
  (10 oz. each) frozen
  asparagus spears,
  cooked
½ cup onion, chopped
½ cup (1 stick) butter
  or margarine
¼ tsp. rosemary
¼ tsp. thyme leaves
¼ tsp. salt
½ cup sauterne or chablis
1 T. parsley, chopped

Cook asparagus to slightly underdone state. Place spears in shallow dish. In a medium skillet saute onions in butter about 4-5 minutes, until soft and tender, but not brown. Stir in herbs and salt. Remove from heat and spoon over cooked asparagus in dish. Pour in wine. Bake uncovered in preheated 400° oven for 5 minutes. At serving time, sprinkle with chopped parsley. Can be made ahead of time, then add wine just before baking.

Mavoureen Briggs (Mrs. Stuart)

BARLEY CASSEROLE

Great with pork chops.

¼ cup margarine
¾ lb. fresh mushrooms
2 medium onions, chopped
½ envelope (½ oz.) onion soup mix
1½ cups barley
2 cups chicken stock

Saute onions and mushrooms in margarine. Mix in remaining ingredients. Place in oblong glass dish. Bake uncovered at 350° for 60 minutes. Stir occasionally while baking.

Jenny Ewing (Mrs. Ted B.)

BOURBON BEANS

10-12 Servings

A great, different flavor.

4 cans (18 oz. each) Boston-type baked beans
1 can (15½ oz.) kidney beans, drained
1 can (8 oz.) kidney beans drained
1 cup brown sugar
½ cup ketchup
2 onions, chopped
¼ cup molasses
⅓ cup black coffee
⅓ cup bourbon
¾ tsp. dry mustard

Mix all ingredients together. Cover and bake at 275° for 1 hour or more.

Betty Reimers (Mrs. Robert)

OLD FASHIONED BAKED BEANS

12 Servings

This is a delicious old family recipe.

1½ lbs. navy beans
Hot water
  ½ tsp. soda
  ½ cup sugar
  1 tsp. dry mustard
  ½ lb. bacon, diced
Salt
Garlic (optional)

Soak beans overnight in water. In morning add soda and par-boil for 30 minutes. Drain. Put beans in bean pot and add hot water to cover beans. Add sugar, mustard, bacon and salt to taste. Cover. Bake at 275° for 4-6 hours. Add water, if needed, while baking. (A sprinkle of garlic powder adds an interesting flavor.)

Mary Phares (Mrs. William)

SAVORY BAKED BEANS

20 Servings

The oregano adds such a unique flavor.

2 cans (1 lb. 13 oz. each)
  pork and beans
1 lb. lean bacon, cut in
  pieces
2 medium onions, sliced
2 large green peppers, cut
  in strips
2 tsp. Worcestershire sauce
1 cup ketchup
1 cup brown sugar
2 T. crushed oregano
Garlic powder, to taste

Combine all ingredients. Bake covered in slow oven (325°) for 2½ hours, stirring occasionally. Uncover and bake 30 minutes more.

Sandy Hass (Mrs. John)

SWISS GREEN BEANS

6-8 Servings

2 pkgs. (10 oz. each)
   frozen green beans
2 T. margarine
2 T. flour
1 tsp. sugar
½ tsp. salt
Pepper
1 tsp. onion, grated
½ cup milk
½ cup sour cream
¼ lb. Swiss cheese
Slivered almonds

Cook green beans and drain well. Melt margarine. Add flour, sugar, salt and pepper. Stir in onion and then milk. Cook over medium heat until smooth. Then stir in sour cream and add Swiss cheese. Cook until cheese is melted. Add sauce to green beans and put in 1½ quart casserole. Top with buttered slivered almonds. Bake uncovered at 350° for 20 minutes, or until bubbly.

Peg Beausang (Mrs. Kenneth)

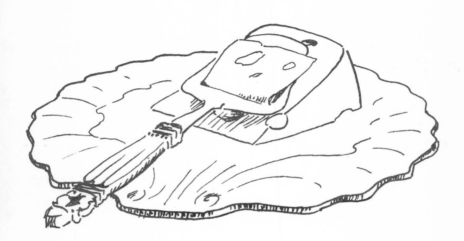

GREEN BEANS IN WINE SAUCE

8 Servings

6 slices bacon, diced
1 medium onion, diced
6 T. sugar
4 tsp. cornstarch
6 T. tarragon vinegar
¾ - 1 cup dry sherry
2 pkgs. (10 oz. each) green
   beans, cooked

Using a small saucepan, saute bacon and onion. Do not drain. Add sugar, cornstarch, (dissolved in small amount of sherry) vinegar, tarragon and remaining sherry. Cook until thickened, stirring constantly. Pour over hot beans, serve. Sauce may be prepared ahead of time and reheated before pouring over beans. You may substitute canned french cut green beans.

Sheila O'Shea (Mrs. John)

BROCCOLI SOUFFLE

6-8 Servings

2 pkgs. (10 oz. each)
    frozen chopped broccoli
1 can (10¾ oz.) cream of
    mushroom soup
¼ lb. processed cheese,
    cubed
3 eggs, slightly beaten
¾ cup real mayonnaise

Cook broccoli just until tender. Drain well. Heat soup and cheese until cheese melts. Combine broccoli with soup and cheese mixture, add eggs and mayonnaise. Place in a well greased 2 quart casserole. Put casserole in pan of water. Bake uncovered at 350° for 1 hour. (Can be prepared in advance.) Also lends itself to spinach, asparagus, carrots, most any vegetable or combination of vegetables.

Marjorie Purcell (Mrs. Donald)

BROCCOLI CASSEROLE

6-8 Servings

¼ cup onion, minced
½ cup margarine
2 T. flour
1 tsp. salt
½ cup water
1 jar (8 oz.) processed
    American cheese
3 eggs, well beaten
2 pkgs. (10 oz. each)
    frozen chopped
    broccoli, thawed
½ cup buttered cracker
    crumbs

Cook onion until tender in margarine, but do not brown. Blend in flour, salt and water. Stir in cheese, eggs and broccoli. Place in a greased 9×9" glass oven-proof dish. Top with cracker crumbs. Bake uncovered at 350° for 40 minutes. (Grated American cheese can be substituted for cracker crumbs.)

Trish Arnold (Mrs. David)

BROCCOLI BLUE-CHEESE CASSEROLE   6-8 Servings

A tangy new flavor for broccoli.

2 pkgs. (10 oz. each)
  frozen chopped broccoli
2 T. butter, melted
2 T. flour
½ tsp. salt
1 pkg. (3 oz.) cream
  cheese, softened
½ oz. or 1 oz. bleu
  cheese, crumbled
1 cup milk
⅓ cup finely crushed
  round Ritz crackers

Cook broccoli and drain well. Meanwhile blend butter with flour, salt and cheeses in sauce pan. Add milk all at once, and cook. Stir in broccoli. Pour into 1 quart casserole, and top with crumbs. Bake uncovered at 350° for 30 minutes.

Mary Ann Linden (Mrs. James S.)

BROCCOLI WITH MUSHROOMS AND CELERY

6 Servings

2 pkgs. (10 oz. each)
  frozen chopped broccoli
  thawed and drained
1 jar (8 oz.) whole
  mushrooms, drained
¾ cup sour cream
1 cup celery, diced
1 tsp. salt
½ tsp. pepper
1 jar (2 oz.) pimento,
  chopped
1 cup sharp cheddar
  cheese, grated

Mix first seven ingredients together in a bowl. Grease a 2 quart casserole with butter and distribute mixture in casserole. Sprinkle cheese on top and spread down the middle of the casserole. Bake uncovered at 350° for 30 minutes. (Depending on taste, up to one cup of cheese may be used.)

Susan Cleaver (Mrs. William)

BROCCOLI CASSEROLE SUPREME

4-6 Servings

2 pkgs. (10 oz. each)
   frozen chopped broccoli
1 can (10¾ oz.) cream of
   mushroom soup
1 cup real mayonnaise
2 eggs, well beaten
1 medium onion, chopped
Salt
Pepper
1 cup cheddar cheese,
   grated
1 cup commercial bread
   crumbs

Cook broccoli just until tender and then drain well. Mix soup and mayonnaise together until smooth. Add eggs, onion, salt and pepper. Add to broccoli and put in 2 quart casserole. Cover with cheese and then top with bread crumbs. Bake uncovered at 350° for 45 minutes.

Sandra McAndrews

BRUSSELS SPROUTS WITH TANGY SAUCE

A super way to fix the lowly Brussels sprout!

2 pkgs. (10 oz. each)
   frozen Brussels sprouts
1 beef bouillon cube
6 slices bacon, fried and
   crumbled
½ cup sour cream
¼ cup real mayonnaise
1 tsp. lemon juice
¼ tsp. Worcestershire
   sauce
½ tsp. paprika
¼ tsp. dry mustard
Salt
Pepper

4-6 Servings

Cook Brussels sprouts in water to cover. Add bouillon cube. Mix rest of ingredients in small saucepan and stir over low heat until heated through. Do not boil. Place drained Brussels sprouts in serving dish and spoon sauce over them. Serve immediately.

Mary Ann Tyler (Mrs. Herb)

CARROTS SUPREME

6-8 Servings

2 pkgs. (10 oz. each)
  frozen carrots
½ cup (1 stick) margarine
½ cup onion, chopped
2 stalks celery, chopped
1 can (10¾ oz.) cream of
  mushroom soup
1 roll (6 oz.) garlic
  cheese spread
1 can (2 oz.) mushrooms,
  drained
1 cup commercial bread
  crumbs

Partially cook vegetable according to package instructions. Drain well. Saute onions and celery in margarine. Add soup, cheese, mushrooms and ½ cup crumbs. Combine ingredients. Place in a greased 2 quart glass baking dish and sprinkle with remaining crumbs. Bake uncovered at 350° for 30 minutes. Can be prepared ahead and refrigerated, then add 15 minutes more to baking time. Green beans, broccoli or asparagus may be substituted in same amount.

Marjorie Magers (Mrs. Tom)

CARROT PUDDING

6-8 Servings

1 lb. carrots, peeled,
  cut in pieces
½ cup water
⅓ cup oil
½ cup sugar
3 eggs
1 tsp. vanilla
½ tsp. salt
1 tsp. grated orange rind
½ tsp. grated lemon rind
1 T. baking powder
1 cup flour

Use blender and grate carrots, adding water. Add remaining ingredients and blend until well pureed. Pour into well greased hot 2 quart casserole. Bake uncovered at 300° for 2 hours. (Grandmother used chicken fat, brown sugar and grated carrots by hand. Mother uses sugar, and grates carrots with a machine.)

Bobbie Galex (Mrs. Martin)

CORN FRITTERS

6 Servings

A favorite old family recipe.

1 can (17 oz.) cream
  style corn
1 cup flour
1 tsp. baking powder
2 tsp. salt
¼ tsp. paprika
2 egg yolks
2 egg whites
1½ cups vegetable
  shortening
Maple syrup

Blend first 5 ingredients. Separate egg yolks and whites, add yolks to the above mixture. Beat egg whites until stiff and fold into mixture. Pour 1 large spoonful of batter into 1½ cups hot vegetable shortening and brown, then turn and brown the other side. Can cook about 3 at a time. Serve with maple syrup. This is nice for a brunch with eggs and bacon, or as a vegetable for dinner.

Ellie Klingbiel (Mrs. Tom)

EGGPLANT PARMESAN

12 Servings

Delicious served with a salad and french bread.

1 large eggplant
3 eggs, beaten
1 cup crackers, crumbled
Oil
Parmesan cheese
Oregano
2 lbs. mozzarella cheese,
  sliced
2 cans (15 oz. each)
  tomato sauce
Garlic powder (optional)

Pare and slice eggplant in ½ inch slices. Dip each slice in eggs, then cracker crumbs and fry in oil until golden brown. Drain on paper towel. Place in 2 quart oblong casserole. Sprinkle with parmesan cheese, oregano and mozzarella cheese. Repeat with another layer. Top with tomato sauce, more oregano and parmesan cheese. Bake uncovered at 350° for 30 minutes. Remove from oven, add more slices of mozzarella cheese and place back in oven until cheese melts.

Mary Jo Hemming (Mrs. Donald)

MYSTERY EGGPLANT AND CHEESE SOUFFLE

Guests can never guess that this is eggplant.

6-8 Servings

1 large eggplant,
  pared and cubed
Water
2 T. butter
2 T. flour
1 tsp. salt
1 cup milk
½ lb. cheddar cheese,
  shredded
2 cups soft bread
  crumbs
1 T. onion, grated
1 T. ketchup
2 egg yolks, well beaten
2 egg whites, stiffly
  beaten

Cook eggplant until tender in small amount of salted, boiling water. Drain and mash. Make white sauce by melting butter and adding flour and salt; blend, making a smooth paste. Gradually add milk and stir until mixture thickens. Add white sauce, cheese, bread crumbs, onion, ketchup and egg yolks to eggplant. Beat egg whites until stiff and fold them into the eggplant and cheese mixture. Bake uncovered in a 2 quart greased casserole at 350° for 1 hour. Delicious, nutritious, and filling.

Served with a salad, this is a good luncheon dish.

Florence Schyberg (Mrs. John A.)
Alice Ann Staak (Mrs. John H.)

GREEN PEPPERS STUFFED WITH CORN

6 Servings

6 green peppers
2 pkgs. (10 oz. each)
  frozen corn, cooked
2 T. butter, melted
½ cup cheese, grated
  (cheddar or American)
½ tsp. salt
¼ tsp. pepper
Water

Prepare peppers for stuffing to stand upright, or cut in half. Remove seeds and boil for two minutes only. Drain. Mix corn with other ingredients. Fill peppers with corn mixture. Place in a shallow baking dish, adding a small amount of water to bottom of dish, and bake at 350° for 20 minutes.

Pat Arp (Mrs. Louis, Jr.)

KENTUCKY DERBY CHEESE GRITS   10-12 Servings

2 cups grits
8 cups water (with 1 tsp. salt)
8 oz. sharp cheddar cheese
½ cup (1 stick) butter or
   margarine
4 egg yolks
4 egg whites, beaten stiff
Paprika

Cook grits in salted water. Add cheese, butter, and beaten egg yolks. Stir until melted. Fold in egg whites, and place in greased 3 quart casserole. Sprinkle with paprika. Bake uncovered at 350° for 45 minutes.

Sally MacMillan (Mrs. Charles)

STUFFED MUSHROOMS   6 Servings

20 large mushrooms
Salt
2 T. butter
2 T. vegetable oil
1 medium onion, finely
   chopped
2 cloves garlic, pressed
Dash of dried thyme
Dash of pepper
1 large tomato, peeled,
   chopped and seeded
3 egg yolks, well beaten
¼ cup grated Swiss or
   parmesan cheese
1 T. parsley

Break stems from mushroom caps. Put caps in a skillet, bottoms up, and sprinkle with salt. Add 1 T. of the melted butter combined with 1 T. oil. Cover. Cook over low heat for 5 minutes. Remove and cool. Chop stems finely, saute with onions in remaining butter and oil. Stir with wooden spoon. Add garlic, thyme, pepper and tomato. Bring to a boil and simmer 12 minutes. Cool slightly. Beat in egg yolks. Bring to a boil and cook, stirring for 1 minute more. Stuff caps with the mixture. Arrange in a shallow oven proof casserole. Cover with cheese. Sprinkle with the parsley. Bake uncovered at 375° until lightly browned, 20-30 minutes.

Barbara Priester (Mrs. Peter)

MUSHROOM CASSEROLE

6 Servings

½ cup onion, chopped
½ cup margarine
1 cup beef boullion
2 T. cornstarch
½ tsp. marjoram
2 cans (6 oz. each)
   mushrooms, drained
2 T. dry sherry
2 T. snipped parsley
½ cup coarsely crumbled
   crackers
2 T. parmesan cheese
1 T. margarine, melted

Cook onion in ½ cup margarine until tender and crisp; blend bouillon with cornstarch and marjoram, add to onion mixture. Add mushrooms and stir and cook until thickened. Remove from heat, stir in sherry and parsley. Pour into 1 quart casserole. Combine cracker crumbs, cheese and margarine, sprinkle over casserole. Bake uncovered at 350° for 20 minutes.

Connie Sauer (Mrs. Ralph)

MUSHROOM-ARTICHOKE CASSEROLE

6 Servings

3 cups fresh mushrooms,
   halved
½ cup sliced green onions
   with tops
4 T. butter
2 T. flour
$^1/_8$ tsp. salt
$^1/_8$ tsp. pepper
¾ cup water
¼ cup milk
1 tsp. instant chicken
   boullion granules
1 tsp. lemon juice
$^1/_8$ tsp. ground nutmeg
1 10 oz. pkg. frozen
   artichoke hearts, cooked
   and drained
¾ cup soft bread crumbs
1 T. butter, melted

Cook mushrooms and onions in the 4 T. butter. With slotted spoon remove vegetables, set aside. Blend flour, salt and pepper into pan drippings. Add ¾ cup water, milk, boullion, lemon juice and nutmeg. Cook and stir until bubbly. Add all vegetables. Turn into 1 quart casserole. Combine bread crumbs and melted butter; sprinkle around edge. Bake at 350° for 20 minutes.

Jean C. McHard

ONIONS SUPREME

8 Servings

This is a West Virginia specialty.

6 cups onions, sliced
(about 8 medium)
¼ cup margarine
1 can (4 oz.) mushroom
stems and pieces,
drained
1 pkg. (2 oz.) almonds,
sliced
1 tsp. sugar
Salt to taste
Pepper to taste
2 cans (10¾ oz. each)
tomato soup
8 round crackers, crushed

Brown and separate onions in margarine in large frying pan. Combine remaining ingredients, except cracker crumbs, and add to onions. Pour into well greased 9×9" glass dish and sprinkle with cracker crumbs. Bake uncovered at 350° for 45 minutes, or until bubbly.

Connie Green (Mrs. George)

HEARTS OF PALM AU GRATIN

8 Servings

3 cans (14 oz. each) hearts
of palm, drained and
cut into 1" pieces
6 T. butter
4 T. flour
1½ cups milk
Dash of Tabasco
½ cup Swiss (or Gruyere)
cheese, grated
½ cup heavy cream
Salt to taste
Pepper to taste
½ cup parmesan cheese,
freshly grated

Preheat oven to 400°. Place hearts in buttered shallow oven-proof casserole. Melt 4 T. butter and stir in flour. Cook 2 minutes over low heat. Heat milk to just below boiling point, add to the flour-butter mixture. Simmer 5 minutes. Add Tabasco, cheese, cream, seasonings and stir well. Pour over hearts. Melt remaining 2 T. butter and pour over hearts. Sprinkle with parmesan cheese. Bake uncovered at 400° for 10-12 minutes. You may substitute 3 pkgs. (10 oz. each) frozen artichoke hearts.

Margaret Stegmaier (Mrs. Otto C.)

FINNISH POTATOES

8 Servings

My husband's mother brought this recipe from Finland.

10 medium sized Idaho
   potatoes, thinly sliced
2 T. onion salt
2 T. peppercorns
1½ cups milk
½ cup (1 stick) butter or
   margarine

Peel and slice potatoes. Allow to stand in bowl of cold water for 30 minutes, then drain and place in 3 quart baking dish. Sprinkle onion salt over potatoes, scatter pepper corns over potatoes, and add milk, also dot with butter. Bake uncovered at 350° for 1 hour or until most of the liquid is absorbed. If you want to be fancy, place the potatoes in rows instead of at random.

Jean Koivin (Mrs. O. Wilhart)

OVEN POTATOES

8 Servings

Easy and delicious.

2 boxes (24 oz. each)
   frozen shredded hash
   browns
Garlic powder
Salt
Pepper
¾ cup butter, melted
1½ cups heavy cream

Thaw hash browns enough to flake. Layer in 2½ quart casserole dish: one layer potatoes, one layer sprinkled garlic powder, lots of salt and pepper, one layer melted butter (⅓ of total butter). Repeat to make three layers. This can be done ahead of time. Just before putting into oven, pour cream over the top of layers. Bake uncovered at 300° for 2½ hours. Mix before serving.

Terry Longval (Mrs. Joe)

BAKED MASHED POTATOES

6 Servings

6 medium potatoes, pared
   cooked and drained
1 tsp. salt
¼ tsp. pepper
1 cup sour cream
1 pkg. (3 oz.) cream
   cheese
3 T. butter
Paprika

Mash potatoes in mixer until light and fluffy. Add seasonings, sour cream, cream cheese and beat until well blended. Taste to check seasoning, adjust if necessary. Put in buttered 2 quart casserole. Dot with butter and sprinkle with paprika. Bake uncovered at 350° for 30 minutes.This freezes well, so can be prepared ahead of time. Defrost before baking.

Alice Ann Staak (Mrs. John H.)

POTATO PANCAKES

6-8 Servings

Wisconsin German style pancakes, serve with applesauce and pork.

3 - 4 large Idaho potatoes, peeled and shredded
3 eggs
1 medium onion, grated
1 tsp. salt
¼ tsp. pepper
4 - 5 T. flour
Vegetable oil

Shred the peeled potatoes. Place in cold water for 30 minutes. Squeeze dry in paper towel. Beat eggs in large bowl, stir in potatoes, onion, salt and pepper. Sprinkle flour on top and stir in. Pour ¼" oil in large skillet. Heat to 350° (medium high), drop mixture by large spoonfuls, flatten. Turn only once, drain on paper towel. Keep warm.

Linda Karwath (Mrs. Robert)

SWEET POTATO CASSEROLE

8 Servings

3 lbs. sweet potatoes, or yams
½ cup sugar
½ tsp. cinnamon
½ tsp. nutmeg
¼ tsp. salt
3 T. butter
1 cup milk
Orange peel, grated
Slivered almonds, roasted

Mash cooked potatoes (or use canned yams, drained well). Add sugar, cinnamon, nutmeg, salt, butter, milk and orange peel to taste, blending well. Place in 2 quart casserole. Top with roasted almonds making a design. Bake uncovered at 400° for 15 minutes.

Hulda Fryxell (Mrs. H.E.)

PERFECT SWEET POTATO PUDDING

6-10 Servings

Yams - allow 1 potato per person
½ - 1 stick butter or margarine
1 can (8 oz.) crushed pineapple
Large marshmallows

Bake yams at 375° until soft. Mash yams well with butter. Add crushed pineapple and if dry, add the juice also. Butter casserole dish and put mixture in it. Bake at 375° for 30 minutes. During final 5 minutes, put marshmallows on top and return to oven to melt.

MR. AND MRS. DANIEL HEIFETZ

100

SHERRIED SWEET POTATOES   8 Servings

8 medium sweet potatoes,
peeled, or 2 cans (22 oz.
each) potatoes, drained
½ tsp. salt
1 cup brown sugar
2 T. cornstarch
½ tsp. orange peel,
grated
2 cups orange juice
½ cup raisins
6 T. butter
½ cup sherry
½ cup walnuts, chopped

Cook potatoes in boiling salted water until just tender. Drain. Cut in half lengthwise and arrange in 2 quart baking dish. Sprinkle with salt. In saucepan combine brown sugar, cornstarch and salt. Blend in orange peel and juice; add raisins. Cook over medium heat, stirring constantly until mixture thickens and bubbles. Cook 1 minute more. Add butter, sherry, and walnuts, stirring until butter melts. Pour over potatoes. Bake uncovered at 325° for 30 minutes. Baste occasionally.

Shan Corelis (Mrs. John)

CELERY-RICE CASSEROLE   12-14 Servings

Excellent side dish with ham or other pork.

2 cans (10½ oz. each)
condensed chicken rice
soup
2 bunches celery, cut in
1" pieces
2 T. flour
¾ oz. slivered almonds
½ tsp. garlic salt
1 cup seasoned croutons

Pour liquid from chicken rice soup and reserve. Place liquid in deep large dutch oven. Add chopped celery to soup liquid. Simmer for 1 hour, covered. Drain liquid and again reserve. Add chicken-rice to celery. Thicken reserved liquid with flour, as you would for gravy. Add thickened liquid, almonds and garlic salt to celery-rice mixture. Put in a 2 quart casserole, top with croutons. Refrigerate until ready to use. Heat uncovered at 350° for 45 minutes.

Linda Karwath (Mrs. Robert)

WILD RICE AND CHEESE CASSEROLE

8 Servings

Makes a fine dinner accompaniment, or main course for a ladies' luncheon.

1 cup wild rice
1 cup cheddar cheese,
  grated
1 cup canned tomatoes
1 cup canned mushrooms,
  drained
½ cup onions, chopped
½ cup salad oil
1 tsp. salt
¼ tsp. pepper
1 cup water, hot

Wash rice well, several times pouring off foreign particles from top. Combine all ingredients and bake uncovered in a 2 quart casserole at 350° for 1 hour.

Annabelle DeCock (Mrs. Dale)

WILD RICE CASSEROLE

6-8 Servings

½ cup (1 stick) butter
1 cup wild rice, washed
  3-4 times
½ cup slivered almonds
3 T. onion, grated
½ lb. fresh mushrooms,
  sliced
3 cups chicken broth

Place first five ingredients in skillet to brown. Place in a 2 quart casserole. Add broth and stir occasionally during baking. Cover and bake at 350° for 1½ hours.

Joanne Loufek

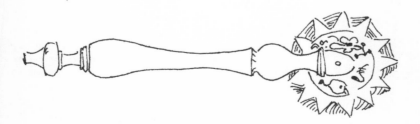

SPINACH-ARTICHOKE CASSEROLE   8 Servings

1 can (14 oz.) water
    packed artichoke hearts,
    drained
4 pkgs. (10 oz. each)
    frozen chopped spinach
20 oz. cream cheese
1½ cups margarine
4 T. lemon juice

TOPPING:
¼ cup butter
1½ cups commercial bread
    crumbs

Rinse and drain artichoke hearts. Cut in bite size pieces and place in a greased 9×13" pan. Cook spinach according to package directions and drain very well. (You may blot it in layers of paper towels.) Place cream cheese, margarine and lemon juice in top of double boiler. Blend well, using a whisk. Mix cream cheese sauce with the spinach and pour over the artichokes.

For topping: Melt butter and add bread crumbs. Mix well and sprinkle over the entire casserole. Bake uncovered at 325° for 25 minutes, or until bubbly.

Bonnie Brotman (Mrs. Jerrel)

SPINACH ON ARTICHOKE BOTTOMS HOLLANDAISE

Worth all the steps to make it, delicious!   6-8 Servings

2 pkgs. (10 oz. each)
    frozen spinach
½ lb. fresh mushrooms
1 can (14 oz.) water
    packed artichoke
    bottoms, drained
4 T. butter

WHITE SAUCE:
2 T. butter
1 T. flour
½ cup milk
½ tsp. salt
¹/₈ tsp. garlic powder

HOLLANDAISE SAUCE
1 cup sour cream
1 cup real mayonnaise
¼ cup lemon juice

Cook spinach according to package directions. Drain very well. Reserve 16 mushroom caps; chop remaining caps with stems and saute in 2 T. of butter. Saute mushroom caps separately in another 2 T. of butter.

For white sauce: Melt butter in saucepan, add flour and cook until bubbly. Add milk stirring constantly until smooth. Add salt and garlic powder.

For Hollandaise sauce: Combine sour cream, mayonnaise and lemon juice thoroughly and heat slowly.

To assemble: Add spinach and chopped mushrooms to white sauce. Mix thoroughly. Place artichoke bottoms in a 7×11" greased glass dish and cover each with a mound of creamed spinach, then with a generous spoonful of sour cream Hollandaise. Top each with a whole mushroom. Bake uncovered at 375° for 20 minutes.

Marilyn Evans (Mrs. Gerald)

SPINACH SOUFFLE CASSEROLE

6-8 Servings

2 pts. small curd cottage
  cheese
6 eggs, well beaten
½ lb. Velveeta cheese,
  cubed
½ cup (1 stick) butter
2 pkgs. (10 oz. each)
  chopped spinach,
  thawed and well drained
6 T. flour

Put cottage cheese in bowl and add beaten eggs. Add cubed cheese and pieces of butter. Fold in the spinach. Sprinkle the flour on top and gently fold together. Place in a buttered 2 quart casserole. Bake at 350° for 1 hour.

Martha Neal (Mrs. David)

SPINACH-CARROT MEDLEY

6-8 Servings

5 medium carrots, cut in
  small pieces (1½ cups)
  cooked and well drained
2 pkgs. (10 oz. each)
  frozen, chopped spinach
  cooked and well drained
1 medium onion, finely
  chopped
3 T. butter
3 T. flour
1½ cups milk
¼ tsp. salt
Dash pepper
1 cup cheddar cheese,
  shredded
Breadcrumbs

Prepare the carrots and spinach. Toss the onion with the spinach, set aside.

Prepare the white sauce: Melt the butter and add flour, blending well and heating until bubbly. Gradually add the milk and stir constantly until thick. Add the cheese and continue to stir until it is melted and blended. Season with salt and pepper.

To assemble: Arrange spinach in an ungreased casserole dish over the entire bottom. Cover with carrots. Pour cheese sauce over all. Sprinkle with buttered bread crumbs. Bake at 350° for 20-30 minutes.

Janelle Stonebraker (Mrs. John)

GREEN TOMATO RELISH

4 Pints

½ cup mixed pickling
  spices
8 cups green tomatoes,
  chopped
2 cups green peppers,
  chopped
2 cups onion, chopped
2 cups cider vinegar
¼ cup salt
2¾ cups sugar

Fashion a bag out of a square piece of lightweight cloth for the mixed pickling spices, secure top with string. Place in the center of pot containing all other ingredients. Simmer 30 minutes, stirring occasionally. Cool. Keep refrigerated. May be frozen in plastic containers.

Sue Ruhl (Mrs. John)

BAKED TOMATO HALVES

8 Servings

Very colorful and attractive.

4 large tomatoes
6 - 8 T. butter
⅓ cup onion, finely
  chopped
2 tsp. prepared mustard
1 tsp. Worcestershire
  sauce
⅓ - ½ cup seasoned
  croutons, crushed
4 T. parsley, chopped

Preheat oven to 350°. Wash fresh tomatoes, remove stems. Cut in half crosswise. Place cut side up in a shallow baking dish. In 3-4 T. butter saute onion until tender. Stir in mustard and Worcestershire sauce. Spread mixture on tomato halves. Melt rest of butter, stir in crumbs and parsley until well blended. Spread over tomato halves. Bake uncovered at 350° for 20 minutes until heated through and crumbs are golden brown.

Janelle Stonebraker (Mrs. John)

BAKED VEGETABLE MEDLEY

8-10 Servings

1½ cups onions, sliced
1½ cups carrots, sliced
¾ of a green pepper cut
   in 1 inch strips
2 tsp. salt
⅛ tsp. pepper
3 T. tapioca
2 cups celery, sliced
2 cups frozen green beans
2 cups canned tomatoes,
   cut up

Combine all ingredients, mixing well. Place in a greased 3 quart casserole, cover tightly. Bake at 350° for 1 hour and 10 minutes.

Mary Loving (Mrs. Roger)

ZUCCHINI-CHEESE CASSEROLE

6-8 Servings

Good for large gatherings. Vegetarians love this one.

3 cups zucchini, thinly
   sliced
2 cups mozzarella cheese,
   grated
1 cup milk
3 eggs, beaten
½ cup (1 stick) butter,
   melted
1 tsp. salt
1½ cups cracker crumbs

Alternate zucchini and cheese in layers in buttered 2 quart casserole. Combine milk, eggs, butter and salt and pour over zucchini and cheese. Put cracker crumbs on top. Bake uncovered at 325° for 30-35 minutes. Allow to cool 10 minutes before serving.

Carol Pedigo

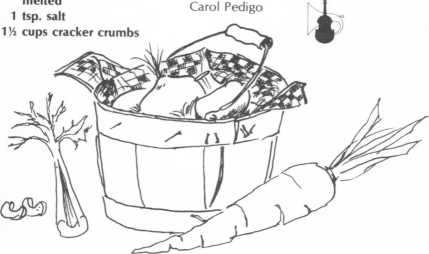

106

FUSILLI WITH CREAMY ZUCCHINI AND BASIL SAUCE

2 lbs. zucchini, cut into
   sticks about 3" long and
   ¼" thick
Vegetable oil
1 lb. fusilli (spiral spaghetti)
   (may substitute macaroni
   with holes or edges to
   catch the zucchini)
4 T. butter
4 T. olive oil
2 tsp. all-purpose flour
1¼ cups milk
½ tsp. salt
1⅓ cups fresh basil, roughly
   chopped
1 egg yolk, lightly beaten
   by fork
1 cup freshly grated
   parmesan cheese
½ cup freshly grated
   romano pecorino cheese

4-6 Servings

Deep fry the zucchini sticks in vegetable oil (380-400° in electric fryer) until light brown in color. Drain well on paper towels. (May be done ahead of time.) Drop fusilli into 4 quarts boiling salted water, stirring with wooden spoon. Fusilli will cook while you prepare the sauce. In skillet, melt half the butter with all of the olive oil. When the butter begins to foam, turn the heat down to medium low and stir in the flour. Cook without browning for 3 minutes. Slowly add the milk, stirring constantly. When fully incorporated, smooth and slightly thickened, add the fried zucchini sticks, the salt and the chopped basil. Stir everything to heat. Remove from heat, swirl in the remaining butter, then the egg yolk and the grated cheeses. Cook fusilli until al dente, (firm to the bite,) drain, transfer to serving bowl. Toss all with sauce and serve immediately.

RICHARD CONTIGUGLIA

Richard & John Contiguglia

RICHARD AND JOHN CONTIGUGLIA, identical twins and duo-pianists, have drawn attention to the large and significant repertoire for two pianos. Since their professional debut in London in 1962, the duo has achieved much acclaim for their unusual programs, and extensive performance of Bartok works. In 1974, the Contiguglias performed Mozart's "Concerto No. 10 in E Flat Major for 2 Pianos" and "Operatic Fantasy on Bellini's 'Norma' for 2 Pianos" by Liszt with the Tri-City Symphony.

ZUCCHINI CASSEROLE

4-6 Servings

½ cup fine bread crumbs
1 T. parsley flakes
¼ tsp. oregano
¼ tsp. sweet basil
2 T. butter, or margarine, melted
1 pkg. (1 oz.) white sauce mix
1 lb. zucchini, sliced and cooked
¼ cup parmesan cheese

Combine bread crumbs, parsley flakes, oregano and basil. Saute lightly in melted butter. Prepare white sauce. Arrange cooked zucchini in shallow casserole. Pour white sauce on top. Sprinkle with cheese, top with bread crumbs mixture. Bake uncovered at 350° for 20 minutes, or until golden brown and bubbly. (Packaged hollandaise sauce substituted for white sauce is also good.)

Helen Maes (Mrs. Frank)

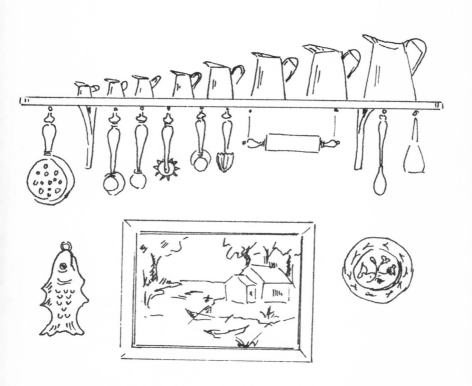

CURRY SAUCE

1 Quart

1 qt. real mayonnaise
1 tsp. salt
2 T. (heaping) curry powder
2 tsp. tarragon vinegar
Juice of ½ lemon
1 T. sugar
1 tsp. paprika
Squirt of Tabasco sauce

Mix all ingredients together well with an electric mixer. Keep well refrigerated, and sauce keeps indefinitely. Also works with raw vegetables for a cocktail dip. Heat slightly and pour over fresh asparagus, broccoli, etc.

Onalee Evans (Mrs. Dick)

CHEESE SAUCE

Yield: 3 Cups

1 can (8 oz.) tomato sauce
  with mushrooms
2 cups cheddar cheese,
  shredded
1 T. flour
1 can (6 oz.) evaporated
  milk
½ tsp. onion salt
¹/₈ tsp. garlic salt
¹/₈ tsp. oregano

Heat tomato sauce to boiling; then reduce to simmer. Toss cheese with flour and add to sauce. When cheese melts, gradually add evaporated milk and seasonings. Simmer, stirring until smooth. Keep hot and serve with bread sticks, or pour over favorite vegetable.

Cindy Peters (Mrs. Randy)

BRUNCH, LUNCH AND ONE-DISH MEALS

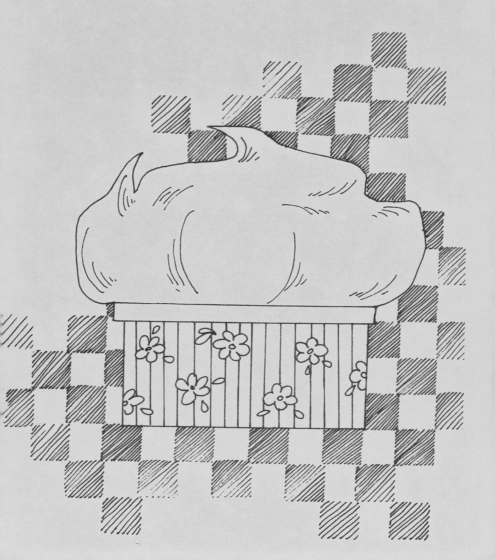

BAKED DEVILED EGGS, ASPARGUS AND HAM

6-8 Servings

3 pkgs. (10 oz. each)
  frozen asparagus, cut
10 hard cooked eggs
2 cans (2¼ oz. each)
  deviled ham
½ tsp. Worcestershire
  sauce
1 tsp. grated onion
¾ tsp. dry mustard
1 T. cream
½ tsp. salt
⅛ tsp. pepper

WHITE SAUCE:
6 T. butter
6 T. flour
3 cups half and half cream
2 cups cheddar cheese,
  grated
¼ tsp. dry mustard
1½ tsp. salt
Dash pepper

TOPPING:
1 cup corn flakes, crushed
2 T. butter

Cook asparagus according to package directions. Drain well. Slice eggs in half, remove yolks. Mash yolks and mix with ham, Worcestershire sauce, onion, mustard, cream, salt and pepper. Refill eggs. Set aside.

For white sauce: Melt butter, add flour and mix well. Gradually add cream, stirring constantly until mixture thickens. Cook about 5 minutes longer over very low heat. Add cheese, dry mustard, salt, and a dash of pepper. Stir until cheese melts.

For topping: Mix corn flakes with butter.

To assemble: Put asparagus in bottom of a shallow casserole, arrange eggs on top, pour sauce over all. Sprinkle with topping. Bake uncovered at 400° for 20 minutes or until sauce bubbles and top is brown.

Diana Normoyle (Mrs. Donald)

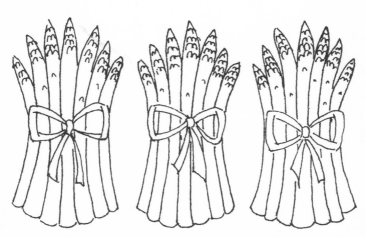

CREAMED EGGS AND ASPARAGUS

4 Servings

1 can (10¾ oz.) cream of chicken soup
¼ cup asparagus liquid
4-6 hard cooked eggs, sliced
1½ cups cooked or canned asparagus tips
½ cup mushrooms, sliced
¼ cup green pepper, sliced
Buttered bread crumbs

Combine soup with asparagus liquid and heat. Alternate layers of eggs, asparagus, mushrooms, green pepper, and soup mixture in a one quart glass casserole. Cover with bread crumbs. Bake at 350° for 15 minutes, uncovered.

Sandy Hass (Mrs. John)

COMPANY EGG CASSEROLE

12 Servings

Family favorite for brunch.

2 dozen eggs
½ cup milk
¼ lb. butter, melted
8 strips bacon
½ cup green pepper, diced
½ cup green onions, sliced
¾ cup sliced fresh mushrooms
2 cups cream of mushroom soup (undiluted)
½ cup white sherry
1 cup cheddar cheese, grated

Combine eggs and milk with whisk or electric mixer. Soft scramble them on top of the stove in the butter. Fry bacon until crisp; crumble. Mix together green pepper, green onions, mushrooms, soup and sherry. Spread half of egg mixture in 9x13" greased glass baking dish and cover with half of soup mixture. Repeat layers and sprinkle cheese over all. Cover and refrigerate overnight. Bake uncovered at 250° for 50 minutes.

Sue Boeye (Mrs. Pryce)
Terry Longval (Mrs. Joe)

OEUFS POCHES TOUT PARIS

6 Servings

Water
1 cup white vinegar
6 eggs (very fresh)

HOLLANDAISE SAUCE:
2 sticks butter, melted
3 egg yolks
2 T. cold water
¼ tsp. salt
Pinch white pepper
1 T. lemon juice
1 tsp. tomato paste
Chopped parsely
Toast rounds

TO POACH EGGS: Put 2 inches of water in a wide skillet, and when it simmers, add 1 cup white vinegar. Break eggs one at a time into simmering water. Cook 2½ minutes, then place eggs in large bowl of salted cold water. Remove when cool and drain on clean, folded towel.

TO PREPARE HOLLANDAISE SAUCE: In a saucepan, melt butter and set aside (keeping warm). In second sauce pan, beat egg yolks with wire whisk. Add water, salt and pepper. Place over very low heat, continuing to whip until mixture attains the consistency of mayonnaise. Remove from heat. Add warm melted butter very slowly. Divide sauce into two parts. Add lemon juice to one, tomato paste to the other.

To serve, place each egg on a small round of toast. Pour lemon sauce over three eggs, tomato sauce over the other three. Sprinkle each serving with chopped parsley.

PRINCESS MARIE BLANCHE DE BROGLIE, PARIS, FRANCE.

L'ECOLE DE CUISINE

This recipe was submitted with best wishes by PRINCESS MARIE BLANCHE DE BROGLIE, PARIS, FRANCE, who conducted the "L'Ecole de Cuisine, 1979" a week-long cooking school in this area to benefit the Annual Development Fund of the Tri-City Symphony Orchestra Association.

EGGS A LA TRISH

8 Servings

4 English muffins, split
½ lb. Old English cheese
   slices
8 slices Canadian bacon
6 eggs
3¼ cups milk
1 T. minced onion
½ tsp. salt
½ tsp. dry mustard

Place 6 muffins in a 9×13" pan; cut remaining 2 muffins in half and fit in pan. Place a slice of cheese and a slice of Canadian bacon on each muffin. Beat eggs, milk, onion, salt and dry mustard and pour over muffins. Cover and refrigerate overnight. Bake at 325° for 1 hour.

Virginia Payton (Mrs. Ed)

EGG-OVEN DISH

8-10 Servings

Good for a brunch--can be made the day before.

3 cups milk
2 T. parsley
¾ tsp. dry mustard
¼ tsp. salt
6 eggs, beaten
10 slices white bread,
   crusts removed and
   cubed
2 cups American cheese,
   cubed or shredded
2 cups ham

Add milk and seasonings to beaten eggs. Stir in bread, cheese and meat. Pour into a greased 9×13" casserole dish. Bake at 325° uncovered for 1 hour or until middle is firm. (Bacon can be used instead of ham - fry and crumble 12 slices)

Ann Payne (Mrs. James)

HAM AND SWISS SANDWICH PUFF   10-12 Servings

2 cups swiss cheese (½ lb.)
2 cups ground cooked
   ham (about 1 lb.)
½ cup mayonnaise
1 tsp. prepared mustard
12 slices sandwich bread,
   toasted
6 eggs
2¼ cups milk
Parsley

Put cheese and ham through the food chopper, using coarse blade. Blend in mayonnaise and mustard. Spread on 6 of the toasted bread slices and top with remaining 6 slices to form sandwiches. Cut each diagonally into quarters. Stand each crust-edge down in a 13×9×2" buttered pan. Beat eggs slightly with milk and pour over sandwiches. Cover and chill at least 4 hours or overnight. Bake for 35 minutes at 325° or until custard sets. Garnish with parsley. Cut between sandwiches and serve immediately.

Babe Neumann (Mrs. Richard)

SAUSAGE STRATA   6 Servings

6 slices bread
1 lb. bulk pork sausage
   (unseasoned)
1 tsp. prepared mustard
1 cup (¼ lb.) swiss cheese,
   shredded
3 eggs, slightly beaten
1½ cups milk
¾ cup light cream
½ tsp. salt
1 T. Worchestershire
   sauce
Dash pepper
Dash nutmeg

Trim crusts from bread and fit in bottom of greased 11×7" baking dish. Brown pork in skillet, drain, stir in mustard. Spoon sausage over the bread. Sprinkle cheese over sausage. Combine other ingredients and pour over cheese. Bake at 350° for 25-30 minutes or until set.

Bonnie Moeller (Mrs. Gerald)

CHEESE PUDDING

8-10 Servings

A delicious side dish--Serve instead of potatoes or bread

¼ lb. butter
¾ lb. sharp cheddar cheese, grated
10 slices bread, crusts removed, broken apart
2 egg yolks
2 egg whites
2 cups milk
¼ - ½ tsp. red pepper
½ tsp. dry mustard
½ tsp. salt

Melt butter and cheese, mix with bread. Separate eggs. Beat whites until stiff and set aside. Beat yolks and add milk and spices. Combine yolk and bread mixtures. Fold in beaten whites. Put into a greased 2 quart glass casserole dish. Refrigerate 12 hours or overnight. Bake at 325° for 40 minutes, then at 350° for 1 hour.

Jane Royster (Mrs. Robert)

CHEESE SOUFFLE

4 Servings

3 T. butter
3 T. flour
1 cup milk
3 egg yolks, beaten
½ tsp. salt
1½ cups shredded cheddar or colby cheese
6 egg whites

Over a medium heat in a medium sized sauce pan, melt butter. Add flour, a tablespoon at a time, stirring constantly. Gradually add milk and stir constantly until sauce thickens. Add egg yolks and salt and stir. Add cheese and stir until melted. Allow sauce to cool slightly. Fold into egg whites which have been beaten stiffly but not dry. Pour into a 1½ qt. ungreased souffle dish, folding a few times. Bake at 350° for 40-45 minutes.

Louise M. Lorimer (Mrs. David)

117

NOODLE KUGEN CHEESE SOUFFLE   15-18 Servings

Yummy!

1 (16 oz.) pkg. flat noodles, cooked
4 eggs, separated
3 T. melted butter or margarine
1 tsp. salt
1 cup sour cream
2 cups small curd creamed cottage cheese

Cook the noodles as directed on the package. Beat egg yolks and whites separately for fluffier souffle. Add melted butter or margarine and 1 tsp. salt. Mix the sour cream and cottage cheese together. Fold all ingredients together softly. Pour into buttered 9×13" casserole. Bake for 40-50 minutes at 350°. (You may add 2 T. sugar, ¼ tsp. cinnamon, and raisins, apples or prunes to make a sweet Kugen.)

JAN D. SLIVKEN

Jan Slivken

JAN SLIVKEN, soprano, has performed lead roles in the "Mikado" and "Madam Butterfly", "Music Man" and "Marriage of Figaro" at the University of Northern Iowa and the University of Iowa. She took part in the Third International Music Festival performances in New York's Lincoln Center and in Kennedy Center, Washington, D.C. in the spring of 1972. In 1975, she performed the role of Kate Pinkerton in "Madam Butterfly" with the Tri-City Symphony. She is currently studying voice under Miss Julia LeVine in Chicago. Mrs. Slivken, a resident of Bettendorf, is a very active member of the Junior Board of the Tri-City Symphony and is especially dedicated to music educational projects, creating and organizing the 1979 String and Wind Ensemble Tour in the local area schools, sponsored by the Junior Board and Musicians' Performance Trust Fund.

SALMON SOUFFLE

4 Servings

1 egg
1 small onion
½ small green pepper
Dash Worchestershire
  sauce
Dash celery seed
Sprig of parsley
Seasoned salt to taste
Pepper to taste
1 cup milk
1 can (10¾ oz.) salmon
1 cellophane pkg. saltine
  crackers, crushed to
  medium sized pieces
2 strips bacon, cut to 1"
  pieces

Place first 9 ingredients into blender container and blend until smooth. Remove from blender and add salmon and crackers and mix well. Place in medium sized greased casserole and top with bacon pieces. Bake covered at 350° for 45 minutes. Uncover and bake for 15 minutes more.

Betty Stevens (Mrs. Dale)

CHEESE SOUFFLE WITH SHRIMP

10-12 Servings

16 slices white bread, crusts
  removed, sliced in half
1 lb. cheddar cheese slices
1 lb. swiss cheese slices
1 pkg. (16 oz.) frozen
  shrimp, cooked
6 eggs
3 cups milk
½ tsp. onion salt
½ tsp. dry mustard
Salt
Pepper
Cornflakes crumbled
3 T. butter, melted

Grease a 9×13" glass baking dish. Layer half of the bread, cheddar cheese, swiss cheese and shrimp into the pan. Mash down and repeat until all is used. Combine eggs, milk, onion salt, mustard, salt and pepper to taste. Pour over casserole and refrigerate overnight. Combine enough mashed cornflakes (to cover casserole) and butter. Sprinkle over top. Bake at 375° for 40 minutes.

Judy Seefeldt (Mrs. Joseph)

QUICHE LORRAINE WITH NO ROLL CRUST 6 Servings

NO ROLL CRUST:
1½ cups flour
1½ tsp. salt
 ½ cup salad oil
 2 T. milk

FILLING:
 1 egg white
 8 slices bacon, fried and
 crumbled
 1 cup green onions,
 minced (include tops)
 ½ lb. swiss cheese, grated
 1 T. flour
 3 whole eggs
 1 egg yolk
1½ cups cream (or 1 cup
 cream plus ½ cup milk)
Salt
Cayenne pepper

For crust: Put ingredients in order given in 9" quiche pan and mix well. Pat in place, covering sides and bottom. Bake at 450° for 5 minutes.

For filling: Brush pie shell with egg white. Sprinkle bacon pieces in bottom of pie shell. Saute onion in small amount of bacon grease until it is limp. Spread over bacon. Dredge cheese in flour and arrange over onion and bacon. Beat together eggs, cream, salt and pepper and pour into quiche shell. Bake at 450° for 10 minutes. Reduce oven to 350° and continue baking for 25 minutes. Remove from oven and cool 10 minutes before serving.

Penny Lounsberry (Mrs. John)

GARDEN QUICHE

4-6 Servings

Good as a supper dish served with onion soup and tossed green salad.

6 eggs, lightly beaten
2 cups light cream
6 T. Dijon mustard
½ cup onion, minced
1 cup swiss cheese, grated
1 cup gruyere cheese,
  grated
½ tsp. salt
¼ tsp. pepper
2 cups fresh spinach, diced
9" unbaked pie shell
Roquefort cheese,
  crumbled (optional)

Combine first 9 ingredients and pour into shell. Sprinkle with roquefort cheese to taste, if desired. Bake at 375° for 45-50 minutes or until knife inserted in center comes out clean.

Jean Steffenson (Mrs. Michael)

FRUITED QUICHE

4-6 Servings

1 cup cooked ham, diced
1 medium green pepper,
  chopped
¼ cup butter
1 pkg. (8 oz.) diced dates
  (or whole dates, cut up)
1 tsp. salt
⅛ tsp. pepper
2 cups evaporated milk
2 eggs, slightly beaten
1 cup cheddar cheese,
  grated
1 cup swiss cheese, grated
9" pie shell, unbaked

Saute ham and green pepper in butter. Add dates and saute 1 minute longer. Season with salt and pepper. Remove from heat. Mix milk, eggs and cheeses. Add to meat-date mixture. Mix well. Pour into pie shell. Bake at 425° for 20-30 minutes, or until knife inserted in center comes out clean. Let stand 10-15 minutes before serving.

Muriel Butler (Mrs. Allen)

TURKEY OR CHICKEN QUICHE

6-8 Servings

½ cup mayonnaise
2 T. flour
½ cup milk
2 eggs, beaten
8 oz. cheese, grated
  (mild cheddar)
2 cups diced turkey
  or chicken
¼ cup green onion,
  chopped (include stalks)
9" deep-dish pie shell,
  unbaked

Combine all ingredients and pour into the unbaked pie crust. Bake at 375° for 35-40 minutes, or until knife inserted in center comes out clean. Serve in wedges.

Marjorie Cooper (Mrs. Steve)

BAKED CHICKEN SALAD

6-8 Servings

4 T. flour
4 T. margarine
1 cup chicken broth
2½ - 3 cups diced chicken
1 cup celery, diced
2 tsp. green onion, minced
½ cup almonds or pecans,
  chopped
2 hard boiled eggs,
  chopped
½ tsp. salt
¼ tsp. pepper
¼ tsp. Worcestershire
  sauce
1 T. lemon juice
¾ cup mayonnaise
2 cups crushed potato
  chips

Make white sauce with flour, margarine and broth. Add chicken and all other ingredients except chips. Mix thoroughly. Line a 1 quart baking dish with half of potato chips. Pour in chicken mixture and top with remaining potato chips. Bake uncovered at 400° for 30 minutes.

Virginette O'Donnell (Mrs. John)

122

CHICKEN-ALMOND CASSEROLE   6-8 Servings

¼ cup butter
¼ cup flour
1 cup chicken broth
1 can (13 oz.) evaporated milk
1 tsp. salt
Dash pepper
2½ cups cooked, diced chicken (1 lg. chicken)
3 cups cooked rice
1 jar (2½ oz.) sliced mushrooms
¼ cup pimento, chopped
¼ cup green pepper, finely chopped
½ cup slivered almonds

Mix butter and flour in saucepan until smooth on low heat. Add chicken broth and evaporated milk to make a white sauce. Add salt and pepper. Remove from heat and add remaining ingredients. Place in a greased 2 quart casserole and bake, covered, at 350° for 30 minutes.

Arlene Tallman (Mrs. Edward)

MOM'S BEST CHICKEN CASSEROLE   12 Servings
Great for Thanksgiving weekend -- Use left-over white meat

12 slices white bread, crusts removed
4 cups cooked white turkey or chicken meat diced
1 can (8 oz.) sliced mushrooms, drained
1 can (8 oz.) water chestnuts, sliced
Butter
1 can (10¾ oz.) cream of mushroom soup
1 can (10¾ oz.) cream of celery soup
½ cup mayonnaise
1 jar (2 oz.) chopped pimento
8 - 10 slices sharp cheddar cheese
4 eggs
2 cups milk
½ tsp. salt
1 pkg. (6 oz.) seasoned stuffing mix
Butter, melted

In a 9×13″ greased baking dish, arrange a layer of bread, chicken, mushrooms, and water chestnuts. Dot with butter. Combine soups and mayonnaise. Pour over layers. Add pimento and cheese over casserole. Mix eggs, milk, salt and pepper. Pour over all. Refrigerate overnight. Bake at 350° for 1 hour and 20 minutes. Remove from oven. Combine stuffing mix and enough melted butter to moisten. Spread over casserole. Return to oven and bake 10 minutes more. Remove and cool 10 minutes.

Penny Lounsberry (Mrs. John)

CHICKEN MUSHROOM CREPES　　16 Crepes

Double the sauce ingredients for extra richness.

2 T. butter
1 clove garlic, crushed
3 lbs. chicken breasts
1 tsp. salt
$1/_8$ tsp. pepper
¼ tsp. cinnamon
½ cup chicken broth
½ cup cooking sherry
1 T. fresh parsley, minced
1 cup fresh mushrooms, sliced
1 cup heavy cream
$1/_8$ tsp. paprika
3 egg yolks
16 warm crepes
Parsley
Pimento

In large skillet, melt butter with garlic. Add chicken, salt, pepper, cinnamon, broth, sherry, parsley, and mushrooms. Cover and cook over low heat until chicken is very tender. Remove chicken from skillet. Cool slightly. Bone and cut meat into small pieces. Set aside and keep warm. Meanwhile, stir cream and paprika into broth. Beat egg yolks and add several tablespoons hot broth to eggs, then stir this mixture into remaining broth. Cook over low heat, beating constantly with a whisk until slightly thickened.

Fill each crepe with about ¼ cup of cooked chicken and one tablespoon sauce. Place folded crepes on a platter and pour remaining sauce over filled crepes. Garnish with a sprig of fresh parsley and slice of pimento. Serve hot.

Mary Greenberg (Mrs. Martin)

CREPES　　32-36 Crepes

4 eggs
¼ tsp. salt
2 cups flour
2¼ cups milk
¼ cup butter, melted

In bowl, combine eggs and salt. Gradually add flour alternately with milk, beating until smooth. Beat in melted butter. Refrigerate batter at least 1 hour.

Lightly butter an 8″ skillet and heat over medium heat until butter is bubbly. Pour a scant ¼ cup of batter into skillet and rotate pan until batter covers the bottom. Cook to a light, golden brown.

CANNELLONI

FILLING:
- ½ lb. sausage
- 1 pkg. (10 oz.) frozen chopped spinach
- ½ cup chicken, ground or chopped, cooked
- ¼ cup parmesan cheese, grated
- ⅛ tsp. thyme
- ⅛ tsp. pepper

CHEESE SAUCE:
- 3 T. butter
- 3 T. flour
- 1½ cup half and half cream
- ½ cup parmesan cheese, grated

1 recipe crepes, page 124

Cook and drain the sausage. Cook spinach until just tender and drain well. Combine sausage, spinach, and all other filling ingredients.

For cheese sauce: Melt the butter and add flour to make a roux. Add light cream and cook over hot water until thick. Stir in parmesan cheese.

To assemble: Spread each crepe with ¼ cup filling mixture. Roll up and arrange in 9×13" glass baking dish. Pour cheese sauce over all. Bake at 350° for 20 minutes then place under broiler until cheese sauce bubbles.

Kath Wilson (Mrs. Charles)

GOOD THINGS -- GOOD TIMES CASSEROLE

This is a great favorite with the String Tour!

- ½ cup onion, chopped
- 2 T. butter
- 3 T. flour
- ½ tsp. salt
- ¼ tsp. pepper
- 1 can (3 oz.) button mushrooms
- 1 cup light cream
- 2 - 4 tsp. dry sherry
- 2 cups diced cooked turkey or chicken meat
- 1 can (6 oz.) water chestnuts, drained and sliced thinly
- 1 cup cooked ham, diced
- ½ cup grated swiss cheese
- 1½ cups soft bread crumbs
- 3 T. butter, melted

6 Servings

Cook onion in butter until tender. Blend in flour, salt and pepper. Add mushrooms, cream and sherry. Cook, stirring constantly until thickened and bubbly. (Liquid from mushrooms may be included in this white sauce). Add turkey, chestnuts, and ham. Pour into a 1½ quart casserole and cover with swiss cheese. Mix bread crumbs with butter and sprinkle over cheese. Bake at 400° for 35 minutes or until the top browns.

Harriet Harmelink (Mrs. Roger)

ICE CURRIED CHICKEN

4-5 Servings

An English recipe

1 T. olive oil
1 small onion, chopped
1 T. curry powder
½ cup chicken stock
1 tsp. (rounded) tomato
    puree
Juice of ½ lemon
2 T. chutney
1 cup mayonnaise
3 T. cream
1 fried or baked chicken,
    cooled
3 cups cooked rice
4 - 6 slices bacon, fried
    and crumbled

Heat oil in saucepan, add onion and fry for 5 minutes, covered. Stir in curry and cook. Add chicken stock, tomato puree, lemon juice and chutney. Stir until boiling and then simmer 5 minutes. Strain sauce and allow to cool. Stir in mayonnaise and cream. Remove flesh from chicken. Spoon rice onto a medium sized platter. Arrange chicken on top of rice and pour sauce over all. Refrigerate for several hours. Before serving, garnish with crumbled bacon.

Betty Reimers (Mrs. Robert)

CHICKEN "HAYSTACK" SALAD

8 Servings

1 cup carrots, shredded
½ cup onions, chopped
    finely
1 cup celery, diced
2 cups cooked chicken,
    diced
1 cup mayonnaise
1 can (4 oz.) shoestring
    potatoes
Egg slices
Olives

Combine carrots, onions, celery and chicken. Moisten with mayonnaise. Add shoestring potatoes to salad just before serving, to prevent them from becoming soggy. Serve on lettuce. Trim with egg slices and olives if you wish.

This recipe makes a fun lunch for your friends. Just add rolls and dessert - - you're all set!!

Virginia Payton (Mrs. Ed)

ARROZ CON VALENCIA
15-20 Servings

A real party dish for a crowd.

½ cup olive oil
30 small onions, canned
  or fresh
2 garlic buds, chopped
5 cans (8 oz. each) tomato
  sauce
Salt
Fresh ground pepper
3 to 4 chickens, cut up
  (no backs, necks, livers)
1½ cups raw rice
3 cups chicken broth
1½ cups cubed ham
2 pkgs. (10 oz. each)
  frozen peas
2 cans artichoke hearts
2 cans pimento, cut in
  strips
2 lbs. shrimp

In a large casserole (or two smaller, deep dishes), put oil, onions, garlic, tomato sauce, and twice as much salt as you think you need. Bake at 350° for 15 minutes. Add chicken pieces, sprinkle with salt. Bake 1 hour. Add rice, broth, ham, more salt. Bake 30 minutes. Sprinkle partly thawed peas in a layer. Wrap strips of pimento around the artichokes, arrange on top. Place shrimp among artichokes, sprinkle with salt. Bake 45 minutes more.

Dorothy Lundahl (Mrs. Arthur)

CASHEW VEAL CASSEROLE
6-8 Servings

½ cup uncooked rice
1½ soup cans water
1½ lbs. cubed veal or beef
1 small onion, diced
3 T. butter
1 can (10¾ oz.) cream of
  mushroom soup
1 can (10¾ oz.) cream of
  chicken soup
1 cup celery, diced
1 cup cashews, chopped

Soak rice in water for 15 minutes. Brown veal and onion in butter. Add rice and water to meat mixture. Add soups, celery and cashews. Pour into 1½ quart casserole. Bake at 325° for 90 minutes.

Bonnie Moeller (Mrs. Gerald)

WILD RICE AND HAM CASSEROLE   6-8 Servings

1 pkg. (6 oz.) long grain
  and wild rice
2 pkgs. (10 oz.each) frozen
  chopped broccoli
12 oz. ham, cut into ½" cubes
1 can (4 oz.) mushroom
  slices
1 cup cheddar cheese,
  shredded
1 can (10¾ oz.) cream of
  celery soup
1 cup mayonnaise
2 tsp. prepared mustard
½ cup parmesan cheese

Cook rice according to package directions. Put in bottom of well greased 9×13" dish. Partially cook the broccoli using the juice from the mushrooms. Drain. Lay broccoli on top of rice. (Fresh broccoli can be used instead of frozen.) Layer ham, mushrooms, and cheddar cheese in dish. Mix together soup, mayonnaise and mustard. Pour on top. Sprinkle with parmesan cheese. Bake at 350° for 45 minutes.

Penny Lounsberry (Mrs. John)

HAM RICE BAKE   4-6 Servings

½ cup evaporated milk
1 can (10¾ oz.) cream of
  asparagus soup
2 - 4 T. onion, minced
1 egg, well beaten
3 cups cooked ham, diced
2 cups cooked rice
½ cup cheddar cheese,
  shredded
¾ cup cornflake crumbs
3 T. butter, melted

Combine milk, soup, onion and egg and fold gently into ham, rice, and cheese. Top with buttered cornflake crumbs and bake in uncovered 1 quart casserole at 375° for 20-25 minutes.

Barbara Jones (Mrs. Robert)

HAM AND BROCCOLI CASSEROLE   8 Servings

12 slices frozen white bread
10 slices sharp processed
  American cheese
1 pkg. (10 oz.) frozen,
  chopped broccoli,
  cooked and drained
2 cups cooked or canned
  ham, cubed
4 eggs, slightly beaten
2½ cups milk
2 T. instant minced onions
¼ tsp. mustard
½ tsp. salt
¼ cup shredded cheddar
  cheese

Cut doughnuts and holes from frozen bread; set aside. Fit scraps of bread in 13×9×2" greased baking dish. Place cheese slices in layer over bread. Add layer of broccoli, then ham. Arrange bread doughnuts and holes on top. Combine remaining ingredients except shredded cheese; pour over bread. Cover; refrigerate for at least 6 hours. Bake, uncovered, 325° for 55 minutes. Sprinkle with shredded cheese; bake 5 minutes longer. Let stand for 10 minutes to firm.

Diann Moore (Mrs. Robert)

CRAB CASSEROLE WITH EGGS AND SUCH

8 slices white bread
2 cups half and half cream
2 cups real mayonnaise
6 hard boiled eggs,
  chopped
2 T. onion, grated
2 T. parsley, chopped
1½ lbs. frozen snow crab,
  well drained
2 tsp. lemon juice
Salt
Pepper
Paprika
Curry
Thyme
1½ cups parmesan cheese
Crushed cornflakes

10-12 Servings

Cut off crusts of bread and cube into cream. Let this set until bread is soft. Add mayonnaise, eggs, onion, parsley, crab, lemon juice, salt, pepper and spices and mix well. Layer in a 3 quart casserole with cheese. Refrigerate overnight. Crush enough cornflakes to cover top of casserole. Bake at 350° for 1 hour.

Sue Katz (Mrs. Martin)

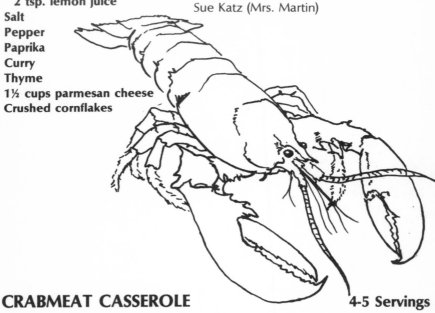

CRABMEAT CASSEROLE

4-5 Servings

May be heated and served in individual sea shells.

1 can (10¾ oz.) mushroom
  soup
¼ cup water
1½ cups chow mein noodles
  (separated)
2 cans (6 oz. each)
  crabmeat
1 cup sliced celery
½ cup salted toasted
  cashews
2 T. onion, finely chopped
Salt

Combine soup with water. Add ¾ cup noodles, crabmeat, celery, nuts and onion. Toss lightly. Place in ungreased 1½ quart casserole baking dish (or shells). Sprinkle remaining noodles on top. Bake at 375° for 15 minutes or until heated through.

Kay Stegmiller (Mrs. Stan)

BAKED SEAFOOD SALAD

8 Servings

1 can (8 oz.) sliced
  mushrooms
¾ cup green pepper,
  chopped
½ cup onion, chopped
4 T. butter
1 can (8 oz.) water
  chestnuts, sliced thinly
2½ cups mayonnaise
1 tsp. Dijon mustard
1½ tsp. salt
½ tsp. cayenne pepper
2 tsp. Worcestershire
  sauce
4 hard cooked eggs,
  chopped
2 cups celery, finely
  chopped
1 lb. shrimp, cooked
1 lb. lump crabmeat
2 cups buttered bread
  crumbs
Paprika

Saute mushrooms, green pepper and onion in butter. Combine with all other ingredients except bread crumbs and paprika. Place in 3 quart casserole dish and sprinkle with bread crumbs and paprika. Bake at 350° for 30 minutes or until heated through. Let stand 5 minutes.

May be served hot or cold.

Ann Spaeth (Mrs. James)

CRAB LOUIS

4 Servings

DRESSING:
1 cup mayonnaise
½ cup heavy cream,
  whipped
¼ cup chili sauce
2 T. onion, grated
2 T. parsley, finely
  chopped
Dash of cayenne pepper

SALAD:
Lettuce, shredded
1½ lbs. lump crabmeat
Hard boiled eggs
Fresh tomatoes
Avocado
Artichoke hearts

Combine all dressing ingredients and refrigerate. Prepare salad by arranging shredded lettuce on a platter. Place flaked crabmeat over lettuce. Garnish with sliced hard boiled eggs, peeled and quartered tomatoes, sliced avocado, and artichoke hearts. Pour the Louis dressing over all.

Crab Louis was created by the chef at the Olympic Club in Seattle. When the Metropolitan Opera Co. played Seattle in 1904, Enrico Caruso kept ordering the salad until none was left in the kitchen.

Ginny Neiley (Mrs. George)

SHRIMP CASSEROLE HARPIN   6-8 Servings

2 lbs. large, fresh shrimp
1 T. lemon juice
3 T. salad oil
¾ cup raw rice
2 T. butter
¼ cup green pepper,
   minced
¼ cup onion, minced
1 tsp. salt.
¹/₈ tsp. pepper
¼ - ½ cup sherry
¹/₈ tsp. mace
½ cup heavy cream (use
   more if needed)
1 can (10¾ oz.) tomato
   soup
½ cup slivered almonds
Paprika

Cook shrimp in boiling, salted water for 5 minutes; drain. Place in 2 quart casserole and sprinkle with lemon juice and oil. Cook rice according to package directions. Saute the pepper and onion in butter for 5 minutes. Add pepper, onion, rice, salt and all other ingredients, except paprika and almonds, to shrimp mixture. Combine well. Sprinkle top of casserole with almonds and paprika. Bake at 350° for 55 minutes.

Pat Gerstenberger (Mrs. Robert)

BAKED SEAFOOD   4 Servings

1 T. flour
1 lb. cooked shrimp or
   thawed scallops
½ cup (1 stick) butter
1 medium onion, grated
½ clove garlic, minced
⅓ lb. fresh mushrooms
Celery salt
1 pint sour cream

Dredge shrimp or scallops in flour (or shake in paper bag). Melt butter in skillet. Add grated onion and fry lightly. Add garlic and mushrooms (sliced). Sprinkle with a dash of celery salt. Add seafood and heat gently. Stir in sour cream last, and cook slowly until heated through, but do not boil. Serve with toast points and green salad.

Sue Staack (Mrs. John)

CRABMEAT MOUSSE

6-8 Servings

1 can (10¾ oz.) tomato
  soup
1 pkg. (8 oz.) cream
  cheese
2 env. unflavored gelatin
  (¼ oz. each)
¼ cup cold water
3 cans (6 oz. each)
  crabmeat
1 cup mayonnaise
¾ cup celery, chopped
  finely
1 med. onion, chopped
1 tsp. salt
½ tsp. paprika
2 dashes Tabasco sauce
1 tsp. Worcestershire
  sauce
2 tsp. white horseradish

Heat soup and cream cheese, stir until cheese melts. Soften gelatin in cold water and dissolve in soup mixture. Cool. Drain crabmeat and fold in all remaining ingredients. Place in a lightly greased mold and refrigerate. (A fish mold is especially attractive.) This can be used as an elegant appetizer with crackers.

Elaine Schneff (Mrs. Warren)

SALMON MOLD PIQUANTE

4 Servings

1 T. unflavored gelatin
¼ cup cold water
1½ tsp. salt
1½ tsp. Dijon mustard
Dash red pepper
2 egg yolks, slightly beaten
¾ cup milk
1½ T. butter, melted
4 T. lemon juice
1 cup flaked salmon
Dill weed
Mayonnaise

Soften gelatin in cold water for 5 minutes. Combine seasonings, egg yolks, and milk in top of double boiler and cook over hot water 6-8 minutes, until thickened, stirring constantly. Add butter, lemon juice, and gelatin, stirring until gelatin is dissolved. Remove from heat and fold in salmon. Turn into mold and chill until firm. Garnish with cucumber slices sprinkled with dill weed and serve with mayonnaise.

Linda Clarke (Mrs. Wade)

LORNA'S SALMON

2 cups cooked rice
2 eggs, beaten
2 cups small curd cottage
cheese
1 can (15½ oz.) salmon,
drained and flaked
1 small onion, chopped
¼ cup green pepper,
chopped
2 tsp. soy sauce
1 cup soda crackers,
crushed

SAUCE:
3 T. butter
1 can (4 oz.) sliced
mushrooms
3 T. flour (heaping)
1 tsp. seasoned salt
1½ cups milk
1½ cups cooked peas
2 T. pimento, chopped

Combine all ingredients, except crumbs, and spoon into buttered 12×7×2" pan. Sprinkle cracker crumbs over top. Bake at 350° for 40 minutes or until firm in the middle.

To prepare sauce: Cook mushrooms in butter for 5 minutes, stir in flour and salt. Gradually add milk and cook until smooth and thickened. Add peas and pimento. Cut casserole into squares and spoon sauce over each serving.

Anne V. Mairet (Mrs. Richard)

TUNA QUADRETINNI

1 pkg. (8 oz.) med. sized
noodles
2 pkgs. (10 oz. each)
chopped broccoli
2 cans (6½ oz. each) tuna
1 clove garlic, minced
1 can (6 oz.) sliced
mushrooms
½ tsp. salt
¼ tsp. basil leaves
½ tsp. liquid red pepper
seasoning
2 cans (8 oz. each) tomato
sauce
½ cup grated parmesan
cheese

Cook noodles as directed on package. Cook broccoli; drain. Drain oil from tuna into skillet. Add garlic and saute lightly. Add mushrooms with liquid, seasonings, tomato sauce and tuna. Let simmer 10 minutes. In greased 2½ quart casserole, layer half the noodles, half the broccoli, and half the tuna mixture. Repeat layers. Sprinkle with cheese. Bake at 375° for 20 minutes.

Lynn Goebel (Mrs. George)

TUNA BROCCOLI LUNCHEON CASSEROLE

¼ cup almonds
1 T. butter
2 pkgs. (10 oz. each) frozen chopped broccoli
1 can (10 oz.) water-packed tuna, drained
1 can (4 oz.) button mushrooms, drained
½ cup dry bread crumbs
½ cup water chestnuts, sliced
½ cup cheddar cheese, shredded
½ cup milk
1 can (10¾ oz.) cream of mushroom soup
¼ cup mayonnaise
¼ tsp. salt
2 T. pimento, chopped (optional)

8 Servings

Toast almonds in butter. Thaw and drain broccoli, arrange in buttered 8×12″ baking dish. Sprinkle tuna, mushrooms, half of bread crumbs, water chestnuts, and cheese over top. Combine milk, soup, mayonnaise, salt and pimento. Pour over tuna mixture. Add remaining bread crumbs to toasted almonds. Sprinkle over casserole. Bake at 350° for 45 minutes.

Ann Green (Mrs. Fred)

TUNA NOODLE CASSEROLE

4-6 Servings

6 oz. wide egg noodles
1 can (6½ oz.) chunk light tuna
½ cup mayonnaise
½ cup sour cream
½ cup milk
1 can (10¾ oz.) mushroom soup
1 cup celery, chopped
1 small onion, diced
¼ cup green pepper, chopped
4 oz. American cheese
¼ cup slivered almonds
¼ cup green olives, chopped

Cook the egg noodles and drain them. Mix the remaining ingredients and fold into the noodles. Place in a greased 2 quart casserole and bake uncovered at 425° for 20 minutes.

Laura Houston (Mrs. Douglas)

TUNAFISH SALAD

3 Servings

1 can (7 oz.) tunafish, drained
½ cup celery, chopped
1 tsp. lemon juice
1 small onion, chopped
$1/_8$ tsp. curry powder
1 can (8 oz.) peas, drained
1 tsp. soy sauce
$3/_8$ cup mayonnaise
Salt, to taste
1 cup chow mein noodles

Mix all ingredients together, except noodles, and refrigerate overnight for best flavor. At serving time, add 1 cup chow mein noodles, toss gently and serve on greens.

Rosalie Murphy

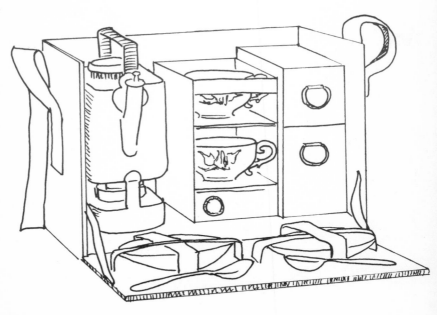

KREATOPITA CEPHALONIKI
(MEAT PIE, ISLAND VERSION)   8 Servings

This recipe, from one of the Ionian Islands, is a traditional dish for Ascension Day.

2½ lb. leg of lamb
 2 onions, chopped
 2 tsp. salt
 ½ tsp. pepper
Water
 ¼ cup rice
 1 T. butter
 2 cloves garlic, chopped
 ¼ cup dry red wine
 1 tsp. finely ground
   orange rind
 ½ tsp. crushed mint
1½ tsp. crushed parsley
 ½ tsp. cinnamon
 3 T. tomato sauce
 2 small boiled potatoes,
   peeled and diced
 ½ cup feta cheese,
   crumbled
 ½ cup ketalotyri cheese,
   grated (may use
   parmesan or romano)
 ½ lb. butter, melted
 ½ lb. fillo pastry
 4 hard boiled eggs, sliced

Wash meat, place in a heavy kettle or dutch oven. Add half of the chopped onion, salt, pepper, and enough water to cover meat. Cover and cook over a medium heat 1½ to 2 hours, or until tender. Skim off the fat. Place meat on a platter to cool. Measure the stock and add water, if necessary, to make 2 cups. In a sauce pan, combine 1 cup stock and rice. Cover and boil for 10 minutes. Melt the butter in a skillet and saute the remaining onion and garlic until golden. Cut the cooked lamb into 1" cubes. In a bowl, combine the lamb, partially cooked rice, sauteed onion and garlic, remaining cup of stock, wine, orange rind, mint, parsley, cinnamon, tomato sauce, diced potatoes, feta cheese and grated cheese. Mix well. Butter an 8×8×2" glass baking dish. Place one sheet of fillo pastry in bottom of dish. Brush with butter. Repeat pastry and butter using ¼ lb. fillo for bottom crust. Add meat filling and arrange sliced eggs over top. Cover with remaining sheets of fillo, each brushed with butter. Pour any remaining butter over the top. Roll all sheets of dough together in towards the center, one side at a time. Score through top layers of fillo into 8 pieces. Bake at 350° for 45 minutes. Let stand for 15 minutes before cutting.

Diana Mihaltse (Mrs. William)

WATERCRESS-SPINACH PITA   12 Servings

This is an authentic Greek recipe.

2 pkgs. (10 oz. each)
  frozen chopped spinach
  or 1 lb. fresh
1 bunch scallions,
  chopped
2 T. butter
2 bunches watercress,
  chopped
½ cup fresh dill, chopped
5 large eggs
2 pkgs. (8 oz. each) cream
  cheese
½ lb. feta cheese
4 oz. cottage cheese
½ tsp. salt
½ tsp. nutmeg
½ cup fresh parsley,
  chopped
½ lb. sweet cream butter
1 lb. fillo pastry

Defrost spinach and drain well. Saute the scallions in butter. Add spinach, watercress and fresh dill and cook until dry. Remove from heat and set aside. Mix eggs, cream cheese, feta cheese, cottage cheese, salt, nutmeg, and parsley. Add spinach mixture. Melt the sweet butter in a small saucepan. Using some sweet butter, butter a 9×13" glass baking dish. Place one sheet of fillo pastry in bottom of pan. Butter well with melted sweet butter. Repeat until there are 7 layers of dough. Add spinach and egg mixture. Layer 7 more buttered sheets of pastry for the top. Generously butter the last sheet all the way to the edges. Roll all sheets of dough together in towards the center, starting with the 9" ends. The result will be a nicely rolled crust edge. Bake at 350° for 30-35 minutes, until golden brown.

Diana Mihaltse (Mrs. William)

GREEK STUFFED TOMATOES   12 Servings

12 tomatoes, ripe and fresh
1 lb. ground beef
½ cup raw rice
1 onion, grated
½ tsp. cinnamon
½ cup raisins
¼ cup walnuts, chopped
Salt
Pepper
Fresh mint
Butter

Cut a thin slice off top of tomatoes, save. Carefully scoop out the pulp and juice, leaving a shell. (Do this over a colander with a bowl underneath to catch the juice.) Chop up the pulp and mix with all other ingredients (except butter). Stuff tomatoes. Butter a 9×12" baking dish and arrange the tomatoes in the dish. Put a pat of butter on each tomato. Put cap on. Pour juice in pan. Bake at 350° for 1 hour, baste with juice.

Green peppers may be used instead of tomatoes.

Eleanor Pappas

ITALIAN SPAGHETTI AND MEATBALLS   8 Servings

This recipe was passed down through 3 generations of Italians.

SAUCE:
2 cans (1 lb. 12 oz.)
   tomatoes
1 can (6 oz.) tomato paste
2 - 2½ cups water
2 - 3 cloves whole garlic
1 tsp. salt
1 tsp. basil
1 T. oregano
Baking soda
¼ - ½ cup brown sugar

MEATBALLS:
1 lb. ground beef
1 lb. plain pork sausage
¼ cup grated parmesan
   cheese
½ cup (or more) bread
   or cracker crumbs
2 eggs
1 medium chopped onion
1 tsp. salt

To prepare sauce: Mix first 7 ingredients together in 4 quart stainless steel pan. Cook over medium heat until simmering well. Add one pinch of baking soda. (This will neutralize the acidity of the tomatoes.) Cook an additional 15 minutes. Add the brown sugar. Cook an additional 30 minutes; add more salt, oregano or basil according to taste. (White sugar or honey may be added at this point if more sweetness is desired.) Continue cooking, uncovered, on low heat until mixture boils down and becomes thick. Stir occasionally. For meatballs: Combine ingredients for meatballs and roll into 1½" balls. Brown in skillet, drain and add to the tomato sauce. Serve over any type pasta.

(Fresh tomatoes may be substituted for the canned tomatoes, tomato paste and water. Use 1 quart home canned stewed tomatoes or 3-4 quarts peeled, cored and quartered home grown tomatoes.)

Peggy Ragona

ITALIAN TORTILLA STACKS   8-10 Servings

1½ lbs. ground beef
1 pkg. (1½ oz.) spaghetti
  sauce mix
1 tsp. seasoned salt
1 can (16 oz.) tomatoes
  (cut in bite-size pieces)
1 can (8 oz.) tomato sauce
½ cup water
1 can (4 oz.) green chiles
  seeds removed,
  chopped
1 lb. ricotta cheese
2 eggs
1 lb. Monterey Jack
  cheese, grated
8 corn tortillas

Brown ground beef until crumbly. Drain fat. Add spaghetti sauce mix, seasoned salt, tomatoes, tomato sauce, water and chilies. Blend thoroughly. Simmer slowly for 10 minutes. Meanwhile, combine ricotta and eggs; blend well, spread evenly on each tortilla. Spread one cup meat sauce in 12×8×2" baking dish. Place 2 cheese topped tortillas side by side in the dish. Spread ⅓ cup of meat mixture and ⅓ cup grated cheese over each. Repeat until each stack contains 4 tortillas layered with meat and cheese. Bake at 350° for 30 minutes. Let stand 5 minutes before cutting into pie-shaped wedges.

Sheri Power (Mrs. Warren)

JOHNNY MASETTI   6-8 Servings

2 lbs. ground beef
1 can (10¾ oz.) tomato
  soup
½ cup water
½ green pepper, chopped
1 large onion, chopped
1 cup cheddar cheese,
  cubed
1 can (4 oz.) mushrooms,
  drained
Salt
Pepper
1 pkg. (8 oz.) noodles
Paprika
American cheese slices

Brown and drain meat. Add soup and ½ cup water. Add pepper, onion, cheese and mushrooms. Stir and cook until cheese is melted. Add salt and pepper to taste. Cook noodles to package directions and drain. In a 3 quart casserole, layer noodles and meat mixture; repeat process. Top with slices of American cheese and paprika. Bake at 350° for 30 minutes.

Judy Dougherty (Mrs. William)

LASAGNE

1 lb. ground beef
1 clove garlic, minced
1 T. dried parsley flakes
1 T. oregano
1½ tsp. salt
1 can (1 lb.) tomatoes
2 cans (6 oz. each)
  tomato paste
9 lasagne noodles
1 carton (1 lb.) small curd
  cottage cheese
2 pkgs. (1 lb. each)
  mozzarella slices

Brown hamburger, add spices, tomatoes and tomato paste. Simmer uncovered until thick, about 1 hour. (Sauce can be made a day ahead.) Cook lasagne noodles according to package directions; rinse in cold water.

To assemble: Place 3 noodles in bottom of 9×13" baking dish; add ½ of meat sauce. Spread ½ of cottage cheese over meat and arrange ½ of mozzarella slices over cottage cheese. Repeat layers ending up with noodles. Bake at 375° for 30 minutes. Let stand for 10-15 minutes before cutting.

Kay Runge (Mrs. Peter)

MAGGIE'S MOSTACCIOLI

1½ lbs. ground chuck
½ cup onion, chopped
¼ cup celery, diced
1 can (4 oz.) mushrooms
½ clove garlic
1 tsp. oregano
1/8 tsp. basil
1/8 tsp. thyme
½ bay leaf
1½ tsp. salt
1/8 tsp. pepper
1 can (1 lb. 12 oz.)
  tomatoes
1 can (6 oz.) tomato paste
½ cup hot water with 1
  beef boullion cube
  dissolved
8 oz. mostaccioli
½ cup parmesan cheese

Brown beef and drain excess liquid. Saute onion, celery, mushrooms, and garlic; (add oil if necessary) add beef. Add all other ingredients except mostaccioli and parmesan cheese. Bring to boil, stirring frequently. Reduce heat and simmer slowly about 1 hour. Cook mostaccioli according to package directions. Mix sauce and noodles. Put in 4 quart casserole and top with parmesan cheese. Bake covered at 350° until bubbling, 45 minutes to 1 hour.

Maggie Collins (Mrs. C. Dean)

CHILIES RELLENO CASSEROLE

4-6 Servings

2 cans (7 oz. each) whole green chilies
1 lb. cheddar cheese, grated
½ lb. Monterey Jack cheese, grated
4 or 5 eggs, beaten
2 T. flour
1 can (13 oz.) evaporated milk
1 can (8 oz.) tomato sauce

Grease a 7x11" pan. Alternate 2 layers of chilies and cheese. Beat eggs, flour and milk together and pour over top. Bake at 375° for 35 minutes. Take out and pour tomato sauce over top. Bake 5 minutes longer.

Darline Streed (Mrs. Warren)

TACO SALAD

6 Servings

A meal in itself

½ cup white rice, cooked and drained
1 can (15 oz.) chili without beans
2 cups taco chips, crushed
1 medium onion, chopped
1 - 2 medium tomatoes, chopped
1 small head lettuce

TOPPING:
2 cups American cheese
4 T. water
2 T. butter

Cook rice and thoroughly heat chili. Meanwhile, make topping.

For topping: Melt all ingredients together until smooth. Keep warm.

To assemble: In a large salad bowl, make a layer of taco chips, rice and chili in that order. Toss onion, tomato and lettuce together and place on top of chips, rice and chili. Pour topping over salad. Serve at once.

Kristyn Mahler (Mrs. Michael)

TACO CASSEROLE

4 Servings

1 lb. lean ground beef
1 can (10 oz.) enchilada sauce
1 bag (7 oz.) cheese flavored corn chips, crushed
1 cup cheddar cheese, grated (may use more)
¼ head lettuce, shredded
1 large tomato, diced

Brown beef and add sauce. Layer half of beef mixture into a 1½ quart casserole, top with half of the chips, and rest of beef. Bake at 350° for 20-30 minutes. Add remaining chips and grated cheese. Bake 5 more minutes. Top with lettuce and tomato.

This recipe is easily enlarged.

Chris Ahlstrand (Mrs. David)

JAMBALAYA

New Orleans favorite

¼ lb. sliced bacon, cut in 1" pieces
½ cup onion, finely chopped
2 medium green peppers, seeded and cut in 1" strips
1 cup raw rice
1 tsp. garlic, finely chopped
1 can (1 lb. 3 oz.) tomatoes, drained and coarsely chopped
½ tsp. thyme
1 tsp. salt
Fresh ground black pepper
1½ - 2 cups chicken stock, fresh or canned
½ lb. cooked smoked ham, cut in 2" by ½" strips
1 lb. medium sized raw shrimp, shelled and deveined
1 T. parsley, finely chopped

Preheat oven to 350°. In a heavy 3 or 4 quart casserole, fry the bacon over moderate heat until it has rendered its fat and is brown but not crisp. Drain on paper towels and reserve. Add the onions to the fat in the pan and cook them for 8-10 minutes, stirring occasionally until they are transparent, but not brown. Mix in the green peppers. They will wilt slightly in about 3 minutes, at which point the rice should be stirred in. Turn the rice about in the hot fat and vegetables over moderate heat until the grains become somewhat opaque and milky. Then add the garlic, tomatoes, bacon, thyme, salt, and a few grindings of black pepper, stirring them together thoroughly. Pour in 1½ cups of chicken stock and bring it to a boil. Add the ham and stir again. Cover the casserole tightly and place in the lower third of the oven. After 10 minutes add the shrimp, pushing them down beneath the rice and continue to cook tightly covered for about 10 minutes longer or until all of the stock is absorbed and the rice is tender. (If at any point during this time the rice appears dry, add a few tablespoons more of the hot stock to it.) Serve directly from the casserole if you wish or mound the jambalaya on a large, heated platter. Garnish with fresh chopped parsley.

Muriel Butler (Mrs. Allen)

BARBECUE HAMBURGERS   20-25 Sandwiches

5 lbs. hamburger
½ cup onion, chopped
1½ cups tomato juice
5 oz. ketchup
2 tsp. chili powder
1 cup barbecue sauce
½ cup sweet pickle juice
¼ cup sugar
1 tsp. salt (or to taste)
1 cup flour

Brown hamburger and onion. Drain off excess fat. Add all ingredients except flour. Stir. Simmer about 10 minutes. Sprinkle flour over meat, stirring constantly until mixture thickens.

Penny Lounsberry (Mrs. John)

BARBECUE BEEF   8 Sandwiches

3 lb. chuck roast
1 small onion, chopped
½ cup beef broth
½ cup ketchup
3 T. cider vinegar
1 tsp. yellow prepared
  mustard
1 tsp. Worchestershire
  sauce
3 tsp. sugar
1 tsp. celery seed

Cook chuck roast and remove meat from bone, set aside. Combine remaining ingredients and cook until onion is tender. Add beef. Simmer 1 hour.

Double or triple this recipe for a great after-the-game supper.

Rose Ann Hass (Mrs. James)

TUNA BUN-STEADS   6 Sandwiches

¼ lb. American cheese,
  cubed
3 hard cooked eggs,
  chopped
1 can (7 oz.) tuna, flaked
2 T. green pepper,
  chopped
2 T. onion, chopped
2 T. green olives, chopped
2 T. sweet pickle, chopped
½ cup mayonnaise
6 long buns
Aluminum foil

Mix all ingredients together. Fill buns with this mixture after slitting along one side. Wrap each bun in aluminum foil. Bake at 325° for 25 minutes or place in electric broiler under moderate heat. Serve at once.

Florence Schyberg (Mrs. John)

ENTREES

MEATS

SWEET-SOUR MEAT LOAF   4 Servings

1½ lbs. ground beef
 1 cup bread crumbs
 1 medium onion, chopped
1½ tsp. salt
 ½ of a (15 oz.) can
   tomato sauce
 1 egg, beaten
 ¼ tsp. pepper
Parsley

SAUCE:
 ½ of a (15 oz.) can
   tomato sauce
 2 T. vinegar
 2 T. prepared mustard
 2 T. brown sugar

Combine all meat loaf ingredients and place in bread pan. Pour combined sauce ingredients over meat. Bake at 350° for 1 hour. After allowing meat to cool about 5 minutes, remove from pan and garnish with parsley sprigs.

Joan Ferguson (Mrs. Wendell)

INDIVIDUAL BARBECUED MEAT LOAVES   8 Servings

 2 lbs. ground beef
 2 eggs, slightly beaten
 ½ cup bread crumbs
 ⅓ cup green pepper,
   chopped
 ¼ cup milk
 ¼ cup ketchup
1½ tsp. salt
 ¼ tsp. pepper

SAUCE:
 ½ cup butter
 ½ cup onion, chopped
 ¼ cup brown sugar
 ½ cup ketchup
1½ tsp. chili powder

Thin onion slices

Mix meatloaf ingredients together and form into 8 individual loaves. Place in 9×13" pan.

For sauce: Melt butter and saute, chopped onions. Add remaining ingredients and simmer for about 5 minutes.

Put onion slices and sauce over each individual loaf. Cover pan with foil and bake at 350° for 45 minutes.

This sauce would be delicious for barbecued chicken, too.

Marcia Keppy

GREEN PEPPER STEAK

Prepare the meat and vegetables ahead of time; then cook directly at the table in a "wok".

1 can (16 oz.) bean sprouts
1 can (8 oz.) bamboo shoots
2 - 3 green peppers, sliced thinly
1 - 2 cups mushrooms, sliced
½ cup sliced onions
½ cup celery, chopped
6 - 8 green onions, cut into 1 inch pieces
1½ lb. sirloin steak, cut into thin strips
¼ cup oil
3 cloves garlic, minced
¼ tsp. pepper
¾ tsp. salt
1½ tsp. sugar
6 T. soy sauce
1 T. cornstarch
2 T. cold water

Prepare meat and vegetables. Heat oil in pan or electric wok. Saute garlic and meat with salt and pepper. Mix soy sauce and sugar and add celery, sliced onions and green pepper. Cook 4-5 minutes stirring twice. Mix cornstarch and water and add. Then add bean sprouts, bamboo shoots and mushrooms. Add green peppers last. Serve immediately over hot rice.

JAN D. SLIVKEN

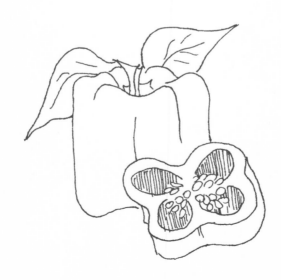

BEEF STROGANOFF

8-10 Servings

Traditional and Elegant

1½ - 2 lbs. lean beef
  (sirloin)
Salt
Pepper
  3 T. butter
  1 cup fresh mushrooms,
    sliced
  1 large onion, chopped
  2 T. flour
  2 cups beef boullion or
    consomme
  3 T. sherry
  2 T. tomato paste
  1 T. dry mustard
  1 cup sour cream

Cut meat into strips, removing fat. Dust strips with salt and pepper; set aside for 2 hours at room temperature. When ready to prepare, melt 2 T. butter in skillet and saute mushrooms until tender (15 minutes); remove from pan. In same pan, saute onions until brown; remove from skillet. Add 1 T. butter. When hot, add beef strips; sear, leaving rare. Remove. In remaining butter in skillet, sprinkle flour and blend, browning well (might need to add more butter). Slowly add boullion; stir to form smooth gravy. Add sherry, tomato paste and dry mustard and blend well. Add mushrooms, onions and meat to gravy; mix together and let mixture simmer very slowly on lowest heat for 20 minutes. 5 minutes before serving, add sour cream; blend thoroughly. Serve with rice or noodles.

Jan McMillan

EASY STROGANOFF

6 Servings

Quick, Easy and Delicious

1½ lbs. boneless sirloin
  2 T. butter or margarine
  1 envelope (1 oz.) onion
    soup mix
1¼ cups water
  1 T. cornstarch, dissolved
    in 2 T. water
  ¼ cup white wine
  1 cup sour cream
Mushrooms (optional)

Cut meat into thin strips, about 2 inches long. In large skillet, melt butter; add meat and brown well on all sides (add mushrooms at this time). Stir onion soup mix and water into skillet. Cover, simmer 30 minutes or until tender. Combine cornstarch with 2 T. cold water and stir into meat. While stirring, heat until thickened. Right before serving, add wine and sour cream. Serve over rice or noodles.

Sandy Hass (Mrs. John)

BOEUF AU LEGUME CASSEROLE   4-5 Servings

**"A hearty stew, in the French manner, where ingredients are simple,
flavor subtle - - especially good during the cold weather of
autumn and winter."**

6 slices bacon
1 lb. lean beef chuck,
   ½" thick
½ cup flour
1 tsp. salt
1 cup dry red wine
2 T. parsley
½ clove garlic
½ tsp. thyme
1 can (10½ oz.) condensed
   beef broth
6 medium potatoes,
   peeled and halved
12 small white onions,
   peeled
3 carrots, sliced
   lengthwise
1 can (4 oz.) mushroom
   stems and pieces,
   finely chopped
Parsley

Cook bacon until crisp; drain on paper towels; reserve drippings. Cut beef into cubes. Shake a few at a time in a paper bag containing flour and salt. Brown cubes on all sides in bacon drippings; remove to 2 quart casserole. Pour wine into electric blender; add parsley, garlic, thyme and beef broth; blend until solid ingredients are pureed. Pour over meat in casserole. Cover casserole; bake at 350° for 1 hour. Stir potatoes, onions and carrots into casserole. Replace cover. Bake 1 hour longer or until vegetables are done. Stir in mushrooms. Crumble bacon; scatter on top with additional chopped parsley.

ARTHUR WHITTEMORE AND JACK LOWE

Whittemore & Lowe

Duo pianists, ARTHUR WHITTEMORE and JACK LOWE, are perennial favorites with the Tri-City Symphony audiences. Universally acknowledged as music's foremost two-piano team, they have accumulated a record of achievement that may never be paralleled in the field of music. In addition to performing with the most acclaimed and major orchestras, they have experienced phenomenal success on radio and television and in recordings. Whittemore and Lowe returned once again to perform Poulenc's "Concerto in D Minor for Two Pianos and Orchestra" with the Tri-City Symphony in October, 1977.

BEEF CURRY

A blend of fruited condiments for group entertaining.

2 lbs. cubed beef, sirloin
   or round steak
6 T. flour
2 oz. vegetable oil
2 medium onions,
   chopped
1 tomato, cut into pieces
2 T. curry powder
2 cups beef stock or
   boullion
Gravy browning (optional)
Rind and juice of ½ lemon
1 T. salt
½ clove garlic, crushed
1 T. coconut flakes
2 tsp. raisins
2 apples (peeled and cut
   up)
1 tsp. brown sugar
Assorted condiments:
   chutney, coconut flakes,
   pineapple bits, raisins,
   sliced bananas, crushed
   peanuts, or chopped egg

Roll meat in flour. Brown meat in oil, then add onions and tomatoes and continue to pan fry. Add curry powder and any remaining flour. Mix and stir in stock. (Add gravy browning to make it darker if you wish.) Add rind and lemon juice, salt, garlic, coconut flakes, raisins, apples and brown sugar. Cover and simmer slowly 4-5 hours.

Serve over white rice with assorted condiments, as suggested.

Pat Agnew (Mrs. Robert)

CURRIED BEEF

6 - 8 lbs. lean chuck
   roast, cubed
1 can (10½ oz.) beef
   consomme
Water
Salt
Pepper to taste
Curry powder to taste
Cornstarch, dissolved in
   cold water

Condiments:
   (chopped finely)
Hard-boiled eggs
Crisp bacon
Celery
Onion
Salted peanuts

Brown beef in own juices and place in large kettle. Add consomme and enough water to cover meat. Season with salt and pepper. Simmer slowly until tender (at least 4 hours). Thicken mixture with cornstarch and cold water. When ready to serve, add curry powder to taste. Serve over rice with condiments sprinkled on top.

Mary Jo Jensen (Mrs. Henry)

SWEET-SOUR BEEF AND NOODLES
6-8 Servings

3 lbs. cubed stew meat
½ cup flour
½ tsp. salt
½ tsp. pepper
2 onions, sliced
1 green pepper, sliced
¾ cup ketchup
2 T. vinegar
2 T. Worchestershire
sauce
¼ cup soy sauce
2 T. brown sugar
¾ cup water

NOODLES:
1 pkg. (8 oz.) thin noodles
Butter
2 eggs, beaten
1 cup milk
1 cup Milnot
1 tsp. salt

Dredge stew meat in flour, seasoned with salt and pepper. Arrange meat in a 2 quart casserole and top with onion and green pepper. Combine remaining 6 ingredients for sauce and pour over meat, onions and pepper. Bake, covered at 300° for 3 hours.

To prepare noodles: Cook and drain noodles, butter lightly and place in greased 2 quart casserole. Combine eggs, milk, milnot and salt and pour over noodles. Bake at 300° for 1 hour.

Virginia Kirk (Mrs. George)

BEEF IN HERB WINE SAUCE
6-8 Servings

3 - 4 medium onions,
sliced
2 T. bacon drippings
or oil
3 lbs. lean beef (sirloin
tip) cut into 1½ inch
cubes
1½ T. flour
1 cup beef bouillon
1½ cups dry red wine
¼ tsp. marjoram
¼ tsp. thyme
¼ tsp. oregano
¼ tsp. salt
½ tsp. freshly ground
pepper
½ lb. fresh mushrooms,
sliced
¼ cup butter

In heavy skillet, saute onions in bacon drippings until transparent, about 5 minutes; remove from pan and set aside. Shake meat cubes and flour together in bag until meat is well coated. Brown meat in drippings. Add ¾ cup beef bouillon, 1 cup wine, the herbs and seasonings. Cover the pan tightly and simmer for 1½ hours. While it is cooking gradually add the remaining bouillon and wine. Meanwhile, saute the mushrooms in butter. Finally add mushrooms and onions to the meat and cook about 20-30 minutes more. Serve with brown rice.

Marilyn Evans (Mrs. Gerald)

STEAK WITH A KICK

4 Servings

4 beef filets
Freshly ground pepper
Fresh clove of garlic
4 T. olive oil
2 oz. port wine
2 oz. cognac
2 oz. sweet cream

Rub steaks with ground pepper and garlic. Heat oil and sear meat on both sides. Pour off excess oil. Add wine and cook for about a half minute; add cognac and cook for a half minute; add cream and cook for a half minute. Serve immediately, with the sauce. Note: The amount of cooking time depends on the doneness desired. I like steak rare, and prefer thick filets. The exact amount of the liquids used is determined by the number of filets used and degree of doneness desired. Basically, the liquids should be reduced to about half their original amount at the end of the cooking process.

LEONARD ROSE

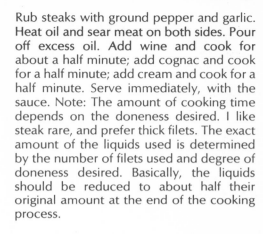

Leonard Rose

LEONARD ROSE, master cellist, has had a most impressive career, beginning at the age of thirteen. He has received many awards and has held the position of solo cellist with the NBC Symphony Orchestra, the Cleveland Orchestra and the New York Philharmonic. Leonard Rose's recordings of the cello repetoire are in demand all over the world. He plays a rare Amati cello circa 1662. His outstanding performance of "Variations on a Rococo Theme" by Tchaikovsky and Saint-Saens' "Cello Concerto No. 1 in A Minor" with the Tri-City Symphony in 1977 will be remembered for years to come.

FILET MIGNON ESSEX

4 Servings

4 filet mignons (approx. 5
  oz. each)
1 T. butter
¼ cup champagne
½ cup brown sauce (this
  can be commercially
  prepared sauce)
1 cup Morels or other
  mushrooms, preferably
  fresh
¼ cup half and half cream
4 slices toast, crusts
  removed

Saute meat in butter for 4-5 minutes or until desired doneness. Remove from pan
and keep warm. Saute mushrooms in remaining butter. Add the champagne,
brown sauce and half and half to the
mushrooms. Heat until boiling. Place toast
on warmed plates. Place filet on top.
Spoon sauce over top of meat. Serve immediately.

Mary Cebuhar (Mrs. Michael)

LONDON BROIL WITH BLEU CHEESE BUNS

A Summertime Favorite

1 cup ketchup
1½ cups water
1 small clove garlic,
  minced
2 T. prepared mustard
2 T. Worchestershire
  sauce
3 T. cooking oil
1 tsp. salt
1 tsp. onion powder
¼ tsp. pepper
2 flank steaks
  (1½ lbs. each)

BLEU CHEESE BUNS:
½ cup (1 stick) butter
3 T. (heaping) bleu cheese
8 buns, sliced in half

8 Generous Servings

Combine the first 9 ingredients to make
marinade. Marinate meat frequently turning for 3-4 hours. Prepare hot coals on out-
door grill. When coals are white hot, grill
steaks. Cook 5-7 minutes on each side,
basting with small amount of marinade.
Heat remaining marinade. Slice meat thinly
on bias (cross grain). Serve on bleu cheese
buns, topped with heated marinade.

Soften butter. Blend in bleu cheese. Spread
on both halves of buns and toast under
broiler until brown and bubbly.

These make a great summertime meal
when served with hash browns and a tossed green salad.

Mary Ann Tyler (Mrs. Herb)

BEEF ROULADES IN RED WINE

6 Servings

1½ lbs. round steak, very
thinly sliced, cut into 6
pieces
1 clove garlic, cut in half
¾ tsp. salt
½ tsp. pepper
¾ lb. ground sausage
2 T. parsley, finely
chopped
2 T. onion, finely chopped
Flour
1½ cups California burgundy
or claret
1½ T. tomato paste
½ cup pitted olives

Rub each piece of meat with cut clove of garlic. Season with salt and pepper. Spread thin layer of sausage on each piece of meat. Sprinkle with parsley and onion. Roll up each piece. Tie at each end. Dredge in flour. Brown well in heavy oven proof skillet. Discard any fat left in pan. Add wine. Mix tomato paste with a little wine. Stir into wine in pan. Cover. (This can be prepared to this point early in the day). Cook at 325°-350°, slowly, 1 hour or until meat is tender. Add olives 15 minutes before meat is done. Serve with brown or wild rice.

Mary Ann Dailey (Mrs. William H.)

SPICED STEAK

4 Servings

1 lb. round steak
¼ cup flour
Salt to taste
Pepper to taste
1 cup ketchup
½ cup water
1 lemon, sliced (or juice
of 1 lemon)
1 green pepper, sliced
1 onion, sliced

Pound flour into round steak; add salt and pepper. Brown each side of steak in small amount of oil. Put browned meat into a roaster. Mix ketchup and water. Pour over steak. Add lemon, green pepper and onion. Bake covered in 350° oven for 1 hour, or until tender.

Joann Hanson (Mrs. James C.)

154

MARINATED CHUCK ROAST

4-6 Servings

4 lb. chuck roast
MSG
⅓ cup wine vinegar
¼ cup ketchup
2 T. cooking oil
2 T. soy sauce
1 T. Worchestershire
  sauce
1 tsp. prepared mustard
1 tsp. salt
¼ tsp. freshly ground
  pepper
¼ tsp. garlic powder

Place the roast in a large flat pan, sprinkle both sides with MSG, and poke with a fork. In a blender or food processor, blend remaining ingredients to make a marinade. Pour marinade over roast and let it stand 3-4 hours (overnight won't hurt). Turn once or twice to insure that marinade reaches all surfaces. Grill on hot coals (length of time depends upon thickness of roast and desired degree of doneness).

Judith Nixon (Mrs. Robert)

FRUITED BEEF POT ROAST

12 Servings

4 - 4½ lb. rolled rump
  roast
2 T. fat
2 tsp. salt
¹/₈ tsp. pepper
¼ cup water
8 - 12 prunes
1 onion, sliced, separated
  into rings
1 can (16 oz.) jellied
  cranberry sauce
2 T. lemon juice
¼ tsp. allspice

Lightly brown meat in fat. Pour off drippings. Season with 1 tsp. salt and all of pepper. Place on rack in Dutch oven or roasting pan. Add water and cover tightly; cook in 325° oven 3-3½ hours. The last 15 minutes of cooking time, add prunes and onion rings. Cover again and continue cooking. Remove roast, prunes and onions from pan, and keep warm. Pour off all but ¼ cup drippings. Mash cranberry sauce into drippings and blend. Add onions, lemon juice, allspice and 1 tsp. salt. Bring to boil and cook over low heat until cranberry sauce is dissolved. Add prunes and cook 5 minutes. Serve carved roast garnished with prunes on hot platter, accompanied with cranberry gravy.

Lynn Goebel (Mrs. George)

SAUERBRATEN

A traditional German recipe.

4 lb. sirloin tip or rolled
   rump roast
1 tsp. salt
1 tsp. ginger
1 cup cider vinegar
3 cups water
1 medium onion, sliced
2 T. mixed pickling spice,
   red pepper removed
2 bay leaves
4 whole cloves
2 T. sugar
2 T. fat
Flour

Rub meat with salt and ginger, put in large deep dish. Combine remaining ingredients except fat and flour; bring to boil; cool; pour over meat. Cover and refrigerate 1½-3 days, depending on preference for spiceness. Turn meat often. Remove meat from marinade and reserve marinade. Pat meat with paper towels; brown in fat. Add 2 cups reserved marinade and ½ of onion and whole spices from marinade. Cover and simmer 3-5 hours on range top, depending upon size of roast, or bake 3 hours at 300-325°. Remove meat and strain liquid; return liquid to pan, heat and thicken liquid with flour mixed with a little cold water. Simmer gravy until thickened, season to taste.

Can cool, even chill, slice and warm in chafing dish with gravy served separately.

Marjorie Purcell (Mrs. Donald)

CALIFORNIA CASSEROLE
WITH BUTTER CRUMB DUMPLINGS   8 Servings

2 lbs. veal or regular
  round steak
⅓ cup flour
1 tsp. paprika
¼ cup salad oil or
  shortening
½ tsp. salt
⅛ tsp. pepper
1 cup water (or part
  onion liquid may be
  used)
1 can (10¾ oz.) cream of
  chicken soup
1¾ cup water
1¾ cup small cooked onions
  (1 lb. can may be used,
  drained)

INGREDIENTS FOR BUTTER
CRUMB DUMPLINGS
2 cups flour
4 tsp. baking powder
½ tsp. salt
1 tsp. poultry seasoning
1 tsp. celery seed
1 tsp. dry onion flakes
1 T. poppy seed, (optional)
¼ cup salad oil
1 cup milk
¼ cup melted butter
1 cup bread crumbs (fine)

INGREDIENTS FOR SOUR
CREAM SAUCE: (optional)
1 can (10¾ oz.) condensed
  cream of chicken soup
1 cup sour cream

To prepare meat; Coat meat with mixture of flour and paprika. Brown meat thoroughly in shortening. Add salt, pepper and 1 cup water. Cover and simmer 30 minutes or until tender. Transfer meat and liquid to 3 quart casserole. Heat chicken soup in the skillet used for browning meat. Blend in 1¾ cups water, gradually, bring to boil, stirring constantly. Pour over meat. Add onions and top with dumplings. Bake uncovered at 425° for 20-25 minutes or until dumplings are a deep golden brown.

To prepare dumplings: Mix first 4 ingredients thoroughly. Add celery seed, onion flakes and poppy seeds. Add oil and milk and stir until moistened. Drop rounded tablespoonfuls of dough into mixture of butter and bread crumbs. Roll to coat thoroughly.

To prepare sour cream sauce: Heat cream of chicken soup mixed with 1 cup sour cream. Use at serving time.

Barbara Davis (Mrs. Richard)

VEAL LUGANESE

4 Servings

3 eggs
¼ cup milk
3 T. grated parmesan
  cheese
1 cup fresh parsley,
  chopped
¾ cup flour
1 tsp. salt
½ tsp. white pepper
4 thin slices veal (approx.
  1½ lbs. veal sirloin or
  veal round steak)
½ cup corn oil
¼ cup butter
1 T. green onions,
  chopped
1 clove garlic
6 medium tomatoes,
  peeled, seeded,
  chopped (may use
  canned

Beat the eggs, milk, cheese and parsley in a bowl. Dip veal into flour, salt and pepper mixture, then in egg mixture, then back into flour mixture. Fry in the oil and butter until golden brown, about 5 minutes on each side. Remove veal and keep warm. Saute onions and garlic in same fat. Add tomatoes and cook for 3-4 minutes. Place veal on serving platter and garnish with tomatoes.

Serve with rice and a green vegetable.

Laura Houston (Mrs. Douglas)

VEAL FLORENTINE

6 Servings

6 veal cutlets
¼ cup milk
1 egg, beaten
Bread crumbs
4 T. butter
1 pkg. (10 oz.) frozen
  chopped spinach
1 T. flour
¼ tsp. salt
⅛ tsp. pepper
Pinch of nutmeg
¼ cup white wine
12 slices swiss cheese
2 T. parmesan cheese
1 can (8 oz.) tomato
  sauce, heated

Pound cutlets until very thin. Dip in milk and egg mixture and then into fine bread crumbs. Let stand 15-20 minutes. Saute cutlets in butter 5 minutes on each side until brown. Put cutlets on large baking sheet with sides, in a single layer. Meanwhile cook spinach and drain well. Combine spinach with flour, salt, pepper, nutmeg and wine. Top each cutlet with spinach mixture. Then place 2 slices of swiss cheese over each cutlet with spinach, and sprinkle with parmesan cheese. Place under broiler until bubbly. Serve on warmed plates with a few tablespoons of tomato sauce.

Kay Kaleba (Mrs. Richard)

BAKED VEAL PARMESAN   4 Servings

½ cup fine dry bread
  crumbs
⅓ cup grated parmesan
  cheese
¼ tsp. salt
Dash pepper
1 egg, beaten
1 T. water
4 veal cutlets (¼" thick)
1 can (15 oz.) tomato
  sauce
½ tsp. dried oregano
½ tsp. sugar
¹/₈ tsp. onion salt
4 oz. grated mozzarella
  cheese

Mix crumbs, parmesan cheese, salt and
dash pepper. Combine egg and water. Dip
veal in egg mixture and then into crumb
mixture. Bake veal in 9×13" baking dish for
20 minutes at 400°. Combine tomato
sauce, oregano, onion, salt and sugar and
mix well in another 9×13" pan. Remove
veal from oven, place in sauce in second
pan, turning baked side down into sauce.
Sprinkle cheese all over and return immediately to oven for 20 more minutes.

Bonnie Brotman (Mrs. Jerrel)

VEAL CHOPS WITH FONTINA CHEESE

8 rib veal chops, from
  the first cut, bone in
  and sliced, ½" thick
4 T. butter
4 T. olive oil
⅔ cup shallots, finely
  minced
1 cup dry white wine
Salt
Pepper
1 tsp. finely minced
  rosemary
8 paper thin slices of
  proscuitto ham
8 slices fontina cheese
  ¹/₈" thick

4-6 Servings (8 chops)

In a large, heavy oven proof skillet, melt
butter and oil. Add chops and cook over
medium high heat 4-5 minutes, until lightly
browned, then turn chops and repeat.
Remove chops from pan and keep warm.
Add shallots and simmer 2-3 minutes until
limp, stirring to prevent burning. Add wine,
salt and pepper, and rosemary. Cook over
medium heat 2-3 minutes. Return chops to
skillet, cover and simmer 25-30 minutes.
Remove from heat. Place a slice of proscuitto ham on each and top with a slice of
fontina cheese. Transfer skillet to a hot
(400°) oven for 5-6 minutes or until cheese
melts. Place on heated plates and serve immediately.

Alice McDonald (Mrs. Donald)

TANGY HAM LOAF WITH MUSTARD SAUCE

8 Servings

1 lb. ground pork
1 lb. smoked ham, ground
½ cup milk
2 eggs beaten
1 cup soft bread crumbs
2 T. chili sauce
1 tsp. minced onion
½ tsp. grated lemon peel
½ tsp. salt
½ tsp. pepper
½ cup canned tomato juice
1 tsp. Worchestershire
  sauce
1½ tsp. cold water
1 T. flour
**INGREDIENTS FOR
MUSTARD SAUCE:**
4 tsp. dry mustard
2 tsp. sugar
1 tsp. salt
2 eggs, slightly beaten
4 T. vinegar
2 T. water
1 T. butter
½ cup heavy cream,
  whipped

Mix all ingredients until well blended. Form into a loaf and bake at 325° for 1½ hours. Serve with mustard sauce.

To prepare mustard sauce: Cook mustard, sugar, salt, eggs, vinegar and water in top of double boiler until creamy. Add butter. Fold in whipped cream. Serve immediately.

Elsie VonMaur (Mrs. Richard, Sr.)

HAM LOAF FOR A LARGE GROUP

25 Servings

2 lbs. ground sausage
1 lb. ground beef
2½ lbs. ground smoked ham
3 eggs
2 cups graham crackers,
  crushed
1 can (20 oz.) pineapple
  slices, reserve juice
Milk
SAUCE:
2 cans (10¾ oz. each)
  tomato soup
2 cups brown sugar
¾ cup vinegar
2 T. dry mustard
Parsley

Combine meats, eggs and graham crackers. Measure juice reserved from pineapple slices and add enough milk to equal 2 cups. Add to meat mixture and blend well. Place in a large pan and bake at 350° for 1 hour. Meanwhile make sauce.

For sauce: Mix all ingredients together and heat slowly until brown sugar dissolves.

After 1 hour of baking remove loaf from oven and skim off excess juices. Pour sauce over loaf and return to oven for another 30-45 minutes. Garnish with pineapple rings and parsley.

Cindy Peters (Mrs. Randy)

HAM BALLS

1½ lbs. ground ham
½ lb. lean ground pork
¾ cup dry bread crumbs
½ tsp. salt
1 egg, beaten
½ cup milk
½ cup tomato juice
Parsley
Pineapple rings

SAUCE:
½ cup brown sugar
¼ cup water
1 T. dry mustard
2 T. vinegar

Combine ham, pork, bread crumbs, salt, egg, milk and tomato juice. Make into about 35 small balls using about 2 T. for each ball. Bake at 350° for 1 hour. Pour sauce over balls.

For sauce: Combine sauce ingredients and pour over balls in pan. Baste balls with sauce 2 or 3 times while baking. Serve on pineapple rings and garnish with parsley.

Bonnie Moeller (Mrs. Gerald)

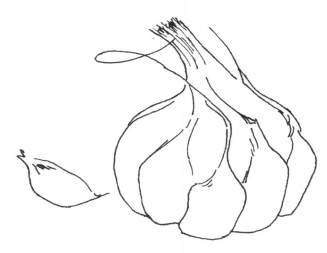

HAM LOAF

8 Servings

2 lbs. fresh ground pork
1 lb. smoked raw ground
  ham (or 1 lb. baked,
  ground ham as a
  substitute)
1 cup crushed, rolled
  cracker crumbs, salted
2 eggs, well beaten
1 cup milk

Mix all ingredients together except milk. Then add milk and mix thoroughly. Mold into loaf pan. Bake at 350° for 1½ hours.

Ellie Klingbiel (Mrs. Tom)

HAM BAKED IN RASPBERRY GRAND MARNIER SAUCE

½ fully cooked bone-in-
  ham, (6 lbs.)
Whole cloves
½ cup yellow mustard
1 cup dark brown sugar
1 cup cream sherry

SAUCE:
  1 orange, unpeeled, diced
  1 cup dark brown sugar
  2 cups raspberry preserves
    or jam
  2 T. yellow mustard
  1 T. Worchestershire
    sauce
  1 cup cream sherry
  ½ cup Grand Marnier
    liqueur

12-16 Servings

Score fat surface of ham; stud with cloves. Combine mustard and brown sugar and spread over ham. Place in baking dish, add sherry to pan. Bake at 325° 1½-2 hours.

To prepare sauce: About ½ hour before ham is finished baking, mix sauce ingredients together. Pour sauce over ham, and finish cooking. Baste every 10 minutes.

To serve, slice ham and serve sauce on the side.

Lee Bettendorf (Mrs. W.E.)

SAVANNAH BAKED HAM

16 Servings

This is a recipe used by my grandmother - originated in Savannah, Ga.

1 uncooked ham, ½ lb. per
  person, proportions
  given here are for an
  8 lb. ham
1 qt. dark molasses
4 qts. weak tea
2 qts. water
1 cup tomato ketchup
½ cup prepared mustard
1 bottle of beer
1 cup brown sugar

Wash the ham well and place in large soup kettle, skin side up. Pour molasses and weak tea over it. Soak the ham in this bath overnight. The next morning, remove the ham from the bath and put it into a steamer, fat side up. (May use a large roasting pan with a trivet in the bottom). Pour 2 quarts of water over the ham, place in 250° oven and steam for 3½ hours. Remove it from the steam, allow it to cool, blot it dry with paper towels. Discard water from the roaster. Skin the ham, rub it with paste made of ketchup and mustard. Return to roaster and 350° oven, baste with beer 3 times, 10 minutes apart. After 30 minutes,, sprinkle with brown sugar and brown. (The last 2 steps should take about 45 minutes.) Serve immediately or allow to cool and serve.

Caroline Nichols (Mrs. Frank R.)

BAKED PORK TENDERLOIN   8 Servings

Tenderloins marinate overnight. So tender!

½ cup bourbon
½ cup soy sauce
4 T. brown sugar
3 whole pork tenderloins,
  trimmed well

SAUCE:
⅔ cup sour cream
⅔ cup mayonnaise
1 T. dry mustard
1 T. onion, grated
½ tsp. vinegar

Combine bourbon, soy sauce and brown sugar. Marinate the pork loins in this mixture over night. Remove meat from marinade and bake in 325° oven for 1½ hours, basting frequently with marinade. Carve into thin diagonal slices and serve with sour cream sauce.

To prepare sauce: Combine all ingredients and heat thoroughly.

Margaret Stegmaier (Mrs. Otto)

BARBECUED LOIN OF PORK   6-8 Servings

1 rolled pork loin roast,
  4-5 lbs.
1 can (10¾ oz.) tomato
  soup
⅓ cup onions, chopped
⅓ cup celery, chopped
1 clove garlic, minced
2 T. brown sugar
2 T. Worcestershire
  sauce
2 T. lemon juice or vinegar
2 tsp. prepared mustard,
  yellow
4 drops Tabasco sauce

Bake pork roast at 325° for 3-4 hours (45 minutes per pound). Combine remaining ingredients to make a sauce. One hour before meat is done, pour off excess drippings. Pour sauce over meat and continue roasting 1 hour longer. Baste with sauce often.

Diann Moore (Mrs. Robert)

WINE-BRAISED PORK CHOPS

4 Servings

4 rib pork chops, 1" thick (1½ lbs.)
1 medium green pepper, sliced crosswise
1 clove garlic, crushed
½ lb. fresh mushrooms, sliced through stem (or 1-6 oz. can, drained)
2 tsp. salt
¼ tsp. pepper
2 medium tomatoes, quartered
⅓ cup white wine

Wipe chops with damp paper towels. Slowly heat large heavy skillet. In hot skillet, brown chops well, about 10 minutes on each side. Remove. Drain all but ½ tablespoon fat from skillet. Add green pepper, garlic and mushrooms; saute, stirring about 5 minutes. Place chops on green pepper mixture; sprinkle with salt and pepper; top with tomatoes and white wine. Simmer slowly; covered, 40-45 minutes, or until chops are tender. Serve with wine sauce.

Heather Gosma (Mrs. John S.)

LEMON-TOPPED PORK CHOPS

6 Servings

6 pork chops
½ cup ketchup
½ cup water
2 T. brown sugar
6 lemon slices

Brown chops. Mix together ketchup, water and brown sugar. Pour mixture over chops. Place lemon slice on each chop. Cover and let simmer 45 minutes to an hour, or until chops are done and tender.

JUDITH AND ALAN HERSH

UNUSUAL BAKED PORK CHOPS

6-10 Servings

6 - 10 thick cut pork chops
1 can (16 oz.) cranberry
  sauce (not jelly)
1 cup orange juice
⅓ cup brown sugar
Fresh orange slices - 2
  per chop

Brown pork chops in a fry pan on stove. Season lightly according to your personal preference (salt, pepper, garlic). Do not overcook. Place chops in casserole. Pour cranberry sauce over chops, spreading evenly. Drain fat from frying pan and add orange juice, mixing the juice well with the pan drippings. Add brown sugar and mix well. Pour over chops. Top each chop with an orange slice. Bake uncovered at 350° for 1 hour. Remove chops to a heated serving platter. Replace orange slices with fresh ones to serve; garnish platter with fresh parsley.

Maggie Collins (Mrs. C. Dean)

SPANISH PORK CHOPS WITH RICE   4 Servings

4 pork loin chops,
  or butterfly pork chops
Salt
Pepper
1⅓ cups rice
  1 green pepper, large
  1 medium onion
1½ cups tomato juice

Brown pork chops about 5 minutes on each side. Salt and pepper to taste. Prepare rice according to package directions. Cut green pepper in four rings and place one ring on each pork chop. Fill each ring with rice and allow the rest of the rice to overflow on to the pork chops and into the bottom of the skillet. Slice the onion in ring pieces and place one ring on top of each mound of rice enclosed by green pepper. Pour tomato juice over rice, onion and pork chops, (If mixture becomes dry, add more tomato juice). Simmer for 1 hour or until tender.

Sue Cleaver (Mrs. William)

PORK CHOPS WITH RICE   6 Servings

6 pork chops - ¾-1 inch
  thick
2 T. cooking oil
1 T. flour
1 T. brown sugar
1 tsp. dry mustard
1 tsp. salt
1 clove garlic, minced
  (optional)
2 medium onions, sliced
½ cup white wine
½ cup water, or as needed
Rice
1 medium green pepper
  chopped
2 - 3 T. pimento, coarsely
  chopped

Brown chops in oil in 10" skillet. Turn to brown well on both sides. Drain off fat. Sprinkle with flour, brown sugar, mustard, salt and garlic. Put onion slice on top of chops and pour in wine. Cover and cook over low heat until chops are tender, about 1 hour. Add water as needed and spoon sauce over chops several times while cooking. Meanwhile, cook rice according to package directions. Add green pepper to pork 15 minutes before end of cooking time. Top with pimento.

To serve: Toss rice lightly with some of the sauce from chops, a little of the green pepper and pimento. Place hot rice on platter and layer pork chops over bed of rice. Serve immediately.

Marlys Wilkinson (Mrs. Tom)

CANTON STIR FRY

2 T. vegetable oil
3 stalks celery, thinly and diagonally sliced
3 medium onions, peeled, quartered and pulled apart
1 large carrot, thinly and diagonally sliced
¼ cup chicken broth
3 pieces preserved ginger sliced, or 2 tsp. ground ginger
12 canned water chestnuts, sliced into thin slivers
1½ - 2 cups leftover pork diced
1 pkg. (6 oz.) frozen snow peas, thawed
½ lb. fresh spinach, washed and blotted dry
¼ cup soy sauce
1 tsp. cornstarch
1 T. water

Have all ingredients prepared before starting. Heat oil over medium heat. Add celery, onion and carrot, turning to coat. Cover and let steam one minute. Add stock and steam 4-5 minutes. Add ginger, water chestnuts and pork, stirring to blend. Cover and cook 4-5 minutes. Vegetables should be tender crisp. Add snow peas, spinach and soy sauce. Blend, cover and steam for 1 minute. Thicken with cornstarch dissolved in water. Stir into mixture until it thickens and bubbles. Serve with rice, passing Chinese noodles and soy sauce.

Sandra Bendixen (Mrs. DeVere O.)

SWEET SOUR PORK

1½ lbs. lean pork, cut into 1" cubes
2 T. shortening
¼ cup water
1 can (20 oz.) pineapple chunks (packed in own juice), drained, reserve liquid
¼ cup brown sugar
½ tsp. salt
¼ cup vinegar
2 T. soy sauce
1 green pepper, cut into strips
1 cup small whole onions
Cherry tomatoes

Brown pork slightly in shortening. Add water, cover and cook slowly on simmer, until tender. Measure juice from pineapple and add enough water to equal 1 cup. In a saucepan, combine brown sugar, cornstarch, salt, vinegar, pineapple juice and soy sauce. Cook over low heat until slightly thickened, stirring constantly. Pour over hot pork and let stand at least 10 minutes. (Can be frozen or refrigerated at this time.) Add green pepper, onion, pineapple chunks and tomatoes and cook 2-3 minutes more. Serve with rice and egg rolls.

Susan Jacobs (Mrs. Steven H.)

HISTORY OF LAMB

Lamb is the meat of sacrifice in Greece and has been so since time immemorial. The priests of pagan Greece would sprinkle it with oregano and thyme that grew wild on the mountainside and anoint the animal with olive oil and lemon juice before roasting it as an offering to the gods.

Women were not allowed to prepare this meat. To this day, every male considers himself a "maygerios" (chef) and will not hesitate to step into your kitchen to check whether the "buti" (leg) has been properly prepared.

Nancy Coin (Mrs. George)

ROAST LEG OF LAMB "ARNI PSITO"

1 leg of lamb
Salt
Pepper
Oregano
Garlic cloves, peeled and
    sliced
2 - 3 oz. butter
½ lemon, or more
1 cup water
Potatoes
Onions
Zucchini

Wash meat well and set aside in roasting pan. In a small bowl, mix salt, pepper, oregano and garlic cloves. Make incisions in lamb with sharp knife and place garlic pieces and a little butter in each cut. Sprinkle rest of spices on meat, rub in well. Melt remaining butter and rub over meat. Pour juice of lemon over meat. Cover roasting pan and bake at 400° for 30 minutes. Lower oven to 350°. After it has roasted for 1 hour, add water to liquid in pan and baste often until meat is brown and done to taste (20-30 minutes per pound). Midway through roasting you may add vegetables to roaster around lamb.

To serve: Remove fat and use remaining liquid for gravy. Serve with red wine, crusty hot bread and a salad tossed with oil and vinegar.

Nancy Coin (Mrs. George)

SULTAN'S SHISH-KA-BOBS

10 Servings

5 large onions, peeled,
  sliced ⅛" thick,
  separated into rings
10 T. imported olive oil
20 T. fresh lemon juice
 3 T. salt
 2 tsp. freshly ground
  pepper
Melted butter
 9 lbs. boneless lamb,
  preferably from the leg
  trimmed of all fat and
  sinew, cut into 2" cubes
 2 pints cherry tomatoes
 4 green peppers, cut into
  2" squares
 1 eggplant, peeled, cut
  into 2" cubes
 2 lbs. small white onions,
  peeled
Olive oil
Butter

Put onion rings, oil, lemon juice and seasonings into large deep bowl. Add lamb and marinate at least 4 hours, at room temperature, the longer the better. Turn to coat occasionally. Prepare charcoal fire. When coals are white hot, remove lamb and string tightly on skewers. Put vegetables on separate skewers, alternating them in a pleasing array. Brush meat and vegetables with a mixture of olive oil and butter, in equal parts. Allow 10 minutes for medium rare lamb; 15 for well done. Serve with a vegetable soup, pilaf and pita bread, with sherbet or fruit compote for dessert.

Sandra Bendixen (Mrs. DeVere O.)

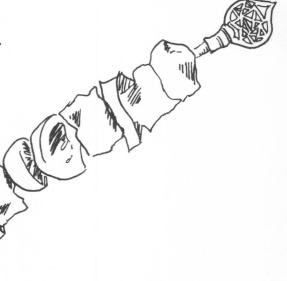

LAMB SHANKS

Individual Servings

Big lamb shanks, 1 per
  serving (remove tendons -
  may be done by butcher)
Concentrated frozen
  orange juice
Salt
Pepper

Lay shank on piece of foil, put 2 T. concentrated orange juice over each shank, sprinkle with salt and pepper. Roll up foil very tightly, using 2 sheets if necessary. Cook in very slow oven (250°) at least 4 hours -- can be left for the afternoon.

Mary Phares (Mrs. William)

GREEK MEATBALLS WITH MINT   4-6 Servings

These fried meatballs, "KEFTETHES" are crisp on the outside and moist on the inside, and are equally delicious hot or cold. The mint gives them a very unusual flavor.

1 lb. ground beef, or lamb or veal or combination
4 slices bread
¼ cup red wine
1 onion finely chopped, or green onions
½ cup parsley, finely chopped
1 egg
2 tsp. spearmint flakes, or 2 T. fresh mint, finely chopped
1 tsp. salt
4 tsp. pepper
1 clove garlic, pressed
1 cup flour
½ cup oil

Put meat in bowl. Dip bread in bowl with wine, making sure it is moist but not dripping. Crumble bread and add to meat with remaining ingredients. Mix together, kneading with hands. Put flour on flat plate. Scoop out a small amount of meat mixture, push onto floured plate and roll into small balls, covering all sides with flour. (Make balls size you prefer. For hors d'oeuvres, teaspoon is a good size.) Heat oil in large frying pan. Drop balls in hot oil and fry 10-15 minutes until crisp and brown on all sides.

Nancy Coin (Mrs. George)

SPANISH STYLE LEG OF LAMB   8-10 Servings

Leg of lamb
Salt
Clove of garlic
Ground pepper
Dry mustard
Paprika
Olive oil

Rub lamb with clove of garlic, and sprinkle with salt and pepper, mustard and paprika and rub well with fingers. Place lamb in oven fat side up. Pour a little olive oil over lamb. Place in oven, uncovered. May roast: 4½-5 lbs. of lamb, boneless - 300° for 4 hours; or start at 400° and finish at 300° for 2 hours; or 2 lb. roast at 300° for 2½ hours, or well done in 3 hours.

Mary Phares (Mrs. William)

POULTRY

ROAST DUCK (TAME)

3 Servings

1 duck (3 lb.)
Dressing of your choice
Orange marmalade

Fill cavity of duck with your favorite stuffing. Cover with orange marmalade, and place on rack in roaster. Cook uncovered in 250° oven for about 6-8 hours. Baste once or twice with marmalade. Drain fat (there is a lot) before making gravy.

Dorothy White (Mrs. F.B.)

WILD DUCK

6-8 Servings

Fixed for years every fall and winter for family and friends.

4 wild ducks, halved
1 cup mushrooms
1 medium onion,
  chopped
2 tsp. ginger
1 tsp. chervil
½ tsp. marjoram
2 cups red wine, preferrably sweet
¼ cup butter
  Salt
  Pepper

Split ducks in half and carefully clean. Remove all fat. Place breast side down in roaster. Cover with mushrooms, onion, ginger, chervil, marjoram and wine. Dot with butter. Bake covered at 350° for 2-3 hours, or until very tender. Toward end of baking time add salt and pepper. Add additional liquid if necessary. Serve with gravy made from drippings and with Orange Sauce, page 173.

Mary Hass (Mrs. Arthur)

171

PHEASANTS IN CREAM SHERRY

8-10 Servings

Serve with Wild Rice Casserole, green salad and dry white wine.

4 - 5 whole pheasant
   breasts, halved, skinned
   and boned
1 cup flour
2 tsp. salt
¼ tsp. pepper
½ tsp. paprika
Butter
Shortening
1 cup cream (half and half)
1 cup sour cream
½ cup sherry
Salt
Pepper

In a paper bag coat pieces with flour, salt, pepper and paprika mixture. In a large, heavy skillet brown breasts in equal portions of butter and shortening. Place in shallow baking dish. Add cream and sour cream to drippings in skillet; bring to a boil to form a slightly thickened gravy, add sherry, salt and pepper to taste; pour over pheasant. Bake covered in slow moderate oven (300°-325°) for 1½-2 hours; remove cover towards the end of the cooking period.

Ann V. Mairet (Mrs. R.A.)

PHEASANT JUBILEE

6-8 Servings

A delicious and attractive main course.

2 pheasants, quartered
½ cup flour
Salt
Pepper
⅓ cup butter

SAUCE:
1 onion, chopped
¼ cup brown sugar
¼ cup seedless raisins
½ cup chili sauce
1 T. Worcestershire sauce
¼ cup water
½ cup sherry
½ cup bing cherries

Roll pheasant in flour, season with salt and pepper, brown in skillet with butter. Remove and place in casserole large enough to lay pieces flat.

For sauce: in skillet brown onion lightly and add all other ingredients except cherries. Blend sauce, tasting for seasoning.

Pour sauce over pheasant. Place cover on casserole. Bake at 325° for 1½ hours. Before serving, add cherries and bake uncovered 15 minutes. Chicken is also delicious prepared this way, but reduce first baking time to one hour.

Charlotte Williams (Mrs. Don E.)

ROAST PHEASANT

4-6 Servings

2 pheasants
Salt
Pepper
Garlic powder
Oregano
1 whole onion
½ cup dry sherry wine
½ cup (1 stick) butter, melted
1 cup water

GRAVY:
1 - 2 T. flour
½ cup sherry
Water
Salt
Pepper

Season birds to taste with first 4 ingredients, inside and out. Place in roasting pan and pour ½ cup of sherry and melted butter over the birds. Add whole onion and water to pan and cover with foil. Place in preheated 400° oven. Baste every 30 minutes. After 2 hours lower oven to 350° and bake 1 hour more. During the last 30 minutes uncover to brown. When ready to serve, remove from pan and keep warm.

For gravy: Add flour to drippings and blend until smooth. Add sherry, water, salt and pepper to taste. Strain if necessary.

Shan Corelis (Mrs. John)

DUCK AND PHEASANT ORANGE SAUCE

2 Quarts

This recipe was given to me by a good hunting friend, Wm. S. Faurot of Chicago, Illinois.

6 jars (8 oz. each) of currant jelly
3 jars (8 oz. each) of crabapple jelly
1 can (24 oz.) frozen orange juice
½ lb. butter
1 tsp. salt
1 tsp. cinnamon
1 cup reconstituted lemon juice
1 jar (8 oz.) pineapple or apricot marmalade
12 oranges
4 lemons
½ bottle walnut brown sherry (approximately 2 cups)

Before starting operations put a band-aid on your right thumb, if right handed, or on left thumb, if left handed! This is important! Place all ingredients, except the oranges, lemons and sherry in a large stew pan. While this is slowly cooking on the stove, grate rind of 12 oranges and 4 lemons, and add to the mix, as well as the juice of these fruits. Boil down well, but be careful not to let the mixture boil over or scorch in the pan. Remove pan from heat, add about ½ bottle of walnut brown sherry. This sauce must be refrigerated, or can be frozen if packed in a plastic container. To serve with cooked game, warm gently!

W.E. Bettendorf

SAUTEED CHICKEN WITH LEMON

4-6 Servings

4 chicken breasts
8 T. salted butter
¼ cup cognac
Rind of 2 lemons, finely
   grated
2 tsp. garlic, finely
   chopped
Salt
Pepper
1 tsp. tomato paste
1 tsp. meat glaze
3 T. flour
1¼ cups chicken stock
1 cup sour cream
1 cup heavy cream,
   whipped
Juice of 1 lemon
2 tsp. sugar
1 tsp. guave jelly

Preheat over to 350°. Bone chicken breasts and cut into bite-sized pieces; brown in 5 T. butter. Heat cognac in a separate pan, ignite and pour over chicken. Remove chicken to baking dish. Heat 3 T. butter and add lemon rind, garlic, salt and pepper. Cook slowly 5 minutes. Remove from heat, stir in tomato paste, meat glaze and flour and mix to a smooth paste. Over low heat, slowly add chicken stock and bring to a boil. Reduce heat to a gentle simmer. In a separate bowl, fold the sour cream with the whipped cream. Stir this mixture into the simmering sauce. Then add lemon juice, sugar and jelly. Pour sauce over chicken. Put in oven, uncovered,, and cook at 350° for 40 minutes. If sauce separates, add a little cold sour cream.

JAMES DIXON

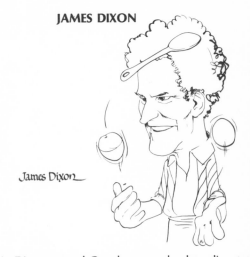

James Dixon

It is JAMES DIXON, Music Director and Conductor, who has directed the Tri-City Symphony Orchestra since 1964 to its enviable reputation. Mr. Dixon has made a national reputation for dedication to and excellence in the performance of contemporary music, conducting the world premiere of more than 30 works by at least 20 American composers. In 1978, he was awarded the Laurel Leaf Award by the American Composers Alliance. His career continues to expand with guest appearances on the podiums of major orchestras around the world, at festivals on both coasts, and awards from several of the music world's most important organizations. In addition to the time Mr. Dixon devotes to conducting the University of Iowa Symphony Orchestra and the Tri-City Symphony, he directs the Tri-City Youth Orchestra and has been an inspiration to many aspiring young musicians.

SUPREME DE VOLAILLE GISMONDA   4 Servings
(Breast of Chicken with Mushrooms and Spinach)

**Served at the White House, May 1961, for
Prince Rainier and Princess Grace of Monaco.**

2 chicken breasts, halved,
  skinned and boned
Salt to taste
Pepper to taste
Flour for dredging
1 T. water
1 egg, beaten
¼ cup grated parmesan
  cheese
¾ cup white bread crumbs
3 T. butter
1 lb. cooked spinach,
  coarsely chopped
¼ lb. mushrooms, sliced
2 T. brown sauce, or
  beef broth
Fresh parsley, chopped

Pound chicken breasts to flatten. Season with salt and pepper and dredge with flour. Add water to beaten egg and dip the meat in this mixture. Combine cheese and crumbs; coat the meat. Heat 2 T. butter in skillet and brown meat about 10 minutes on each side. Make a bed of coarsely chopped spinach on serving platter, arrange chicken breasts on top and keep hot. To the skillet add remaining butter (1 T.) and saute mushrooms until tender. Spoon over chicken, pour brown sauce over chicken and sprinkle with chopped parsley.

Louise L. McCarty (Mrs. Harvey)

CRANBERRY CHICKEN   6-8 Servings

Easy recipe for large group - - zesty flavor!

1 bottle (8 oz.) French
  dressing
1 can (8 oz.) crushed
  pineapple
1 can (16 oz.) whole
  cranberries
1 tsp. dry mustard
1 pkg. (1 oz.) onion
  soup mix
2 chickens, cut up

Mix dressing, pineapple, cranberries, mustard and onion soup together. Place chicken pieces in 9×12" baking dish. Cover with sauce. Bake at 350° for 1 hour.

Laura Houston (Mrs. Douglas)

CRAB-STUFFED CHICKEN

The crab stuffing blends delightfully with the chicken flavor.

4 large chicken breasts
halved, skinned
and boned
3 T. butter or margarine
¼ cup flour
¾ cup milk
¾ cup chicken broth
or stock
⅓ cup dry white wine
¼ cup onion, chopped
1 T. butter or margarine
1 can (7½ oz.) crab meat
drained, flaked and
cartilage removed
1 can (3 oz.) chopped
mushrooms, drained
½ cup coarsely crumbled
saltine crackers (10)
2 T. parsley, snipped
½ tsp. salt
Dash pepper
1 cup (4 oz.) shredded
process Swiss cheese
½ tsp. paprika

Have all ingredients prepared before beginning.

Place one chicken piece, boned side up, between 2 pieces of waxed paper. Working from center out, pound chicken lightly with meat mallet to make cutlet about 1/8-inch thick (8x5 inches). Repeat with remaining chicken. Set aside. (This can be done ahead and refrigerated.)

In saucepan, melt the 3 T. butter or margarine; blend in the flour. Add milk, chicken broth, and wine all at once; cook and stir until mixture thickens and bubbles. Set aside.

In skillet, cook onion in the remaining butter until tender, but not brown. Stir in crab, mushrooms, cracker crumbs, parsley, salt and pepper. Stir in 2 T. of the sauce. Top each chicken piece with about ¼ cup crab mixture. Fold sides in, roll up. Place seam side down in 9×12" baking dish, or comparable ovenproof serving dish.

Pour remaining sauce over all. Bake covered, with aluminum foil if necessary, in 350° oven for 1 hour, or until chicken is tender. Uncover; sprinkle with cheese and paprika. Bake 2 minutes longer or until cheese melts, watch carefully!

LANCE O. WILLETT

Lance Willett

LANCE O. WILLETT, Orchestra Manager of the Tri-City Symphony since 1976, has been a constant source of support and enthusiasm to the symphony family. Outside the symphony office, he is gaining additional recognition for his culinary talents as well.

CHICKEN BREASTS GOURMET   8 Servings

Absolutely delicious, very easy and fast.

4 - 5 chicken breasts,
  halved, boned and
  skinned
1 cup sour cream
1 can (10¾ oz.) golden
  mushroom soup
½ cup cream sherry
Extra mushrooms, if
  desired

Place chicken breasts in 9×13" pan. Mix together thoroughly sour cream, golden mushroom soup, cream sherry and extra mushrooms. Pour over chicken breasts and bake at 350° for 1½ hours. Serve with wild rice.

Mary Loving (Mrs. Roger)

CHICKEN CAMBRIDGE   4 Servings

Can be made one day ahead - delicious combination using wine and ham.

1 large chicken (fryer),
  cut in pieces
Flour
Salt
Pepper
½ cup (1 stick) butter
¼ cup green onions,
  chopped
1 can (4 oz.) mushrooms,
  drained
1 cup ham, chopped
1 clove garlic, minced
1 cup red wine

Shake chicken in sack with flour, salt and pepper. Brown chicken in butter and place in 4 quart casserole. Mix remaining ingredients, plus 2 T. pan drippings together and pour over chicken. Place in refrigerator overnight. The next day, spoon liquid over chicken and bake at 350° covered, for 1½ hours. Can be baked the same day, but reduce cooking time to 1 hour. Very easy and a good way to use left over ham.

Katie Ainsworth (Mrs. Gordon)

TANGERINE PEEL CHICKEN   4 Servings

This dish goes nicely with plain rice and Chinese-style stir-fried vegetables.

PART I
 2 whole chicken breasts,
   with wings
 1 onion, sliced
 3 slices fresh ginger root
 1 T. dry sherry
 1 T. soy sauce
 1 tsp. salt

PART II
 6 T. vegetable oil

PART III
 Peel of 1 large tangerine,
   grated
 ½ tsp. hot red pepper
   flakes

PART IV: SAUCE
 2 T. dry sherry
 2 T. soy sauce
 2 tsp. wine vinegar
 Juice from tangerine
 Pinch of black pepper
 2 tsp. cornstarch
 Sesame seeds

PART I:
Split chicken breasts and detach wings. Cut wings into three pieces and discard tips. Cut remaining breasts through bones into small pieces (approximately 6 pieces per split breasts). In a bowl, combine chicken with sliced onion, fresh ginger, sherry, soy sauce and salt. Rub this marinade well into chicken and leave for several hours. Toss chicken pieces several times during marinade period. Remove onion and ginger and dry chicken on paper towels. Before proceeding, make sure chicken is at room temperature.

PART II:
In wok or frying pan, heat oil until very hot. Add one-third of chicken pieces and cook until lightly browned. Turn and toss chicken as it cooks. Cooking time is approximately 4-6 minutes, but this may vary depending on heat of oil and temperature of chicken. When done, remove with slotted spoon and drain on paper towels. Keep warm while cooking other batches of chicken. Between cookings, let oil heat to hot frying temperature.

PART III:
After all chicken pieces have cooked, and drained, pour off oil. To residual oil, add tangerine peel and red pepper flakes. Stir-fry over high heat about 15 seconds.

PART IV:
Mix all ingredients for sauce. Make sure cornstarch is completely dissolved. Add the sauce to wok or pan and cook over high heat until sauce thickens and is translucent. Immediately add drained chicken pieces and toss over high heat until chicken is well coated and hot. Sprinkle sesame oil over chicken; toss and serve.

John Contiguglia

COCONUT MACADAMIA CHICKEN 8-10 Servings

This recipe originated in Hawaii!

5 chicken breasts, halved, skinned and boned
Salt
Pepper, freshly ground
4 T. butter
½ cup green onions with tops, thinly sliced
1 T. brown sugar
¼ tsp. salt
⅛ tsp. MSG
⅛ tsp. dried thyme, crumbled
⅔ cup golden raisins
2 T. fresh lemon juice
1 jar (4 oz.) pimento, sliced

COCONUT CRUST:
5 T. butter, melted
2 T. fresh lemon juice
¼ tsp. salt
¼ tsp. pepper, freshly ground
1½ cups flaked coconut
2 T. fresh parsley, chopped
¾ cup macadamia nut bits

Season chicken generously with salt and pepper. Gently brown chicken in butter with loose corners folded under on all sides. Arrange in shallow baking dish. Add onions to fry pan and stir. Stir in brown sugar, salt, MSG, thyme, raisins, lemon juice and pimentos. Pour this sauce over the chicken. Cover and bake at 375° for 45 minutes.

For coconut crust: Combine all ingredients, except nuts. After chicken bakes for 45 minutes, remove cover and sprinkle with the coconut crust. Top with macadamia nuts. Bake uncovered 10 minutes more. Spoon sauce from pan over chicken as you serve.

Doris Mueller (Mrs. August)

SWISS CHICKEN 4 Servings

Extremely easy and very rich in flavor.

2 chicken breasts halved, skinned and boned
6 slices American cheese
1 can (10¾ oz.) cream of chicken soup
½ cup cooking sherry
2 cups pre-seasoned croutons
¼ cup butter, melted

Place chicken in 9×9" glass pan. Cover with cheese slices. Combine soup and wine, pour over cheese. Coat croutons with melted butter and sprinkle on top. Bake at 325° for 60-75 minutes.

Terri Lischer (Mrs. Michael)

CHICKEN BREASTS IN WINE SAUCE

4 Servings

½ cup flour
½ tsp. salt
$\frac{1}{8}$ tsp. black pepper
2 large chicken breasts, split and skinned
4 T. butter or margarine
½ lb. sliced mushrooms
1 medium onion, chopped
¼ cup chopped parsley
1 cup dry white wine
2 cups cooked rice

Combine flour, salt and pepper. Coat chicken with this mixture. Shake off and reserve excess flour. Melt half the butter or margarine in large skillet over medium heat. Brown the chicken and remove from skillet. Add remaining butter and the mushrooms, onion and 2 T. chopped parsley. Saute until onion is transparent. Remove from heat. Stir in reserved flour. Blend in wine. Return to heat and bring to a boil, stirring frequently. Add chicken. Cover, reduce heat and simmer 25 minutes. Serve over rice and garnish with remaining parsley.

MR. AND MRS. DANIEL HEIFETZ

Daniel Heifetz

DANIEL HEIFETZ was hailed by the New York Times for his 1970 debut performance in Philharmonic Hall of the Tchaikowsky Violin Concerto with the National Symphony of Washington, D.C. Since then, he has been touring extensively throughout the United States, Europe, Central and South America. Tri-City Symphony audiences were delighted with his performance of "Concerto in D Minor for Violin" by Sibelius in 1975. In 1979, Mr. Heifetz returned to perform Bruch's "Violin Concerto No. 1, in G Minor, Op. 26."

CHICKEN IN WINE   6-8 Servings

8 chicken breasts, halved,
  skinned and boned
Flour for dredging
½ cup (1 stick) butter
1 medium onion, chopped
2 cans (10¾ oz. each)
  cream of chicken soup
1 can (10¾ oz.) cream of
  mushroom soup
¼ cup sour cream
½ cup sauterne
1 can (4 oz.) whole
  mushrooms

Coat chicken with flour and brown in butter. Remove and place in large baking dish. Pour off all but 2 T. drippings and saute onions. Add soups, sour cream, sauterne and blend. Add mushrooms and warm mixture only until smooth. Pour over chicken. Cover and bake at 350° for 40 minutes. Uncover and continue baking 30-40 minutes longer. Serve with wild rice. Chicken thighs can also be used.

Chris Ahlstrand (Mrs. David)
Vicki Patramanis (Mrs. Mike)

DUTCH OVEN CHICKEN   4 Servings

1 whole chicken
1 tsp. salt
1 can (10¾ oz.) cream of
  chicken soup
8 medium carrots
4 medium potatoes
3 T. cooking sherry

Choose lean chicken and remove excess fat before cooking. Wash chicken, dry and sprinkle inside and out with salt. Mix soup and sherry in dutch oven. Place chicken, in dutch oven, breast side down, and baste with soup, cover. Bake at 350° for 1 hour, basting once. Turn chicken breast up and place peeled carrots and potatoes in pan. Lightly salt and baste the vegetables. Bake approximately 1¼ hours more, covered. Baste once. Water can be added to soup if you want a gravy.

Jean Appier (Mrs. William)

SUSANN McDONALD'S FAVORITE CHICKEN RECIPE

8 chicken breasts, boned
1 cup raw rice
1 T. butter, melted
1 can (10¾ oz.) cream of
   mushroom soup
1 can (10¾ oz.) cream of
   celery soup
1 can (10¾ oz.) cream of
   chicken soup
½ cup sherry
Grated cheddar cheese
Sliced almonds

8 Servings

Bone chicken breasts. Set aside. Melt butter; put rice in casserole dish and stir in butter. Pour ½ can of each of the three soups over rice. Place chicken over top of rice and soup mixture. Mix remaining soup together with sherry and pour over chicken. Sprinkle grated cheese and almonds over all. Bake at 350° 1½ hours covered, then ½ hour uncovered.

SUSANN McDONALD

Susann McDonald

One of the very few internationally known harp virtuosos, SUSANN McDONALD's interpretations of vast repertoire and superb musicianship delighted audiences in Europe, Israel, North and South America, the Orient and the South Pacific. Always a favorite with Tri-City audiences, she last appeared with the Tri-City Symphony in 1977, performing the "Harp Concerto in E Flat Major" by Gliere.

DOLLY'S CHICKEN KAPAMA

6-8 Servings

2 chicken fryers cut in
 pieces
Salt
Pepper
Garlic salt
¼ cup butter
¼ cup margarine
1 can (6 oz.) tomato
 paste
1 can (8 oz.) tomato
 sauce
2 - 3 cans water
Cinnamon
Juice of 2 lemons
1 whole onion
Pasta
Fresh romano cheese

Salt and pepper chicken, then sprinkle with garlic salt on just one side. Melt butter and margarine in skillet and brown chicken on both sides. Remove chicken pieces. Add tomato paste, tomato sauce and 2-3 cans of water to pan drippings. Bring this to a boil and blend. Add cinnamon, to taste, and the juice of 2 lemons. Place chicken in roaster with onion, pour sauce over chicken, and cook over low heat (simmer for 1 hour. Prepare favorite shape of pasta (mostaccioli or macaroni are good) according to package directions. Remove chicken from sauce, keep warm. Bring sauce to a boil. Place pasta on platter then chicken, cover with sauce, top with freshly grated romano cheese.

Shan Corelis (Mrs. John)

MISSISSIPPI RIVER BOAT CHICKEN

12 Servings

My favorite "do at home and serve on board" recipe.

6 chicken breasts, halved
12 strips bacon
½ lb. chipped beef
1 can (10¾ oz.) mushroom
 soup
1 cup sour cream
Sliced almonds

Wrap each breast with bacon strip diagonally. Cover bottom of 9×12" pan with chipped beef. Place chicken on the beef. Cover with a mixture of soup and sour cream. Sprinkle top with almonds. Do not salt, as the chipped beef seasons it. Bake at 250° for 3½ hours. Cover the last hour. If it starts getting dry add a bit more sour cream. "Past presidents" and busy mothers appreciate this delicious recipe for guests.

Barb Heninger (Mrs. Ralph H.)

CHICKEN AMBASSADOR

6-8 Servings

3 - 4 large chicken breasts, halved
1 T. salt
1 tsp. poultry seasoning
Paprika
½ cup (1 stick) butter, melted
1 can (10¾ oz.) beef consomme
½ cup sherry
½ lb. fresh mushrooms, sliced
3 T. butter
2 cans (10 oz. each) artichoke hearts, packed in water, drained and quartered
2 T. flour

Season chicken with salt, poultry seasoning and sprinkle with enough paprika to give them a good color. Spread out in a 9×13" roasting pan, skin side up. Baste with melted butter and consomme mixture. Bake in 325° oven for 1 hour, basting every 20 minutes. Add sherry and continue baking 30 minutes longer. Meanwhile, saute mushrooms in butter. When ready to serve, remove chicken breasts and keep warm. Add 2 T. flour to pan drippings. Add sauted mushrooms and drained artichoke hearts to drippings. Heat thoroughly. To serve: pour sauce over chicken arranged on platter.

Connie Sauer (Mrs. Ralph)

HUNGARIAN CHICKEN WITH WINE

6-8 Servings

¼ cup chicken broth or boullion
½ cup onion, chopped
1 3½ lb. chicken or pieces (whole chicken should be cut up)
1 cup dry white wine
1 tsp. salt
⅛ tsp. pepper
6 cups cabbage, shredded
½ tsp. salt
1 tsp. lemon juice
1¼ cup chopped pimiento

Preheat oven to 400°. Heat chicken broth in small pan over moderate heat. Add chopped onion and cook until tender. Place chicken pieces in 5 quart baking dish. Add wine, salt and pepper to onion and broth. Pour over chicken. Bake uncovered for 45 minutes, basting occasionally. Add cabbage, salt, and lemon juice. Cover, cook until cabbage is done (30-45 more minutes). Stir in pimiento, bake 5 more minutes. Serve hot.

Jan McMillan

SEAFOOD and FISH

SHRIMP "SAVOIA BEELER" (BROCHETTES OF SCAMPI)

6 Servings

24 peeled raw shrimp
   (medium large)
Salt
Pepper
24 small stemmed
   mushroom caps
24 slices boiled ham, lean
24 chunks mozzarella
   cheese (1"x1"x½")
½ tsp. dried thyme
½ cup (1 stick) butter
   melted
1 T. lemon juice

Wipe shrimp clean and devein, and sprinkle with salt and pepper. Thread on each of 12 skewers 2 each of the following: shrimp, mushroom, ham slice folded in fourths and cheese. Add thyme to butter and brush over the skewered food. Place skewers in a shallow pan. Cook in preheated moderate oven (350°) 10-20 minutes, basting 2 times with butter and lemon juice. Carefully remove the skewers and arrange the shrimp, etc., on a heated platter. Serve with rice pilaf.

Heather Gosma (Mrs. John S.)

SHRIMP-SCAMPI

6 Servings

This can be used as a first course.
Serve on small seafood plates, garnished with lemon.

3 lbs. raw shrimp, shelled,
   deveined and dried
10 - 12 oz. olive oil
Salt
Pepper
3 cloves garlic, finely
   chopped
½ cup fresh parsley, finely
   chopped

Saute shrimp in ¼" of olive oil over high heat, shaking skillet for 5 minutes, or just until shrimp are bright pink (do not overcook). Season with salt and pepper. Remove to a hot platter, leaving oil in pan. Add the finely chopped parsley to oil in pan. Shake pan over high heat for a few seconds. Pour sauce over shrimp. Serve immediately.

Kay Kaleba (Mrs. Richard)

SHRIMP CANTONESE

6 Servings

Beef, chicken or pork may be substituted for shrimp.

2 lbs. fresh shrimp, shelled, deveined
2 T. butter
1½ cups water
2 T. soy sauce
1 pkg. (1 oz.) onion soup mix (use less if preferred)
2 T. cornstarch
¼ cup water
1 cup fresh mushrooms, sliced
1 can (6 oz.) water chestnuts, sliced thinly
1 pkg. (10 oz.) frozen Chinese pea pods

Brown shrimp in butter. Add to shrimp 1½ cups water, soy sauce and onion soup mix. Stir together, cover and cook over a low heat 30 minutes, or until shrimp is tender. Blend 2 T. cornstarch in ¼ cup water. Add to shrimp mixture and cook, stirring constantly until thickened. Add mushrooms, water chestnuts and pea pods. (the pea pods should be separated, but not defrosted.) Cover and cook over low heat 7 minutes more. Serve with rice.

Mary Cebuhar (Mrs. Michael)

SHRIMP CREOLE

2-3 Servings

4 strips bacon, diced
2 small onions, chopped
2 T. flour
1½ cups canned tomatoes, drained
½ cup green pepper, chopped
1 tsp. salt
¼ tsp. ground marjoram
½ tsp. ground oregano
½ cup hot water
1 pkg. (12 oz.) frozen shrimp, cooked

Dice bacon and fry in heavy pan until crisp. Add chopped onions and brown lightly. Sprinkle with 2 T. flour and stir in tomatoes, green pepper, salt, marjoram, oregano and hot water. Bring to a boil and add cooked shrimp. Cover and simmer just until tender. Correct seasoning. Serve over cooked rice.

Jan Crow (Mrs. David)

BAKED STUFFED SHRIMP   4 Servings

As served at Christopher's, Rock Island.

1 lb. green shrimp (raw,
  unpeeled)
Melted butter
Seafood stuffing

STUFFING INGREDIENTS:
4 oz. butter
1 small onion, finely
  chopped
1 tsp. fresh garlic,
  minced
4 oz. raw shrimp, coarsely
  chopped
4 oz. crabmeat, coarsely
  chopped
⅛ cup brandy
⅛ cup sherry
Dry bread crumbs
  (approximately ½ lb.)
Salt to taste
White pepper to taste

Note: If possible buy green
  shrimp that are large,
  15-20 per pound.

To prepare stuffing: Melt butter in skillet or saucepan. Add onion, garlic, shrimp and crabmeat. Saute until seafood is cooked. Add brandy and sherry. Remove from heat. Stir in bread crumbs until all liquid is absorbed and mixture is loose and flaky. Season to taste with salt and white pepper.

To prepare shrimp: Peel shrimp, but let tail remain on. Slit back of shrimp almost completely through and remove vein. Wash under cold water. Place shrimp attractively in a shallow casserole or individual casseroles. Cover shrimp with stuffing, but allow shrimp tails to protrude above the stuffing. Drizzle with melted butter. Bake in hot (400°) oven for 20 minutes or until shrimp are nicely cooked and stuffing is browned. Garnish with fresh chopped parsley and serve immediately.

Robert E. Wechsler

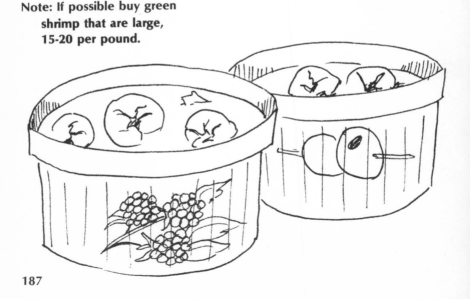

ORIENTAL SHRIMP

6-8 Servings

2 cans (20 oz. each)
  pineapple chunks
½ cup vinegar
1½ cups water
½ cup brown sugar, firmly
  packed
2 T. honey
1 tsp. soy sauce
¼ tsp. ginger
$1/_8$ tsp. nutmeg
¼ tsp. curry
$1/_8$ tsp. cloves
$1/_8$ tsp. savory
½ tsp. dry mustard
1 tsp. salt
¼ tsp. white pepper
2 T. butter
2 large green peppers,
  cut into 1" pieces
½ lb. fresh mushrooms,
  sliced
2 stalks celery, cut into
  1" pieces
2 lbs. shrimp
¼ cup cornstarch

Drain pineapple chunks and reserve 1 cup syrup. Combine pineapple syrup and next 13 ingredients. Heat to boiling. Reduce heat and simmer 3 minutes. In a large skillet melt butter. Add green pepper, mushrooms, celery, shrimp and pineapple chunks. Cover and cook over high heat for 10 minutes. Occasionally, pour off excess liquid and add to the sauce. Mix cornstarch with equal amounts of cold water. Stir into sauce and cook, stirring constantly until thickened. Pour sauce over shrimp mixture. Serve over rice.

Shan Corelis (Mrs. John J.)

EASY METHOD FOR COOKING FISH FILETS

Fish filets
Sliced onion
Butter
Tarragon
Lemon Juice
Salt

Use all according to
individual preference.

Individual Servings

Cook onion slices in butter. Place fish filets in onion-butter. Season with tarragon, lemon juice, and salt. Cover and simmer on low for 20 minutes. Serve immediately.

Gladys Ryan (Mrs. Ben, Jr.)

188

POLYNESIAN FISH

3 lbs. fish
1 tsp. ginger
1 tsp. soy sauce
1 tsp. salt
½ tsp. MSG
1 tsp. sherry
¹/₈ tsp. pepper
¼ cup margarine, melted
Cornstarch

SAUCE:
1 can (8 oz.) pineapple
  chunks
Orange juice
1 T. sugar
½ tsp. ginger
½ tsp. salt
1 T. cornstarch
1 carrot, thinly sliced
1 red or green pepper,
  cut into strips
1 stalk celery, sliced
  thinly on a diagonal
3 T. sweet pickles, sliced
  thinly
1 tomato, diced

To prepare fish: Sprinkle fish with ginger, soy sauce, salt, MSG, sherry and pepper, and rub into the fish. Let stand at least 1½ hours. Roll fish in cornstarch and bake in melted margarine in a 9×13" cake pan for 10-15 minutes at 450°.

To prepare sauce: Drain pineapple and measure juice. Add enough orange juice to equal 1 cup. Add sugar, ginger, salt, cornstarch, carrot, pepper, celery and pickle. Cook, until thick and add tomato and pineapple chunks. Keep sauce warm and serve with the fish.

Kristyn Mahler (Mrs. Michael)

ASPEN TROUT

1 trout per person,
  ¾-1 lb. each
Fresh lemon
2 tsp. salt
½ tsp. thyme
1½ tsp. powdered caraway
1 tsp. celery seed
1 tsp. fennel
¼ tsp. cayenne
½ tsp. garlic powder
¹/₈ tsp. Fines herbes
Thick-sliced bacon strips,
  1 per fish

On a lightly oiled cold broiling pan sprinkle trout generously with fresh lemon juice (insides, too). Combine spices and dust trout liberally on both sides. Broil 10 minutes, one inch from heat. Turn trout, lower grill to 3 inches from heat. Lay 1 strip country style bacon on each trout and broil until bacon is crisp. Serve immediately with pan juices.

Kristyn Mahler (Mrs. Michael)

FLORENTINE SOLE

6-8 Servings

3 pkgs. (10 oz. each)
frozen, chopped spinach
2 cups sour cream
3 T. flour
½ cup green onions, finely
chopped (include some
of the tops)
Juice of one lemon
2 tsp. salt
1½ - 2 lbs. thin filets of
sole (may use halibut)
Paprika
2 T. butter

Cook spinach slightly and drain very thoroughly. Blend sour cream with flour, green onion, lemon juice and salt. Combine half of this mixture with spinach and spread evenly over bottom of a shallow baking dish (9×13" or larger). Arrange fish on spinach, overlapping as necessary. Dot with some of the butter. Spread remaining sour cream mixture evenly over fish, leaving a border to show spinach if you like. Dust with paprika. (At this point, you can refrigerate until ready to cook.) Bake in moderately hot oven (375°) for 25 minutes, or until fish flakes when broken with a fork.

Harriet Harmelink (Mrs. Roger)

FILET OF SOLE MORNAY

6-8 Servings

This recipe is a variation of one learned from the Cordon Bleu while living in Paris.

3 lbs. sole or flounder
filets, fresh if possible
Juice of 2 lemons
2 bay leaves
2 sprigs of thyme (or a
pinch of dried)
White wine

MORNAY SAUCE:
2 cups milk
1 dash of garlic powder
2 sliced onions
10 peppercorns
¼ cup butter
3 T. flour
Salt
Pepper
4 T. cream
1½ cups grated sharp
cheddar cheese

To prepare the fish: Rinse the filets in lemon water (using 1 lemon) and pat dry with paper towel. Fold ends of fish under and put in a well-buttered baking dish. Add lemon juice from second lemon, bay leaves thyme and a little white wine. Bake in 350° oven for 15 minutes.

To prepare Mornay sauce: Put milk, onion slices, garlic powder and peppercorns in saucepan and bring to a boil, slowly. Melt butter in separate pan. Remove from heat and add flour. Strain hot milk mixture and add it to the butter and flour mixture; stir over heat until sauce begins to boil. Add cream; simmer for a few minutes, then add grated cheese reserving a small amount of cheese.

Final preparation: Using a baster, drain liquid from fish. Cover fish with sauce and sprinkle remaining grated cheese on top. Bake at 350° until done, approximately 30 minutes more.

Fish can be prepared through first 2 steps in the morning and refrigerated until final baking time.

Linda Clarke (Mrs. Wade)

ELEGANT MUSKIE OR NORTHERN PIKE

1 whole muskie, northern
  pike, or similar game fish
Bacon strips
Heavy aluminum foil
Melted butter
Fresh lemons
Fresh parsley

Wild Rice Dressing

1 lb. per person

To freeze a muskie: Don't wash off any of the outer protective slime, and do not remove entrails. Wrap in plastic wrap, then freezer paper; tape lightly, then freeze.

To prepare fish: Thaw fish. Scale, cut off head, remove entrails. Cut off tail and all fins at skin line with scissors. Leave bones in fish. Set fish with back up and pour small quantities of boiling water the length of the fish. Scrape fish immediately with a knife, removing all pigments and residue. Rinse thoroughly. Flour inside of fish and sprinkle with salt and pepper. Stuff with wild rice dressing; insert aluminum foil in head cavity to hold dressing. Sew fish with needle and string about ½" from edge of opening to avoid string from pulling out. Lay bacon strips side by side over top of fish, which will act as a self-baster. Make a foil boat of heavy duty aluminum foil on a large cookie sheet by overlapping 2 or 3 layers and crinkling the edges. Place stuffed fish with back up inside the boat. Cover with foil. Bake at 450°, removing foil the last 10 minutes to crisp bacon. To estimate baking time, stand fish on flat surface and measure depth. Allow 10 minutes per inch. For example, a 6" fish would bake for 60 minutes.

To serve the fish: With a sharp knife, cut the fish lengthwise down the center of the back, only to the bone. Starting on either side, cut every 2 inches from top to bottom, leaving bones intact. Serve each guest individually, removing fish from bone with a pie server starting at the back bone and gently lifting the meat away. After each serving is removed, a serving of dressing is accessible. Serve with melted butter to which fresh lemon juice has been added. Garnish with fresh parsley.

John S. Gosma

WILD RICE DRESSING FOR STUFFING WHOLE FISH

1 large onion, chopped
1 cup mushrooms,
    chopped
4 celery stalks with some
    tops, chopped
½ cup butter
Salt
Pepper
Beau Monde seasoning
  2 cups pure wild rice
1½ slices fresh bread, cut
    in small pieces
Poultry seasoning

Saute onion, mushrooms, and celery in butter. Add salt, pepper and Beau Monde. Boil rice for about 45 minutes until ends pop. Pour into colander and rinse thoroughly with hot water. Combine all ingredients with bread pieces. Sprinkle lightly with poultry seasoning. Allow to cool and stuff cavity of fish, leaving room for expansion. Any extra stuffing may be heated in a separate casserole.

John S. Gosma

SAUMON, STYLE NORVEGIENNE

8-10 Servings

COURT BOULLION:
1 qt. white wine (dry)
1 qt. water
2 carrots
2 onions
Bouquet garni of:
6 sprigs parsley
4 green celery tops
2 large bay leaves
1 sprig thyme
Juice of 1 lemon
2 whole cloves
12 bruised peppercorns
1 T. salt

8 lb. salmon, whole and
fresh
Cheesecloth
String

3 cups of rich cream sauce
using Mei Yen Seasoning
instead of salt (use your
favorite recipe)

3 hard boiled eggs
Paprika

For court boullion: Bring wine, water, carrots, onions and bouquet garni ingredients to a boil and simmer for 30 minutes, covered.

For salmon: Wrap salmon in cheesecloth and secure with string. Place on rack in fish poacher or covered roaster rack. Simmer the salmon for 30 minutes to an hour, fish should flake easily when touched with table fork. Turn off heat and leave salmon in stock, covered, for another half hour. Lift out fish, drain well, carefully remove cheesecloth and string and place on heated platter. Pour rich cream sauce over fish. Put hard-cooked eggs through ricer over top of sauce. Sprinkle with paprika.

GRANT JOHANNESEN

Grant Johannesen

GRANT JOHANNESEN, appeared with the Tri-City Symphony in 1957. This distinguished American-born virtuoso made a fine reputation for himself not only in America but abroad. His shining performances won him acclaim from critics and audiences alike. Tri-City audiences enjoyed his performance of Saint-Saëns "Concerto for Piano and Orchestra No. 4 in C Minor".

193

SAUMON EN BRIOCHE

10 Servings

Prepare brioche dough the day before serving.

BRIOCHE CRUST:
- 1 pkg. (¼ oz.) dry active yeast
- 3½ cups flour
- 2 eggs
- ½ cup peanut oil
- ¾ tsp. salt

- 4 lb. salmon

STUFFING:
- ½ cup bread crumbs
- 3 T. chicken stock
- 3 shallots, minced
- 3 T. butter
- 1 lb. mushrooms, minced
- 1 egg yolk
- Salt
- Pepper

- 2 small eggs
- Water

- Butter, melted
- Lemon juice
- Salt
- Pepper

For brioche crust: Prepare the brioche dough in food processor the day before this dish is to be served.

To prepare salmon: Cut off the fins of the salmon and a little of the tail.

To prepare stuffing: Mix bread crumbs with the stock. Cook the minced shallots in butter until they are soft. Add the minced mushrooms and saute them. Combine them with the bread puree, egg yolk; the mixture should be stiff. Season. Fill the fish with the stuffing, then sew up the side opening.

To assemble: Beat 2 small eggs with water. Roll the brioche pastry longer and wider than the fish. Place the fish in the center. Fold the edges of the pastry up the sides of the fish. Brush with the beaten eggs on the outside of the pastry. Bake in a preheated 400° oven for 45 minutes. When it is done, the fish can rest a good half hour in the turned off oven with the door ajar. Serve with melted butter, lemon juice, salt and pepper.

PRINCESS MARIE BLANCHE DE BROGLIE, PARIS, FRANCE

L'ECOLE DE CUISINE

This recipe was submitted with best wished by PRINCESS MARIE BLANCHE DE BROGLIE, PARIS, FRANCE, who conducted the "L'Ecole de Cuisine, 1979" a week-long cooking school in this area to benefit the Annual Development Fund of the Tri-City Symphony Orchestra Association.

AUNT JANE'S POACHED SALMON   8 Servings

1 large onion, peeled
1 stalk celery
2 carrots
1 bay leaf
½ cup vinegar
Water
1 5-7 lb. fresh salmon,
    whole or half (not steaks)

SAUCE:
4 T. vinegar
8 T. oil
2 T. sugar
1 tsp. salt
1 tsp. dry mustard
2 tsp. Worchestershire
    sauce
½ cup chili sauce

Simmer onion, celery, carrots and bay leaf in vinegar and add enough water to cover vegetables. Cook until tender. Add salmon and simmer 20 minutes more. (You may need to add additional water at this point to cover salmon.) Allow to remain in stock while cooling.

For sauce: Combine all ingredients. Serve over salmon.

Martha Neal (Mrs. David)

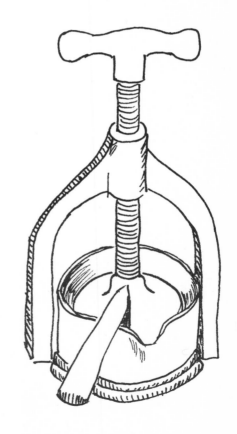

DESSERTS

APPLE PIE SQUARES

20 Servings

2½ cups flour
1 cup lard
1 egg yolk
Milk
1 cup cornflake crumbs
6½ cups apples, peeled
    and sliced
1 cup sugar mixed
    with cinnamon
1 egg white

FROSTING:
Powdered sugar
Milk, warmed
Vanilla

Blend flour and lard together with pastry blender. Put 1 egg in a measuring cup and add enough milk to equal ⅔ cup. Add this to flour mixture and mix well. Divide dough in half. Roll out half of dough and line a jelly roll pan (11×15"). Spread cornflake crumbs on bottom crust. Add apples tossed with sugar. Roll out other half of dough and cover apples, pinch edges together. Beat egg white and spread over top crust. Bake at 350° for 1 hour.

For frosting: Mix ingredients together according to personal preference. Spread this on dessert while still warm. Cut into squares to serve.

Margie Voss (Mrs. Fritz)

APPLE PUDDING

4-6 Servings

¼ cup butter or margarine,
    softened
1 cup sugar
1 egg, well beaten
½ tsp. cinnamon
½ tsp. nutmeg
¼ tsp. baking soda
½ cup flour, sifted
2 cups apples, peeled
    and sliced

Whipped cream or
    ice cream

Cream softened butter with sugar and add well-beaten egg. Sift together cinnamon, nutmeg, baking soda and flour and add to creamed mixture. Fold in the sliced apples. Turn into greased 1½ quart baking dish. Bake at 350° for about 35 minutes. Serve warm with whipped cream or ice cream.

Gail A Diehl (Mrs. David)

APPLE DUMPLINGS

12 Servings

This recipe is of German origin, and was passed on to my mother.

SYRUP:
2 cups sugar
¼ tsp. nutmeg
¼ tsp. cinnamon
2 cups water
¼ cup butter

DOUGH:
2 cups flour
2 tsp. baking powder
1 tsp. salt
¾ cup shortening
½ cup milk

FILLING:
6 apples, peeled and
finely cut
½ cup sugar (depending
on tartness)
Nutmeg
Cinnamon

For syrup: Combine syrup ingredients and bring to boil. Set aside.

For dough: Sift flour, baking powder and salt into mixing bowl. Cut in shortening as for pie dough. Stir in milk. Roll out on floured board to about ¼" thick. Cut out 5" circles.

For filling: Mix apples with sugar and spices, to taste.

To assemble: Place a large spoonful of filling in center of each circle. Fold over one side like a turnover. Wet edges and press together to seal. Place dumplings in a greased pan. Pour the syrup over the top. Bake at 375° for 35-45 minutes or until golden brown.

Mary Kae Waytenick (Mrs. Paul)

OLD FASHIONED APPLE CRISP

6-8 Servings

This recipe won 3rd place in a special Apple Judging Day at the Indiana State Fair in 1965. It comes from the one-room schoolhouse hot lunchroom in Miles, Iowa, population 450, where I grew up.

½ - ¾ cup sugar
1 tsp. cinnamon
4 cups Johnathan apples,
peeled and sliced

TOPPING:
½ cup sugar
½ cup flour
½ cup butter
½ cup uncooked oatmeal

Ice cream or whipped cream
or cheddar cheese slices

Combine sugar and cinnamon with apples and place in greased 9×9" pan.

Blend together with pastry blender the sugar, flour, butter and oatmeal until the mixture resembles small peas. Sprinkle on apples. Bake at 350° for 30-45 minutes or until apples are tender, and top is lightly browned. Serve hot with ice cream, whipped cream or sharp cheddar cheese slices.

Theona Fahl (Mrs. John W.)

199

APPLE SLICES

8-12 Servings

2 cups flour
1 tsp. salt
⅔ cup shortening
1 egg yolk, beaten
½ cup milk
5 - 6 cups apples, peeled
   and sliced
2 T. flour
1½ cups sugar
½ cup (1 stick) butter
1 egg white

Ice cream

Blend flour, salt and shortening with a pastry blender. Add egg yolk and milk and mix well. Roll out half of dough and place in bottom of 9×12″ pan. Add apples. Mix flour and sugar together and sprinkle over apples. Slice butter over apples and sugar. Roll out remaining dough and cover apple mixture. Brush dough with slightly beaten egg white. Bake at 375° for 45 minutes. Can be frosted. Delicious served with ice cream.

Sue Boeye (Mrs. Pryce)

CHERRY PUDDING

6-8 Servings

A family recipe from grandmother.

1 cup sugar
1 T. butter
1 egg, well beaten
1 cup flour
1 tsp. baking soda
1 pint tart, pitted cherries,
   drained (reserve juice)

Whipped Cream

Cream butter and sugar well. Add well-beaten egg. Add flour and soda mixture. Fold in cherries and mix well. If too dry, add a little cherry juice. Put in well greased and floured 9×9″ pan. Bake at 350° about 45 minutes or until it looks dark brown. Serve slightly warm with whipped cream.

Karen Brooke (Mrs. Charles)

RHUBARB DREAM DESSERT   6 Servings

CRUST:
1 cup flour, sifted
5 T. confectioner's sugar
½ cup butter or margarine

FILLING:
1½ cups sugar
¼ cup flour
¾ tsp. salt
2 eggs, beaten
2 cups rhubarb, finely
   chopped

Cream, whipped or plain
   or ice cream

For crust: Blend together flour, sugar and butter. Press mixture into ungreased 7×11" pan. Bake at 350° for 15 minutes.

For filling: Sift together dry ingredients and mix together with eggs and rhubarb. Spoon onto crust and bake at 350° for 35 minutes. Top with cream, plain, whipped, or ice cream. To serve 12, simply double all ingredients and use a 9×13" pan.

Trish Arnold (Mrs. David)

RHUBARB MERINGUE SQUARES   18 Servings

CRUST:
1 cup plus 2 T. butter
2 cups flour

FILLING:
3 cups rhubarb, cubed
3 egg yolks, beaten
1 cup sugar
2 T. flour
$1/_8$ tsp. salt
½ cup canned milk or
   cream

MERINGUE:
3 egg whites
¼ tsp. cream of tartar
⅓ cup sugar
½ tsp. vanilla

For crust: Blend ingredients like pie crust. Press into bottom and sides of 9×13" pan. Bake at 350° for 10 minutes.

For filling: Mix all ingredients together and pour over baked crust. Bake at 350° for 40-45 minutes.

For meringue: Beat egg whites until foamy and add sugar gradually to make stiff mixture. Add cream of tartar and vanilla and beat until blended. Spread on baked rhubarb and bake at 350° for 10-15 minutes. Coconut or nuts may be added as a topping.

LaVonne Monson (Mrs. Larry)

RHUBARB DESSERT

HARD SAUCE:
½ cup butter, softened
1 cup powdered sugar, sifted
½ tsp. vanilla

RHUBARB:
2 cups rhubarb, diced
1 cup sugar
1 egg

TOPPING:
1 cup flour
¼ cup sugar
1 T. baking powder
¼ tsp. salt
¼ cup butter
½ cup milk
1 egg

For hard sauce: Cream butter until fluffy and gradually beat in powdered sugar. Stir in vanilla and chill about 1 hour.

For rhubarb: Combine rhubarb, sugar and egg and pour into a baking dish.

For topping: Sift together dry ingredients of topping. Cut in shortening. Combine milk and egg and stir into dry ingredients. Drop by spoonfuls onto rhubarb. Bake at 350° for 50-55 minutes. Serve warm with hard sauce.

Elsie VonMaur (Mrs. Richard, Sr.)

NUT SHORTCAKE

6-8 Servings

Makes individual servings to use with fruit. So moist & tender!

½ cup sour cream
1 egg
⅓ cup margarine
½ cup broken walnuts
1½ cups flour
¼ cup sugar
1 tsp. baking powder
½ tsp. salt
¼ tsp. soda

Sliced fresh fruit
Whipped cream

Beat sour cream, egg and margarine. Add walnuts and mix. Sift remaining dry ingredients and add to sour cream mixture. Stir until all ingredients are moist. Drop by tablespoons onto greased cookie sheet. Make 6-8 mounds, depending on size desired. Bake at 400° for 15 minutes. Slice in half and layer with fresh fruit, such as strawberries or peaches. Top with whipped cream. (Can be stored in refrigerator 2-3 days in an airtight container. They become more moist and tender.)

Bonnie Brotman (Mrs. Jerrel)

CHOCOLATE "OMELET" SOUFFLE   6 Servings

4 egg whites
2 T. water
4 egg yolks
¾ cup chocolate chips,
  melted and cooled
  slightly
½ cup sour cream
¼ cup powdered sugar,
  sifted
1 T. butter

½ cup whipping cream
2 T. cream de cocao

Beat egg whites until frothy. Add water and beat to stiff peaks. Beat yolks until thick and lemon-colored. Beat chocolate, sour cream and sugar into yolks. Fold yolk mixture into whites. Melt butter in oven-proof skillet on stove. Heat until water drop sizzles. Pour "batter" in and spread to sides. Reduce heat to low and cook 6 minutes. Finish in 325° oven for 10 minutes or till knife inserted off-center comes out clean. Loosen around edges and invert on warm platter. (Will deflate a little.) Sprinkle with powdered sugar. Whip cream until stiff, fold in cream de cocao, and serve on wedges of omelet.

Sue Jacobs (Mrs. Steven)

CHOCOLATE AMARETTO   8-10 Servings

1 box (12 oz.) vanilla
  wafers
1 cup butter
2 cups powdered sugar
6 egg yolks
2 squares (1 oz. each)
  semi-sweet baking
  chocolate
1 tsp. vanilla
6 egg whites
½ tsp. unflavored gelatin
3 T. Amaretto liqueur
1 cup salted almonds,
  chopped

Whipped cream

Crush the vanilla wafers; set aside. Cream the butter and powdered sugar. Add the egg yolks one at a time and beat well. Melt chocolate and add to above. Add vanilla. Beat egg whites until stiff but not dry and fold into chocolate mixture. Soften gelatin in Amaretto, stir into chocolate. Chop nuts, mix with crumbs. Put half of crumb mixture in bottom of 10" round springform pan. Add filling. Sprinkle remaining crumbs and nut mixture on top of filling. Serve with whipped cream.

Sue Staack (Mrs. John)

203

MINT CHOCOLATE CUPS FOR THE FOOD PROCESSOR

1 cup butter, softened
2 cups powdered sugar
4 squares (1 oz. each)
   bitter chocolate, melted
3 eggs, extra large
2 T. vanilla
½ tsp. peppermint extract
   or more to taste
1 cup vanilla wafer crumbs

12 Servings

With steel knife, cream butter and powdered sugar. Add chocolate and beat until blended. Add eggs, one at a time, beating well after each addition. Add flavorings. Sprinkle half of wafer crumbs in bottom of individual aluminum-lined paper baking cups. Spoon mixture on top and sprinkle with remaining crumbs. Freeze. Can be done the day before.

Rose Ann Hass (Mrs. James)

BLENDER POT DE CREME   6 Servings

1 pkg. (6 oz.) semi-sweet
   chocolate chips
2 T. sugar
Salt
1 egg
1 tsp. vanilla
¾ cup milk

Whipped cream
Cherries

Place first five ingredients in an electric blender. Heat milk just to boiling. Pour over ingredients in blender and cover. Blend 1 minute. Pour immediately into 6 small serving dishes and chill for 3 hours. Recipe also works well when doubled. May substitute brandy or creme de menthe for vanilla. Garnish with whipped cream and a cherry.

Lois Florence (Mrs. Donald)

FUDGE PUDDING

1 cup all-purpose flour,
  sifted
1½ tsp. baking powder
½ tsp. salt
¼ cup butter or margarine,
  softened
⅔ cup granulated sugar
½ cup milk
1 square (1 oz.)
  unsweetened chocolate
  (melted)
1 tsp. vanilla extract
¾ cup nuts, coarsely
  chopped
½ cup brown sugar, packed
½ cup granulated sugar
3 T. cocoa
¼ tsp. salt
1½ cups boiling water

Cream, whipped or plain,
  or ice cream

Preheat oven to 350° (if glass baking dish is used, set at 325°). Sift flour, baking powder, ½ tsp. salt. Cream butter with ⅔ cup granulated sugar until light and fluffy, add flour mixture with milk, stirring just enough to blend. Add chocolate, vanilla, nuts; turn into 8×8" baking pan. Combine brown sugar, ½ cup granulated sugar, cocoa, ¼ tsp. salt; sprinkle over batter. Pour boiling water over batter (do not stir). Bake 1 hour (pudding will separate into cake and sauce layers). Cool slightly in pan. Cut into squares; serve warm with sauce over it. Can be served with cream, ice cream or whipped cream.

Charlotte Griggs
Onalee Evans (Mrs. Richard)

CHOCOLATE CHIP ANGEL FOOD DESSERT

9 oz. chocolate chips
4 egg yolks
Dash of salt
4 egg whites
2 T. sugar
1 tsp. vanilla
½ cup walnuts, chopped
1 pint whipping cream
1 large angel food cake

Whipped cream
Cherries

Melt chocolate chips in top of double boiler. Add beaten egg yolks and salt. Stir until thick and well blended. (Mixture will be very thick.) Let cool. Beat 4 egg whites. Add sugar. Beat until stiff and add vanilla. Fold into chocolate mixture. Add nuts. Whip cream until stiff and fold in. Break up cake in bite sized pieces. Make layer of cake and chocolate mixture, starting with cake, in 9×13" pan. Make day before or chill at least 6 hours. Serve with whipped cream and garnish with a cherry.

Dorothy Oliver (Mrs. Thomas)

CHOCOLATE OR CHRISTMAS PLUM PUDDING

Served at Christmas for at least 50 years in my family.

2 level T. unflavored
   gelatin
1 cup cold water
2 cups milk
1 cup seeded raisins
½ cup currants
1½ squares semi-sweet
   chocolate
1 cup sugar
Salt
½ tsp. vanilla
½ cup nuts
¾ cup chopped dates
3 egg whites
Whipped cream
Red and green cherries

12 (½ cup) Servings

Soak gelatin in cold water, five minutes. Put milk and fruit in top of double boiler. When hot, add chocolate which has been melted with part of the sugar and a little milk to make a smooth paste. Add soaked gelatin, sugar and dash of salt; remove from heat and when mixture begins to thicken, add vanilla, chopped nuts and dates. Beat egg whites until very stiff; fold into mixture. Turn into wet 3 quart mold decorated with whole nut meats. Chill. Unmold. Fill center with whipped cream decorated with maraschino red and green cherries cut to make poinsettias. Chill overnight.

Margaret Becker

PLUM DUFF

8-10 Servings

A Neuman Family Christmas Tradition.

1 cup brown sugar
   (packed)
½ cup butter or shortening,
   melted
2 eggs, beaten
Salt
1 cup flour
1 tsp. baking soda
1 T. milk
2 cups chopped prunes,
   pre-cooked

HARD SAUCE:
1½ cups powdered sugar
1 whole egg, beaten
5 T. butter, melted
1 T. vanilla
1 cup heavy cream,
   whipped

Cream butter and sugar. Add eggs, dash of salt and flour. Dissolve soda in milk and add to mixture. Fold in prunes. Pour batter into heavily buttered 2 quart ring mold. Cover mold with foil. Place mold on a rack in large pot or steamer, containing boiling water in bottom. Cover pot and steam on top of stove for 1 hour. Replenish boiling water as necessary. Turn pudding out onto platter. Serve warm with hard sauce. May do pudding day ahead; resteam during dinner (15-30 minutes) and serve warm with sauce.

To prepare hard sauce: Fold all ingredients into whipped cream. May do ahead and refrigerate.

Eloise Smit (Mrs. Jack)

DATE NUT PUDDING

6 Servings

Butter (size of an egg)
1 cup sugar
1 T. flour
⅔ tsp. baking powder
1 egg, beaten
1 cup dates, diced
1 cup pecans
1 cup milk

Cream butter and sugar. Add flour, baking powder, egg, dates, nuts and milk. Pour into greased 9×9" pan. Bake at 350° for 40-45 minutes. Very good warm, but can also be done ahead.

Mary Andrews (Mrs. Charles)

FROZEN GRASSHOPPER TORTE

8-12 Servings

CHOCOLATE CRUST:
1 cup chocolate cookie crumbs, finely crushed
2 T. butter, melted

FILLING:
1¼ cups half and half cream
2½ cups whole marsh-mallows, firmly packed
½ cup green creme de menthe
⅓ cup white creme de cocoa
2 egg whites
3 T. sugar
1½ cups heavy cream, whipped
Semi-sweet chocolate curls

For crust: Mix cookie crumbs and butter together and press evenly on bottom of an 8" or 9" springform pan.

For filling: Put cream and marshmallows in enamel pan and cook, stirring until marshmallows are melted. (Don't turn your back on this mixture, it will foam up and over in a twinkling of an eye.) Set pan in cold water and stir until mixture is cooled. Blend in liqueur. Chill mixture until it begins to thicken. Beat egg whites until stiff, then gradually beat in the sugar and continue whipping until whites hold short, distinct peaks. Whip cream until stiff. In large bowl, thoroughly fold marshmallow mixture and whites into whipped cream. Pour over crust. Cover and freeze until firm - 8 hours or longer. Remove from freezer one half hour before serving. Remove pan sides by wrapping a towel dipped in hot water for 30 seconds and then running a sharp knife around sides. Garnish with semi-sweet chocolate curls (use potato peeler).

Bobbie Searles (Mrs. John M.)

GREEK RICE PUDDING

6 Servings

⅓ cup water
⅓ cup rice (long grain)
1 qt. milk, hot
Salt
¾ cup sugar
2 eggs
¼ cup butter
1 tsp. vanilla
½ tsp. cinnamon

Cook rice (use a 1 quart heavy kettle), in ⅓ cup boiling water on low heat, until water is absorbed. Add hot milk, and dash of salt and cook slowly until rice is tender. Add sugar and heat until sugar is dissolved. Remove pan from heat. Beat eggs and stir a little of the hot mixture into eggs, add butter and stir until melted and blended. Pour this into rice mixture. Replace pan on heat and stir until creamy. Add vanilla. Mix and pour into dessert dishes and sprinkle with cinnamon. Cool. Refrigerate if not used within 4 hours.

Vickie Patramanis (Mrs. Mike)

PINEAPPLE PUDDING-CUSTARD

6-8 Servings

¾ cup butter
1 cup sugar
4 eggs
1 can (20 oz.) pineapple, crushed, (drained)
5 slices bread, cubed

Cream butter and sugar. Mix in eggs, one at a time. Add pineapple and bread cubes. Mix well. Put in greased casserole. Bake at 350° for 60-80 minutes, or until golden brown and crusty. Also good as a side dish with a main course, especially pork.

Trish Arnold (Mrs. David)

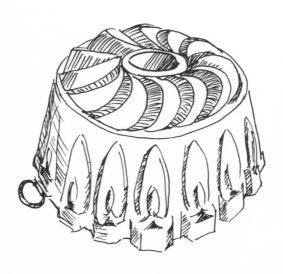

MELON BALL COMPOTE

6-8 Servings

1 cantalope
1 small honeydew melon
¹/₈ watermelon
1 cup fresh blueberries
⅔ cup sugar
⅓ cup water
1 tsp. lime rind
6 T. lime juice
½ cup light rum

Prepare melons with melon baller. Boil sugar and water for 5 minutes over medium heat. Add rind and let cool to room temperature. Stir in lime juice and rum. Pour over combined melon balls and blueberries. Chill. Looks beautiful served in a clear glass dish.

Jan Crow (Mrs. David)

STRAWBERRIES OR RASPBERRIES ROMANOFF

Very tasty! Pretty!

8-10 Servings

2 qts. berries
Sugar
1 pt. vanilla ice cream
1 cup heavy cream,
  whipped
1 lemon
¼ cup Cointreau
2 T. light rum

Clean berries; sweeten with sugar. Put aside. Whip ice cream slightly. Whip cream and fold into ice cream. Add juice of 1 lemon, Cointreau, and rum. May serve at once over berries. I like to make Romanoff several hours ahead of time and store in refrigerator, then flavors really ripen.

Ginny Neiley (Mrs. George)

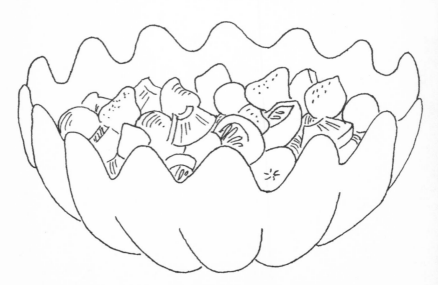

SOUFFLE A L' ORANGE

8 Servings

8 large oranges, cut in
  half
2 cups milk
5 egg yolks
⅓ cup sugar
2 T. flour
½ tsp. vanilla
Grated rind of 1 orange
¼ cup orange liqueur
6 egg whites, beaten
4 T. Confectioner's sugar

Using a spoon, scoop out the flesh of each orange half, being very careful not to break skin. Bring milk to boil in saucepan. Mix egg yolks, sugar and flour in a bowl, pour over the boiling milk. Put mixture back in saucepan, whisking constantly, until it boils and thickens. Remove from heat and add vanilla, rind and liqueur. Fold in egg whites. Fill orange shells with the souffle mixture and place in preheated 425° oven. After 8 minutes, dredge souffles with confectioner's sugar and return to oven. After they have risen about half-inch above the rim of the orange and the sugar has carmelized (takes about 4 minutes), remove the souffles from oven and serve at once.

**PRINCESS MARIE BLANCHE DE BROGLIE
PARIS, FRANCE**

L'ECOLE
DE
CUISINE

This recipe was submitted with best wishes by PRINCESS MARIE BLANCHE DE BROGLIE, PARIS, FRANCE, who conducted "L'Ecole de Cuisine, 1979" a week-long cooking school in this area to benefit the Annual Development Fund of the Tri-City Symphony Orchestra Association.

LEMON SCHAUM TORTE

12 Servings

Takes time to make, but so delicious!

MERINGUE SHELL:
 4 egg whites
 ¼ tsp. cream of tarter
 1 cup sugar

LEMON CUSTARD:
 4 egg yolks
 ½ cup sugar
 3 T. lemon juice
 2 tsp. grated lemon rind

1½ cups heavy cream,
 whipped

For meringue: Beat egg whites until frothy. Add cream of tartar. Gradually add sugar. Beat until stiff peaks form and sugar is dissolved. Bake in 9" greased pan at 275° for 20 minutes. Raise heat to 300°, and bake 40 minutes more.

For custard: Beat yolks until thick and lemon colored. Add sugar, juice and rind in top of double boiler, and cook until thickened. Whip the cream. To assemble, put half of whipped cream on meringue shell. Spread lemon mixture over cream. Cover with remainder of cream. Chill overnight or longer.

Linda Clarke (Mrs. Wade)
Helen DeKalb (Mrs. James)

LEMON PUDDING DESSERT

10-12 Servings

It's a cool and refreshing dessert to top off dinner, or serve with coffee.

LAYER 1:
 ½ cup margarine, melted
 1 cup flour
 ½ cup chopped nuts

LAYER 2:
 8 oz. cream cheese
 1 cup powdered sugar
 1 cup heavy cream or
 topping, whipped

LAYER 3:
 2 pkgs. (3½ oz. each)
 instant lemon pudding
 mix
 3 cups milk

LAYER 4:
 ½ cup heavy cream,
 whipped

For layer 1: Melt margarine and combine with flour and nuts. Bake in 9×13" pan at 350° for 15 minutes. Cool.

For layer 2: Combine ingredients and pour over layer 1.

For layer 3: With electric mixer, blend pudding and milk, until smooth. Pour over layer 2.

For layer 4: Whip cream and spread over layer 3. Chill overnight.

For variation, you may use instant coconut or chocolate pudding in place of lemon.

Jan Illingsworth (Mrs. R.N.)
Kathryn Quiram (Mrs. William A.)

211

CREPE SUZETTE SAUCE FOR FOOD PROCESSOR

26 Crepes (your favorite recipe)
Rind of 1 orange, cut into strips
¼ cup sweet butter, room temperature
Juice of ½ orange
3 T. sugar
3 T. Grand Marnier Liqueur
Powdered sugar
Additional Grand Marnier

26 Crepes

Make crepes. Set aside. See page 124.

With steel blade, chop orange rind and set aside. With plastic blade, cream butter. Add orange rind, orange juice, sugar and Grand Marnier. If the butter will hold, add a little more juice. Scrape the sauce into a container and refrigerate.

Before serving time, bring crepes and sauce to room temperature. Spread a heaping teaspoon of sauce on one side of crepe. Fold in half, then in half again (to form a triangle). Place crepes in a buttered baking dish. Sprinkle with a little liqueur and powdered sugar. Bake at 350° for 5 minutes. Note: Do not flambe, as it destroys the subtle flavor.

MARGHERITA ROBERTI NOBIS

COLD LEMON GRAND MARNIER SOUFFLE

¼ cup cold water
1 envelope (¼ oz.) unflavored gelatin
4 T. fresh lemon juice
4 T. Grand Marnier
1½ cups sugar
3 eggs, separated
1 tsp. vanilla
¼ tsp. almond extract
2 cups heavy cream, whipped
1 T. fresh orange rind, grated

Berries for garnish

6-8 Servings

Soften gelatin in water for 10 minutes. Heat lemon juice and Grand Marnier; add to gelatin, beating at a high speed until well blended. Add sugar, egg yolks, vanilla and almond extract and blend well. Cool until just starting to congeal. Whip cream and fold into egg mixture, along with orange rind. Beat egg whites until stiff and fold into mixture. Pile into souffle dish and chill. Serve on individual dishes and garnish with a few fresh raspberries or sliced strawberries.

Beverly Walker (Mrs. Douglas)

BANANA SPLIT DESSERT

15-18 Servings

CRUST:
- ½ cup (1 stick) butter, melted
- 2 cups graham cracker or vanilla wafer crumbs

FILLING:
- 2 eggs
- 2 cups powdered sugar
- ¾ cup butter, softened
- 1 can (13 oz.) pineapple, crushed
- 3 medium bananas, sliced

TOPPING:
- 1 qt. whipped topping
- ½ cup maraschino cherries, chopped
- 1 cup walnuts, chopped

For crust: Combine butter and crumbs and press on bottom of 9×13" pan. Chill.

For filling: Beat eggs, sugar and butter until fluffy and spread evenly over crust. Drain pineapple well and spread over filling. Next, place sliced bananas on top of pineapple.

For topping: Spread whipped topping over all. Garnish with cherries and walnuts. Chill at least 2 hours. (Crust can be made the night before.)

Miriam Thor (Mrs. John)
Dorothy Oliver (Mrs. Thomas)

SHERRIED CHEESECAKE

8-10 Servings

CRUST:
- ½ cup (1 stick) butter, melted
- ⅓ cup sugar
- 11 graham crackers, crushed

FILLING:
- 6 large eggs
- 4 pkgs. (8 oz. each) cream cheese, room temp.
- 2 cups sugar
- 1 T. lemon juice
- 2 oz. cream sherry

For crust: Mix sugar and graham cracker crumbs with butter. Press into 10" springform pan (bottom only).

For filling: Beat eggs thoroughly with lemon juice and 2 oz. sherry (or to taste). Slowly beat in cheese. Add sugar and beat until very smooth. Pour into 10" springform pan. Cook at 325° for 1½-2 hours. Center will be firm to the touch. Cool. May top with pie filling (cherry or blueberry) if desired. Refrigerate at least 6 hours.

Sue Van Scoy

DINNER PARTY DESSERT PUDDING
12 Servings

A family recipe - the children can help.

LAYER 1:
1 cup flour
1 stick corn oil margarine
1 cup pecans, chopped

LAYER 2:
1 pkg. (8 oz.) cream
cheese
1 cup powdered sugar
6 oz. of 13 oz. Cool Whip
(thawed)

LAYER 3:
3 cups cold milk
2 pkgs. (4½ oz. each) instant
chocolate pudding

LAYER 4:
Remaining Cool Whip
1 bar (4 oz.) milk chocolate

Combine flour and margarine thoroughly and add chopped nuts. Press into bottom of 2 quart rectangular pyrex dish. Bake at 350° for 20 minutes. Cool.

Cream powdered sugar and cream cheese. Fold in 6 oz. Cool Whip. Spread over the cooled crust layer. Refrigerate until firm.

Beat milk with pudding mix for 2 minutes. Spread onto cheese mixture and cover with plastic wrap. Refrigerate until firm.

Cover with Cool Whip and decorate with chocolate curls. Refrigerate until serving time; then cut into squares and serve.

Note: Each step is simple, but cooling and refrigerating takes time.

WILLIAM WALKER

HOT FUDGE TOPPING
About 1 Quart

A must for homemade ice cream, or any ice cream for that matter!

1 cup butter
2½ oz. baking chocolate
3 cups sugar
1 can (13 oz.) evaporated
milk
1 tsp. vanilla
½ tsp. salt

Blend all ingredients in saucepan and cook until thickened. (This is approximately the soft ball stage on a candy thermometer.) Can be refrigerated, but is best served warm.

Annabelle DeCock (Mrs. Dale)

SNOW ICE CREAM

3 Quarts

Such fun for the children!

2 eggs, beaten well
½ tsp. salt
3 tsp. vanilla (or more)
2 cups milk
1½ cups sugar
Copious amounts of fresh,
    fluffy snow

Beat eggs at high speed. Add other ingredients. Spoon snow into egg mixture, and blend well. Freeze.

Tested and devoured during January blizzard of 1979.

Jan Crow (Mrs. David)

ORANGE SHERBET

4-6 Servings

Makes a refreshing dessert in the warm summer months.

Juice of 2 oranges
Juice of 4 lemons
  3 cups sugar
2½ qts. of whole milk

Mix all ingredients together and place in hand or electrically operated ice cream freezer, and follow its instructions for freezing. This recipe has been in my family for years.

Diann Moore (Mrs. Robert)

CARAMEL ICE CREAM

3 Quarts

3 cups sugar
6 whole eggs, slightly
  beaten
Pinch salt
2 qts. heavy cream
1 T. vanilla

Caramelize 2 cups of sugar in a heavy sauce pan by melting and boiling sugar until a clear, amber color. Stir with wooden spoon and do not touch or splatter as it becomes extremely hot. Place eggs, 1 cup of the sugar, salt and 4 cups heavy cream in top of a double boiler. Cook stirring constantly, until thickened. Add the caramelized sugar while very hot. Strain and cool. Add the vanilla and the other quart of heavy cream. Freeze and ripen as per manufacturer's instructions on either electric or hand ice cream freezer.

RICHARD CONTIGUGLIA

215

PASTRIES

GRANDMA'S PIE CRUST

Flaky, tender and delicious.

1 CRUST:
1½ cups flour
½ cup lard
1 tsp. salt
3 - 5 T. ice water

2 CRUSTS:
3 Cups flour
1 cup lard
2 tsp. salt
6 - 7 T. ice water

Cut lard into flour and salt with pastry blender until mixture is size of small peas. Add enough water to form a ball. Roll out between 2 sheets of heavy plastic or waxed paper. Add very little additional flour to keep from sticking. If baked crust is needed, prick with fork gently and bake at 450° for 12 minutes. (If home or farm rendered lard is available, it will be ever so much more tender.)

Rose Ann Hass (Mrs. James)

PERFECT PIE PASTRY

Flaky and works together easily.

1¼ cups flour, sifted
¼ tsp. baking powder
⅜ tsp. salt
⅓ cup lard
⅜ tsp. vinegar
2½ T. cold water
2 T. egg, beaten

Sift dry ingredients together. Cut in lard with pastry blender until pieces are size of small peas. Blend vinegar, cold water, and egg. Stir liquid into dry ingredients with fork. Add only enough to hold dough together. Work quickly. Wrap in waxed paper until ready to roll out. Form 2 balls, one large and one small. Roll dough thin. Place in pan. Add filling. Roll top crust, cut lattices and place on filling. Seal edge and bake at 425° for 30 minutes.

Bonnie Moeller (Mrs. Gerald)

GRAHAM CRACKER COCONUT CRUST   1 Crust

¾ cup graham cracker
  crumbs
¾ cup sweetened flaked
  coconut
⅓ cup butter or margarine,
  melted
¼ cup pecans, finely
  chopped
2 T. sugar

Heat oven to 375°. Mix all ingredients. Press mixture evenly on bottom and sides of 9″ pie plate. Bake until golden, about 8 minutes. Cool on rack.

Kay Stegmiller (Mrs. Stan)

DUTCH APPLE PIE   6-8 Servings

Recently rediscovered, this recipe is a childhood favorite!

1 9″ pie shell, unbaked
1 cup sugar
2 T. plus 1 tsp. flour
½ tsp. cinnamon
6 cups apples, peeled
  and sliced (6-8 medium
  sized tart cooking apples)
2 T. butter
1 egg yolk
¼ cup heavy cream, or
  half and half

Mix well sugar, flour and cinnamon in a large bowl. Add apples and toss until evenly coated. Fill pie shell with apple mixture, dot with butter. Bake at 400° for 30 minutes until apples are tender. Remove pie from oven, reduce temperature to 350°. Beat egg yolk. Add unwhipped cream. Stir and pour cream-egg yolk mixture over pie, pressing apples with a fork to allow cream to ooze down into filling. Bake 15 minutes longer until crust is browned and filling bubbly. Cool to room temperature before cutting.

Mary Cleaveland (Mrs. Harry)

CRANBERRY-APPLE PIE

6-8 Servings

1 9" pie shell, unbaked
1 9" lattice pie crust
1½ cups cranberries
½ cup raisins
½ cup chopped nuts
2 large apples, sliced
1 T. butter
1 cup sugar
2 T. flour
2 T. water
1 tsp. cinnamon
½ tsp. orange extract
½ tsp. lemon extract

Prepare pastry. Wash and drain cranberries. Add remaining ingredients and mix together. Put into a 9" unbaked pie shell. Arrange lattice crust on top. Bake at 400° for 45-50 minutes.

SHERRILL MILNES

Sherrill Milnes

Baritone SHERRILL MILNES, became a star overnight after his debut with the Metropolitan Opera in December, 1965. Besides his outstanding operatic and concert apperances, Mr. Milnes has made a number of recordings including the operas, "Traviata", "Cosi Fan Tutti", "Travatore", "Aida", "Don Carlos" and "Salome". He appeared with the Tri-City Symphony in November, 1970.

FRUIT TARTS   5 Dozen Tiny Tarts

Served at the Annual Meeting of the Sr. Board of the Tri-City Symphony at Elsie Von Maur's, June 1978.

Tart pans: Round 2½" and Oval 3¼x1¼" or one large tart or flan pan

CREAM FILLING:
2 cups milk
6 egg yolks
½ cup sugar
½ cup flour
3 T. butter
1 T. vanilla or (half vanilla and half rum, Kirsch or Cognac)
Pinch of salt

CRUST:
1¾ cups unbleached flour
Salt (pinch)
2 T. sugar
9 T. cold butter (1⅛ sticks)
2½ T. cold shortening
A scant ½ cup liquid (consisting of 1 egg yolk plus ice water to make the ½ cup)

For cream filling: Heat milk in small saucepan until hot. Meanwhile beat yolks and gradually add sugar until mixture is thick and pale yellow. Beat in flour. Very gradually add about ⅔ of the hot milk. Cook over moderate heat in heavy bottomed pan beating constantly with mixer or whisk until it boils. Beat vigorously to smooth it. Thin with hot milk as it cooks. (It should resemble thick mayonnaise.) Lower heat and cook 2 more minutes. Remove from heat and beat in butter, one tablespoon at a time. Add flavoring and salt. (If too stiff, beat in a little heavy cream by driblets.) COOL.

For crust: Place flour, salt and sugar in mixing bowl (or food processor bowl). Cut butter into ¼ inch pieces, shortening also. Add to flour mixture. Beat for a minute or so in mixer (or 3 seconds in processor) until texture is that of coarse cornmeal. Add ⅓ cup liquid and mix a few seconds - - add rest by drops until mass is formed (in processor - - add all but 2 T. liquid at first.) Scrape onto lightly floured working surface. Form into a flat 5" ball. Flour lightly - - wrap in plastic wrap and place in plastic bag and refrigerate for 2 hours.

To form crusts: Remove dough from refrigerator and beat with rolling pin to soften and roll about 3/16" thick. Place in molds and prick bottoms with fork. (Or, place a buttered piece of aluminum foil in each crust and fill with dried beans to keep pastry from puffing.) Bake at 450° for 7-8 minutes. Remove liners and return to oven and bake 2-3 minutes more. Lower oven to 400° and bake 2-3 minutes until pastry begins to color and is set.

APRICOT GLAZE:
 2 jars (12 oz. each)
  apricot jam, strained
 ¼ cup sugar

For apricot glaze: Bring apricot jam and sugar to a boil and cook for 8-10 minutes until it is thick and sticky. Keep warm.

FRESH FRUIT:
Strawberries, sliced
Grapes, sliced
Peaches, sliced
Bananas, sliced and dipped
  in lemon juice

To assemble: Paint baked shells with apricot glaze. Fill with ½" of COOLED pastry cream. Arrange choice of fruit slices over cream. Spoon warm glaze over fruit. Refrigerate until serving time.

Winifred Pheteplace (Mrs. Willard)

STRAWBERRY ALMOND CREAM PIE   6-8 Servings

A truly beautiful dessert!

CREAM FILLING:
- ½ cup sugar
- 3 T. cornstarch
- 3 T. flour
- ½ tsp. salt
- 2 cups milk
- 1 egg, slightly beaten
- ½ cup heavy cream, whipped
- 1 tsp. vanilla

GLAZE:
- ½ cup fresh strawberries
- ½ cup water
- ¼ cup sugar
- 2 tsp. cornstarch
- Red food coloring

- 1 10" pie shell, baked and cooled
- ½ cup blanched, slivered almonds, toasted
- 2 cups fresh strawberries, sliced in half

For cream filling: Combine sugar, cornstarch, flour and salt. Gradually stir in milk. Bring to a boil, stirring constantly. Lower heat and cook and stir until thickened. Stir a little of the hot mixture into the beaten egg, return to remaining hot mixture. Again bring just to boil, stirring constantly. Cool, then chill thoroughly.

For glaze: Crush; ½ cup strawberries, add water and cook 2 minutes, sieve. Combine sugar and cornstarch; gradually stir in strawberry juice. Cook stirring constantly until thickened and clear. Tint to desired color with red food coloring. Cool slightly.

To assemble: Cover bottom of pie shell with almonds. Complete cream filling: Beat custard; fold in whipped cream and vanilla. Place into shell. Pile strawberries on top of filling. Pour glaze over the halved strawberries. Refrigerate until serving time.

This filling is delicious in cream puffs, too, or as a base for banana cream pie.

Margaret Becker

MILE HIGH STRAWBERRY PIE   6-8 Servings

1 10" graham cracker crust
2 egg whites
1 cup sugar
1 pkg. (10 oz.) frozen
  strawberries, partially
  thawed
½ T. lemon juice
½ tsp. salt
1 cup heavy cream,
  whipped
1 tsp. vanilla

GARNISH:
Fresh strawberries
Mint leaves

Beat egg whites until frothy, add sugar and continue beating until stiff. Add strawberries, lemon juice and salt. Beat for 20 minutes at high speed. (This mixture mounds to almost overflowing in large bowl of mixer.) Whip cream and vanilla. Fold cream into egg white-strawberry mixture. Fill pie shell. Freeze at least 4 hours, or overnight. To serve, garnish with a fresh strawberry, or a few mint leaves. Serve slightly thawed.

Jenny Ewing (Mrs. Ted B.)

FRESH PEACH PARFAIT PIE   6-8 Servings

Delicious and the crust is scrumptious!

CRUST:
1 cup quick rolled oats
½ cup sliced almonds
½ cup brown sugar
⅓ cup butter, melted

FILLING:
1 pkg. (3 oz.) orange or
  peach flavored gelatin
1 cup water, boiling
1 pt. vanilla ice cream,
  softened
2 cups fresh peaches,
  thinly sliced

For crust: Toast oats in shallow pan at 350° for 5 minutes. Add almonds and toast 5 minutes more. Add sugar and melted butter. Blend thoroughly and press into a 9" pie pan; reserving ½ cup of mixture for garnish. Chill.

For filling: Add water to gelatin. Stir until dissolved. Add ice cream and stir until smooth. Fold in peaches. Pour into crust. Sprinkle reserve crumbs around edge of top. Chill several hours. If peaches are tart, sweeten with a little sugar before adding them to gelatin mixture.

Diann Moore (Mrs. Robert)

CONCORD GRAPE PIE

6-8 Servings

So unique and flavorful.

4 cups concord grapes
¾ cup sugar
1½ T. fresh lemon juice
½ T. orange rind, grated
2 T. "quick" tapioca
1 9" pie shell, baked
Whipped cream

Slip pulp from grapes, save skins. Cook pulp in a little water until seeds loosen. Push through a fine colander. Add skins to pulp along with juice, rind and tapioca. Let stand 15 minutes. Pour into pie crust. Bake at 450° for 10 minutes. Lower oven to 350° and bake 20 minutes more. Chill in refrigerator for several hours before serving. Garnish with whipped cream.

Eleanor Pappas

BANANA SPLIT PIE

6-8 Servings

This is my mother's favorite luncheon dessert - ladies love it!

CRUST:
1 cup flour, sifted
½ cup butter or margarine
3 T. sugar
⅛ tsp. salt

FILLING:
1½ cups powdered sugar, sifted
½ cup (1 stick) butter or margarine
1 pkg. (3 oz.) cream cheese, softened
2 eggs
1 T. vanilla
2 T. sweet chocolate, grated
½ cup nutmeats, chopped

2 bananas, medium sized
1 T. lemon juice
Whipped cream
Maraschino cherries

For crust: Mix flour, butter, sugar and salt until crumbly. Press into 9" greased pie pan. Bake at 350° until lightly browned, about 10 minutes. Cool.

For filling: Cream sugar and butter. Add cream cheese. Add eggs one at a time and beat 3 minutes after each addition. Add vanilla, and fold in chocolate and nuts.

To assemble: Slice bananas and dip into lemon juice. Place bananas in baked pie shell. Pour filling over top. Chill 2-3 hours. Serve garnished with whipped cream and cherries.

Bonnie Moeller (Mrs. Gerald)

LEMON CUSTARD PIE

6-8 Servings

1 8" pie shell, unbaked
3 egg yolks,
½ tsp. salt
6 heaping T. or ¾ cup
  sugar
1 tsp. lemon extract
1⅔ cup milk
3 egg whites
1 T. sugar

Beat egg yolks, salt and sugar until light and lemon colored. Add lemon extract and blend. Add milk, (that has been preheated a little) gradually until thoroughly blended. Take 2 T. egg white and beat until fluffy, but not stiff and fold into the custard mixture. Pour into unbaked pie shell. Bake at 350° until firm, about 45 minutes to one hour. Remove from oven. Beat remaining egg whites until frothy, but not too stiff. Add 1 T. sugar and blend. Spread over pie and bake until meringue is light brown.

Karen Hanson

LEMON CREAM PIE

6-8 Servings

1 9" graham cracker crust
½ pt. heavy cream,
  whipped
1 can (14 oz.) sweetened
  condensed milk
¼ cup lemon juice
1 qt. fresh strawberries,
  halved

Prepare your favorite graham cracker crust and pat into bottom and sides of a 9" pie pan. Whip cream. Mix sweetened condensed milk and lemon juice in separate bowl. Fold into whipped cream. Put into pie crust. Chill over night. Top with fresh strawberries before serving.

Miriam Thor (Mrs. John)

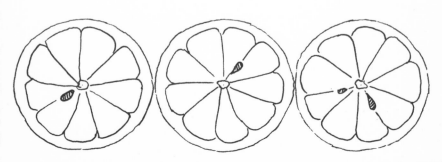

LEMON ICE CREAM PIE

6-8 Servings

CRUST:
1 cup cornflakes, crushed
¼ cup sugar
⅓ cup butter, melted

FILLING:
½ cup lemonade
  concentrate, thawed
1 qt. vanilla ice cream,
  softened

HOT SAUCE:
1 lemon, large
½ cup water
⅔ cup sugar

For crust: Combine ingredients and press into a 9" pie pan. Chill or freeze.

To prepare filling: Combine lemonade concentrate and ice cream. Spoon into chilled crust. Freeze until serving time.

For sauce: Peel lemon with an apple peeler. Cut the peeling into fine toothpick-like strips. Cut to ½" lengths. Cook strips in water over low heat for 10 minutes. Add sugar and boil slowly another 10 minutes, uncovered. At serving time reheat sauce in double boiler and pour over pie slices. (For ease in serving any cereal crust pie: Remove from freezer or refrigerator and place pan on cloth rinsed in hot water. The warmth will loosen the crust just enough to remove servings easily from pan.)

Marlys Wilkinson (Mrs. Tom)

KEY LIME PIE

6-8 Servings

An easy, but "true" key lime pie.

1 9" graham cracker crust
3 egg yolks
1 can (14 oz.) sweetened
  condensed milk
¾ cup fresh lime juice
3 egg whites
6 T. sugar

Whip 3 egg yolks with sweetened condensed milk. Gradually beat in lime juice, and pour into pie shell. Whip 3 egg whites until stiff. Whip in sugar 1 T. at a time. Pile on top of pie. Brown 3-4 minutes at 425°. Chill 6 hours. Pie has pale yellow color. (You may substitute bottled lime juice.)

Sue Jacobs (Mrs. Steven)

RHUBARB CREAM PIE

1 9" pie shell, unbaked
1½ cups sugar
¼ cup flour
¾ tsp. nutmeg
3 eggs, slightly beaten
4 cups (1 lb.) rhubarb
   cut into ½" pieces
2 T. butter

Blend sugar, flour and nutmeg. Add eggs. Beat until smooth. Stir in rhubarb. Pour into pie shell. Pat with butter. Cover with lattice crust, or leave uncovered. Bake at 375° for 45-60 minutes.

Mary Kae Waytenick (Mrs. Paul)
Eloise Smit (Mrs. Jack)

RHUBARB BUTTER-CRUNCH PIE

6-8 Servings

1 9" pie shell, unbaked

FILLING:
4 cups fresh rhubarb, cut
   into 1" pieces
1 cup sugar
3 T. flour

TOPPING:
½ cup brown sugar
½ cup oatmeal
¾ cup flour
½ cup (1 stick) butter

Mix together rhubarb, sugar and flour. Place into unbaked 9" pie shell. Top with mixture of brown sugar, oatmeal, flour and butter. Bake at 375° for 40 minutes.

Chris Ahlstrand (Mrs. David)

LEMON-PINEAPPLE PIE   6-8 Servings

Can be used in meringue shells or spooned over angel cake slices.

1 8" pie shell, baked
  and cooled
1 cup sugar
1¼ cup water
1 T. butter
¼ cup cornstarch, mixed
  with 3 T. water
6 T. lemon juice
3 egg yolks, mixed with
  2 T. water
1 cup canned crushed
  pineapple, drained

In saucepan, (do not use aluminum as it will discolor filling) combine sugar, water, butter, and cornstarch blended with water. Cook slowly over medium heat, stirring constantly until thick and clear, about 8 minutes. Add lemon juice and cook 2 minutes. Slowly add egg yolks which have been beaten with 2 T. water. Bring to a boil. Remove pan from burner. Cool. Beat while cooling with wire whisk. Add drained pineapple. Pour into cooled pie shell, or can be refrigerated and stored in a covered container to be used next day.

Shirley Harris (Mrs. Zeivel)

PECAN CHIFFON PIE   6-8 Servings

Came from Mrs. Jeannie Warwick, who formerly ran Jean's Diner in Laurinburg, N.C. which was on Duncan Hines' list of good eating places in the United States.

1 9" pie shell, baked
½ cup milk
3 egg yolks, beaten
½ cup sugar
Pinch of salt
1 envelope (¼ oz.)
  unflavored gelatin
¼ cup cold water
1 tsp. vanilla
1 T. rum
3 egg whites, beaten
  to soft peaks
½ cup sugar
½ cup pecans, finely
  chopped and toasted

In top of double boiler combine milk, egg yolks, ½ cup sugar and salt. Beat well and cook until mixture coats a spoon-thin custard stage. Dissolve gelatin in cold water. Add to custard mixture. Cool. Add vanilla and rum. Set aside until slightly congealed. Beat egg whites to foamy stage and gradually beat in sugar. Continue beating to soft peak stage allowing sugar to dissolve completely. Fold custard mixture into egg whites. Fold in pecans. Pour into pre-baked 9" pie shell. Chill. Serve with whipped cream.

Mollie Montgomery (Mrs. Thomas)

229

PRALINE PUMPKIN PIE

6-8 Servings

PRALINE CRUNCH:
- ¼ cup butter
- ½ cup sugar
- 1 cup pecans, coarsely chopped

FILLING:
- 1 pkg. (¼ oz.) unflavored gelatin
- ½ cup cold water
- ¾ cup brown sugar, firmly packed
- 1 can (16 oz.) pumpkin
- ¼ cup milk
- ½ tsp. salt
- ½ tsp. cinnamon
- ¾ tsp. nutmeg
- 1 cup heavy cream, whipped

1 9" pie shell, baked
Whipped cream for garnish

For crunch: Melt butter in a small skillet. Stir in sugar. Add pecans. Cook over medium heat, stirring constantly until sugar mixture begins to turn golden, about 3 minutes. Remove from heat; turn out onto a piece of foil. Cool. Crumble into small pieces.

For filling: Sprinkle gelatin over water in saucepan. Place over low heat, stirring constantly until gelatin dissolves; 2-3 minutes. Remove from heat, add brown sugar, stirring until dissolved. In mixing bowl, combine pumpkin, milk, salt, cinnamon and nutmeg. Gradually blend in gelatin mixture until smooth. Whip cream until stiff and fold into mixture.

To assemble: Sprinkle ¾ of the praline crunch over bottom of baked pastry shell. Pour pumpkin mixture into shell. Chill until firm. At serving time, garnish with whipped cream and praline crunch.

Jean Midkiff (Mrs. Tom)
Kay Stegmiller (Mrs. Stan)

CHOCOLATE SILK PIE

6-8 Servings

CRUST:
- 15 vanilla wafers
- 2 T. butter

FILLING:
- 2 squares (1 oz. each) semi-sweet chocolate
- ½ cup (1 stick) butter or margarine
- ¾ cup sugar
- 2 eggs
- 1 tsp. vanilla

½ cup heavy cream, whipped

For crust: Roll wafers to crumbs and add melted butter. Pat into 9" pie tin and bake at 350° for 10 minutes. Cool.

For filling: Melt chocolate over low heat, cool. Cream butter and sugar well. Add chocolate. Add one egg and beat for 5 minutes. Add second egg and vanilla and blend well. Pour into shell. Chill overnight. Serve right from refrigerator; top with whipped cream.

Marian Dauber
Donna Strieder (Mrs. Henry L.)

GRASSHOPPER PIE

6-8 Servings

Super easy to make and a very popular dessert!

CRUST:
24 chocolate sandwich
   cookies with filling,
   crushed
¼ cup butter, melted

FILLING:
¼ cup Creme de Menthe
1 jar (7 oz.) marshmallow
   creme
2 cups heavy cream,
   whipped

For crust: Combine the crushed chocolate sandwich cookies and melted butter. Press into a 10" pie pan. Reserve 1 T. for topping.

For filling: Gradually add the Creme de Menthe to the marshmallow creme and mix until well blended. Whip cream until stiff. Fold in the whipped cream. You may add a couple drops of green food coloring to darken the color. Pour into pie pan and sprinkle with the remaining crumbs. Freeze at least 4 hours before serving, longer is better. This may be made the night before.

If desired, use ¼ cup milk, a few drops of peppermint extract, and a few drops of green food coloring instead of the Creme de Menthe. Remove from freezer 10 minutes before serving.

Judy Petersen (Mrs. David)

FUDGE PIE

6-8 Servings

This dessert is especially good topped with peppermint ice cream.
It tastes like a chewy brownie.

2 squares (1 oz. each)
   semi-sweet chocolate
½ cup margarine
2 eggs
1 cup sugar
¼ cup flour

Grease and flour 9" pyrex pie pan, (no crust). Melt the chocolate and margarine together and set aside. Beat eggs, add sugar and flour and beat well. Mix the chocolate mixture into this. Pour into a glass pie pan. Bake at 350° for 20 minutes. Serve warm or cold, top with ice cream.

Peg Beausang (Mrs. Kenneth)

FUDGE SUNDAE PIE

6-8 Servings

1 cup evaporated milk
1 pkg. (6 oz.) chocolate
   morsels
1 cup miniature
   marshmallows
¼ tsp. salt
Vanilla wafers, left whole
1 qt. vanilla ice cream
1 pkg. (4 oz.) whole
   pecans

Put milk, chocolate morsels, marshmallows and salt in heavy 1 quart pan. Stir over medium heat until chocolate and marshmallows melt and mixture thickens. Take off heat and cool. Meanwhile, line bottom and sides of 9" pie pan with whole vanilla wafers. Spoon half of 1 quart ice cream over wafers. Cover with half the chocolate mixture. Repeat ice cream layer and chocolate layer. Place pecans on top. Freeze 3-5 hours, or over night. May double the recipe and put in a 9x13" pan to serve up to 20 small servings.

Elaine Schneff (Mrs. Warren)

CAKES
AND
FROSTINGS

WALDORF RED CAKE

12-16 Servings

A beautiful Valentine cake when baked in heart shaped pans.

½ cup (1 stick) butter
1½ cups sugar
2 eggs
2 oz. red food coloring
1 tsp. vanilla
2 tsp. cocoa
1 tsp. salt
1 cup buttermilk
2¼ cups cake flour
1 tsp. soda
1 tsp. vinegar

FROSTING:
3 T. flour
1 cup milk
1 cup butter
1 cup sugar
1 tsp. vanilla
Pinch of salt

Cream butter, sugar, and add eggs. Mix together vanilla, coloring and cocoa. Add this to the eggs, sugar and butter. Add salt and cake flour alternately with buttermilk. Mix soda and vinegar together, add to batter. Bake at 350° for 30 minutes in two 8" greased round cake pans. (I also line the bottom of the pans with wax paper so the cake is easier to remove.) Remove cooled cake from pans and slice to make 4 layers. Frost between each layer and the top only.

For frosting: Cook flour and milk until thickened and let cool. Cream butter, sugar, vanilla and salt together and blend into cooked mixture.

This is always the birthday cake at our house.

Annabelle De Cock (Mrs. Dale)

WEST VIRGINIA POUND CAKE

12-16 Servings

Given to me by my mother from Huntington, W. Va.

1 cup butter
½ cup shortening
3 cups sugar
5 eggs
3 cups all purpose flour
½ tsp. baking powder
1 cup milk
2 tsp. vanilla

Cream butter, shortening and sugar together. Beat in eggs one at a time. Sift flour and baking powder. Add alternately with milk to creamed mixture. Beat in vanilla. Bake in greased and floured 10" tube pan for 1 hour and 10 minutes at 350°. Turn out as soon as cooled. Sprinkle with powdered sugar.

Beverly VanHook (Mrs. Don)

MISSISSIPPI MUD CAKE

12-15 Servings

Very delicious and very rich - - kids love it!

1 cup butter
⅓ cup cocoa
1 tsp. baking powder
2 cups sugar
1½ cups flour
4 eggs
1 can (3 oz.) coconut
1 cup nuts, chopped

FROSTING:
2½ - 3½ cups miniature
    marshmallows or 1 (7
    oz.) jar marshmallow
    cream
½ cup soft butter
½ cup powdered sugar
⅓ cup cocoa
¼ cup milk
1 tsp. vanilla

Melt butter. Add remaining ingredients and mix until blended. Pour into greased 9×13" pan. Bake at 350° for 40-50 minutes. Remove cake from oven and immediately cover the hot cake with marshmallows. Press them down. When melted, cover with frosting.

For frosting: Beat butter, sugar and cocoa until mixed. Add milk and vanilla. The muddy look is obtained by swirling the frosting over the marshmallows.

Vera Scheeper (Mrs. Leroy)

SAUERKRAUT CHOCOLATE CAKE

12-16 Servings

⅔ cup margarine
1½ cups minus 2 T. sugar
3 eggs
1 tsp. vanilla
½ cup unsweetened cocoa
1 tsp. baking powder
2 cups sifted flour
¾ tsp. salt
1 cup water
⅔ cup sauerkraut

Thoroughly cream together sugar and margarine. Beat in eggs and vanilla. Sift together dry ingredients; add alternately with water. Mix thoroughly. Stir in sauerkraut which has been rinsed in water, coarsely chopped and thoroughly drained. Turn into two 8" round greased and floured cake pans. Bake at 350° for 30 minutes. Frost with Butter Cream Frosting, page 248. .

Meg Elliott (Mrs. William)

STRAWBERRY CAKE AND FROSTING   12-16 Servings

Special cake at our house - - also devoured rapidly when taken to college dorms.

1 box (18.5 oz.) white
  cake mix
1 box (3 oz.) strawberry
  flavored gelatin
½ cup water
3 T. flour
1 cup cooking oil
3 large or 4 small eggs
½ cup frozen strawberries,
  thawed

FROSTING:
1 box (1 lb.) powdered
  sugar
½ cup (1 stick) butter
½ cup frozen strawberries,
  thawed

Mix all ingredients together except eggs. Add eggs one at a time, mixing well after each one. Continue to beat with mixer at least 4 minutes more. Pour batter into 3 well greased and floured 8" cake pans or use one 9×13" cake pan. Bake at 350° for 25-30 minutes, longer for 9×13". Cool cake before frosting. Cake and frosting freeze well.

For frosting: Beat all ingredients with mixer until fluffy and smooth. Spread between layers, on top and sides of cake.

Maggie Collins (Mrs. C. Dean)

OATMEAL CAKE   15-18 Servings

1¼ cups boiling water
1 cup oatmeal
½ cup shortening
1 cup brown sugar
1 cup white sugar
2 eggs
¼ tsp. salt
1 tsp. cinnamon
1 tsp. nutmeg
1½ cups flour
1 tsp. soda
1 tsp. vanilla

Pour boiling water over oatmeal. Let stand 20 minutes. Cream shortening and sugars, add eggs, salt, cinnamon and nutmeg. Add oatmeal to batter. Sift together and add flour and soda. Add vanilla. Mix well. Pour into well greased and floured 9×13" pan. Bake at 350° for 30-40 minutes or until toothpick comes out clean when inserted in middle of cake. Frost with Coconut-Almond Frosting, page 248.

Marcia Keppy

CHOCOLATE SHEET CAKE   36 Servings

2 cups sugar
2 cups flour
½ cup oil
1 cup water
½ cup margarine
4 T. cocoa
½ cup buttermilk
2 eggs
1 tsp. vanilla
1 tsp. baking soda
½ tsp. salt

FROSTING:
4 T. cocoa
½ cup margarine
⅓ cup milk
1 box (1 lb.) powdered
  sugar
1 tsp. vanilla
½ cup ground nuts

Sift sugar and flour together and place in a large bowl. Put oil, water, margarine and cocoa in saucepan and bring to a boil. Pour over the sugar and flour mixture. Mix the remaining ingredients into the bowl with a mixer. Pour mixture into well greased 11×15" jelly roll pan. Bake at 350° for 25 minutes. While cake is warm, frost with sheet cake frosting.

For frosting: When cake has baked 15 minutes, start making frosting. Bring first three ingredients to a boil. Remove from stove and add the remaining ingredients. Beat well (approx. 2 minutes) and frost cake immediately when taken from oven. Cool well before cutting.

Amy Hockridge

BANANA CAKE   12 Servings

A great way to use up very ripe bananas.

½ cup butter
1½ cups sugar
2 eggs
2 cups flour
½ tsp. salt
1 tsp. baking powder
¾ tsp. soda
½ cup sour milk
1 cup mashed bananas,
  very ripe (about two
  large bananas)
1 tsp. vanilla

Cream butter and sugar. Add eggs; beat until smooth. Sift together flour, salt, baking powder and soda. Add flour mixture to creamed butter alternately with sour milk, banana and vanilla. (To sour milk, add 1½ tsp. vinegar to ½ cup milk.) Pour batter into well greased 9×12" glass cake pan. Bake at 350° for 30-35 minutes until golden brown. Cool. Frost with Butter Cream or Cream Cheese frosting, page 248.
Also makes great cupcakes.

Marie Lindsay

GRAHAM CRACKER CAKE

12-16 Servings

1 cup sugar
½ cup butter
2 eggs, well beaten
½ lb. (24) graham crackers, finely crushed
2 tsp. baking powder
½ cup chopped nuts
1 cup coconut, shredded
¾ cup milk
1 tsp. vanilla

Heavy cream, whipped and sweetened

Cream together sugar and butter. Add eggs and beat well. Add remaining ingredients and mix until well blended. Pour into 2-8" cake pans and bake at 350° until middles spring back when lightly touched, approximately 40 minutes.

Frost with sweetened whipped cream. Refrigerate.

Patty Barnard (Mrs. Franklin L.)
Nan Power (Mrs. Gordon)

ZUPPA INGLESE

Zuppa Inglese means "English Soup" in Italian.
This famous Italian dessert is a sort of Italian "transcription"
of the venerable English trifle.

PART I - CAKE:
2 9" layers of sponge cake
prepared according to
your favorite recipe.

PART II - CUSTARD:
1 cup cornstarch
½ cup sugar
5 cups whole milk
10 egg yolks
2 tsp. vanilla
1 tsp. grated lemon peel
3 oz. bittersweet
chocolate (melted over
hot water)

PART III - ZUPPA:
½ cup Rosolio (red Italian
liqueur, available from
stock distillery)
¼ cup dark rum
¼ cup brandy
Chocolate curls, or ½ oz.
bitter chocolate, grated

PART I - PREPARE SPONGE CAKES
I prefer a Genoise for this. Whatever recipe
you choose, do not use more than 1 cup
sugar for the two layers. The cake does not
want to be too sweet.

PART II - TO PREPARE CUSTARD:
In a saucepan, mix cornstarch and sugar
together. Add milk and stir until dissolved.
Heat mixture to boiling and boil for about
20 minutes, stirring constantly, until all
taste of uncooked cornstarch is gone. In a
mixing bowl, beat egg yolks until blended.
Gradually, beat in hot cornstarch mixture a
little at a time. Pour egg yolk-cornstarch
mixture into a clean saucepan and cook
over low to medium heat for about 10
minutes or until custard is very thick (candy
thermometer should be 170°), stirring constantly. Scrape bottom of pan often to
make certain custard does not scorch on
pan. Strain half of custard into a bowl. To
the custard in bowl, add 1 tsp. vanilla and
the grated lemon peel. To custard in
saucepan, add melted chocolate and 1 tsp.
vanilla. Stir until smooth and thoroughly
blended. Strain into another bowl. Cover
both bowls with plastic wrap touching surface of custard. Cool. Refrigerate until
ready to assemble Zuppa.

PART III - TO ASSEMBLE ZUPPA:

Split cooled layer cakes in half horizontally. Place one split layer of cake in center of serving dish, cut side up, and sprinkle with ¼ cup Rosolio. Spread with half of chocolate custard. Place second split layer on top, cut side up, and sprinkle with ¼ cup rum. Spread with half of vanilla custard. Place third split layer of cake over, cut side up, and sprinkle with ¼ cup brandy. Spread with remaining chocolate custard. Sprinkle cut surface of last split layer of cake with remaining ¼ cup Rosolio and place cut side down over custard. Cover top and sides of Zuppa with remaining vanilla custard. Decorate top with chocolate curls or with grated chocolate. Cover entire cake with plastic wrap and refrigerate at least 6 hours, or better still, overnight.

JOHN CONTIGUGLIA

Richard & John Contiguglia

JOHN AND RICHARD CONTIGUGLIA, identical twins and duo-pianists, have drawn attention to the large and significant repetoire for two pianos. Since their professional debut in London in 1962, the duo has achieved much acclaim for their unusual programs and extensive performance of Bartok works. In 1974, the Contiguglias performed Mozart's "Concerto No. 10 in E Flat Major for 2 Pianos" and "Operatic Fantasy on Bellini's 'Norma' for 2 pianos" by Lizst with the Tri-City Symphony.

CAKE!!!

Tastes best the next day - - serve with dollop of whipped cream.

1 cup chopped dates
1 cup hot tap water
1 cup margarine
1 cup sugar
2 eggs
2 squares (1 oz. each)
  unsweetened chocolate,
  melted
1¾ cups all purpose flour
1 tsp. baking powder
1 tsp. baking soda
1 cup chocolate chips
½ cup chopped walnuts

Mix dates and hot water in dish and set aside. Cream margarine and sugar; add eggs and beat thoroughly. Add melted chocolate and cooled date mixture. Sift dry ingredients, and mix them thoroughly. Add to cream mixture. Fold in chocolate chips and nuts. Bake in greased and floured bundt pan at 350° for 35-45 minutes. Cool for 10 minutes. Turn out on wire rack after 10 minutes. Very moist - - requires no frosting.

Anne V. Mairet (Mrs. Richard A.)

DATE CAKE

16 Servings

1 cup boiling water
1 cup whole dates,
  chopped
1 tsp. soda
1 cup granulated sugar
½ cup shortening
1 egg
1½ cups flour
1 tsp. salt
½ tsp. baking powder
1 tsp. vanilla

Pour boiling water over dates and soda; let stand. Cream sugar and shortening; add remaining ingredients to the date mixture. Pour into greased and floured 9×13" pan. Bake at 350° for 50 minutes. Immediately after baking, spread coconut-almond frosting on cake and broil until lightly browned. For variation, this cake may be baked in a 9×4" loaf pan. Turn out onto a heat proof platter. Pour icing over top and sides and broil. It is a very elegant dessert. Coconut-Almond frosting, page 248.

Anne V. Mairet (Mrs. Richard A.)

PUMPKIN SHEET CAKE

36 Servings

2 cups sugar
1 cup salad oil
4 eggs
1 can (16 oz.) pumpkin
2 cups flour
2 tsp. baking powder
1 tsp. soda
½ tsp. salt
2 tsp. cinnamon
1 tsp. pumpkin pie spice
1 cup nuts

Mix sugar, oil, eggs and pumpkin. Add remaining dry ingredients and mix well. Add nuts. Bake in well greased 11×15" jelly roll pan at 375° for 20 minutes. When cool, frost with Butter or Cream Cheese Frosting, page 248.

Chris Ahlstrand (Mrs. David)

MY MOTHER'S MINCEMEAT CAKE

12-15 Servings

Always taken to the family potlucks and holiday dinners, as far back as I can remember.

½ cup shortening
1 cup sugar
1 cup sour milk
1 cup mincemeat
2 cups flour
1 tsp. soda
½ tsp. salt
1 cup black walnuts

Cream shortening and sugar. Add sour milk and mincemeat and stir. (To sour milk: 1 T. vinegar or lemon juice to 1 cup less 1 T. lukewarm milk. Let stand 5 minutes.) Add remaining ingredients. Pour into 9×12" glass cake pan. Bake at 350° for 35-40 minutes. Frost with Black Walnut Frosting, page 249.

Mary Andrews (Mrs. Charles)

HEAVENLY WALNUT-APPLE CAKE   12-16 Servings

Marvelous served warm with whipped cream.

1½ cups vegetable oil
2 cups sugar
4 eggs
1 tsp. vanilla
3 cups flour
1 tsp. baking soda
1¼ tsp. cinnamon
½ tsp. salt
3 cups apples, peeled,
  cored and diced
½ cup black walnuts,
  chopped

Preheat oven to 325°. Lightly grease and flour 10" tube pan. Combine oil, sugar, eggs and vanilla. Sift flour with baking soda, cinnamon and salt. Add flour mixture to the oil mixture and blend well. Stir in apples and nuts and pour into prepared cake pan. Bake at 325° for 1 hour and 20 minutes. Cool on wire rack 10 minutes, then turn out on rack to cool longer.

Karen Getz (Mrs. Thomas)
Sue Wurbs

DIVINE PECAN CAKE   16-18 Servings

This is a heavy, moist, rich cake.

1 cup butter
1 cup margarine
3⅓ cups sugar
6 eggs
4 cups flour
1 tsp. baking powder
2 tsp. vanilla
1 cup milk
2 cups pecans, chopped

Cream butter, margarine and sugar until light and fluffy. Add eggs and beat well. Sift flour with baking powder and add to batter alternately with milk and vanilla. Stir in pecans. Pour into a greased and floured 10" tube pan. Bake at 325° for 1¾-2 hours. Insert straw to test for doneness. Cool. No need to frost.

Bonnie Brotman (Mrs. Jerrel)

APPLE RICOTTA REFRIGERATOR CAKE   10-12 Servings

"An Old Italian Recipe"

1 frozen pound cake
1 lb. ricotta cheese
½ cup sugar
2 squares (1 oz. each)
   unsweetened chocolate,
   grated
1 cup raw apple, freshly
   grated
Few drops of almond extract
1 cup heavy cream,
   whipped
½ cup broken walnuts

Thaw pound cake; cut lengthwise, from end to end in several long thin slices. Combine ricotta and sugar, mix well. Stir in chocolate, apples and almond extract. Spread mixture generously between cake slices, putting back together in loaf shape. Chill several hours or overnight. Just before serving, whip cream, frost top and sides of cake. Sprinkle walnuts over top. To serve, slice from top to bottom.

JUDITH AND ALAN HERSH

Judy & Alan Hersh

JUDITH AND ALAN HERSH, are duo pianists, now residing in Bettendorf. Judith grew up here and has appeared as a recitalist and accompanist, as well as with her husband. Alan Hersh has perfomed extensively throughout the East and Midwest as a recitalist, as a soloist with band and orchestra, as a vocal accompanist and in many chamber music ensembles. He is currently an Associate Professor of Music and Chairman of the Music Department at Augustana College. In 1978, the Hershs delighted the family audiences with their performance of "Carnival of the Animals" with the Tri-City Symphony Youth Orchestra.

CARROT CAKE

2 cups sugar
1 cup cooking oil
½ cup pineapple juice
4 eggs
2 cups flour
2 tsp. baking powder
1½ tsp. soda
1 tsp. salt
1 - 2 tsp. cinnamon
1 can (8 oz.) crushed
  pineapple
2 cups carrots, grated
1½ cups nuts (optional)

Drain pineapple reserving ½ cup liquid. Mix sugar, oil, pineapple juice and eggs thoroughly. Add sifted dry ingredients. Fold in carrots, pineapple and nuts and mix well. Pour into a 9×13" metal pan or a 7×11" glass pan and an 8×8" glass pan. Bake at 325° for 40-50 minutes. Frost with Cream Cheese Frosting, page 248.

Joan Ferguson (Mrs. Wendell)

PLUM GOOD CAKE

A moist cake - good to serve any time of day, for brunch or a dinner dessert.

2 cups self-rising flour
2 cups sugar
1 cup oil
3 eggs
1 tsp. cinnamon
1 tsp. cloves
2 jars (3½ oz. each) plum
  with tapioca, strained
  baby food

Grease and lightly flour a 10" bundt pan. Mix all ingredients for 3 minutes at medium spead and turn into pan. Bake at 350° for 1 hour or until toothpick comes out clean. Cool 15 minutes or until pan is cool enough to handle. Invert on cake rack and remove cake from pan. When cool, sprinkle with powdered sugar, or serve plain.

Ann Green (Mrs. Fred)

ORANGE CHIFFON CAKE
12-16 Servings

This cake has a delicate flavor and texture.
My married daughter still requests this cake on her birthday!

2¼ cups cake flour
1½ cups sugar
 1 T. baking powder
 1 tsp. salt
 ½ cup vegetable oil
 5 egg yolks, unbeaten
 ¾ cup liquid (juice of two
   oranges plus water)
 3 T. orange rind, grated
 7 egg whites
 ½ tsp. cream of tartar

Sift flour, sugar, baking powder and salt together. Make a well and add in order: oil, egg yolks, liquid and orange rind. Beat with spoon until smooth. Beat egg whites and cream of tartar in large mixing bowl until whites form stiff peaks. Pour egg yolk mixture gradually over beaten whites, gently folding with rubber scraper just until blended. Pour into ungreased 10" tube pan. Bake at 350° for 45-50 minutes. Invert on funnel to cool. Frost with butter icing made with orange rind and juice of fresh orange as liquid.

Marie Lindsay

CHOCOLATE ANGEL FOOD CAKE
12-16 Servings

1⅓ cups egg whites
1⅓ tsp. cream of tartar
 ½ tsp. salt
1½ cups sugar
1¼ tsp. almond extract
 1 cup minus 2 T. cake flour
 2 T. cocoa

Beat egg whites, cream of tartar and salt until they hold a point. Add 1 cup of the sugar and the flavoring, and blend well. Sift cake flour and cocoa 3 times. Fold flour and cocoa in by hand. Add remaining ½ cup sugar and fold in by hand. Place in ungreased 10" tube pan and bake at 350° for 45-50 minutes. Cool and frost with Seven Minute Frosting, page 248.

Mary Hass (Mrs. Arthur)

CREME DE MENTHE CAKE WITH SPREAD

Easy and attractive cake.   **12-16 Servings**

1 white cake recipe
3 T. creme de menthe

Mix favorite white cake according to directions, adding 3 T. creme de menthe and bake in 9×13" well greased pan. Cool.

SPREAD:
1 can (16 oz.) fudge topping
1 container (9 oz.) whipped
   topping
3 T. creme de menthe

Spread cake with fudge topping (you will not use the entire can). Then top with whipped topping mixed with 3 T. creme de menthe. Refrigerate.

Amy Hockridge

246

TWINKIE CAKE FILLING

Great treat for youngsters.

1 yellow or chocolate cake

FILLING:
  5 T. flour
  1 cup milk
  1 cup sugar
  ½ tsp. salt
  ½ cup solid vegetable
    shortening
  ½ cup (1 stick) margarine
  1 tsp. vanilla

Bake your favorite yellow or chocolate cake recipe in a 9×13" pan or in two 8" round cake pans. If using 9×13" pan, cut cake into two halves to make two layers. Cut two round cakes into four layers.

For filling: Gradually add milk to flour. Cook over medium low heat until thickened, stirring constantly. Cool. Beat rest of ingredients in large mixing bowl until fluffy. Add cooled milk mixture and beat again until fluffy. Spread filling between layers. Store covered at least 24 hours. Do not refrigerate. Top can be sprinkled with powdered sugar.

Chris Ahlstrand (Mrs. David)

CHOCOLATE CHERRY CAKE FILLING

Delicious and very easy to prepare.

1 chocolate cake recipe
1 cup maraschino cherries,
  chopped

FILLING:
  1 container (9 oz.)
    whipped topping
  ½ cup sifted powdered
    sugar
  1 cup (8 oz.) cherry yogurt
  Red food coloring

Prepare favorite chocolate cake according to directions. Fold in cherries. Pour into two well greased and floured 9" cake pans. Bake at 350° for 25-30 minutes. Cool 10 minutes. Loosen edges and remove from pans. Cool thoroughly. Cut both layers in half, horizontally, making four layers.

FILLING: Gradually add sugar to whipped topping. Fold in yogurt and a few drops of food coloring. Place bottom layer of cake on serving plate. Spread 1 cup whipped mixture over bottom layer. Top with second layer and 1 cup mixture. Repeat layering, ending with whipped topping mixture. Garnish with chocolate curls and maraschino cherries. Refrigerate until serving time. Serve with ice cream flavor of your choice.

Sheila O'Shea (Mrs. John)

BUTTER CREAM FROSTING

2 Cups

¼ cup butter
3 cups powdered sugar
1½ tsp. vanilla
3 T. cream

Cream butter and sugar well. Add vanilla and cream, and mix until smooth. May add more or less cream for right consistency.

Mildred Schnekloth (Mrs. H.A.)

CREAM CHEESE FROSTING

2 Cups

1½ T. butter
4 oz. cream cheese
1½ cups powdered sugar
1½ tsp. vanilla

Blend. Add water if too thick. Spread on cooled cake.

Rose Ann Hass (Mrs. James)

COCONUT ALMOND FROSTING

4 Cups

½ cup (1 stick) butter, melted
½ cup brown sugar
4 T. milk
1½ cups coconut
1½ cups slivered almonds

Combine all ingredients. This makes a large quantity.

Anne V. Mairet (Mrs. Richard A.)

SEVEN MINUTE FROSTING

2 Cups

1 cup sugar
¼ tsp. salt
3 T. water
½ tsp. cream of tartar
2 egg whites
1 tsp. vanilla

Combine all ingredients in the top of a double boiler. When water boils, place parts of double boiler together. Beat over heat with electric beater on high speed for 7 minutes, or until stiff. Be sure to reach all sections.

Mary Hass (Mrs. Arthur)

BLACK-WALNUT FROSTING

2 Cups

⅓ cup butter or margarine,
  melted
¼ cup black coffee
¼ tsp. vanilla
1 box (1 lb.) powdered
  sugar
1 - 1½ cups black walnuts

Combine first 4 ingredients and mix well. Fold in walnuts. Consistency should be spreadable, not too thick.

Mary Andrews (Mrs. Charles)

BROWNIE FROSTING

2 Cups

1½ cups white sugar
½ cup (1 stick) margarine
⅓ cup milk
½ cup chocolate chips

Bring first 3 ingredients to a boil in a 2 quart saucepan. Boil for one minute. Remove from heat. Add ½ cup chocolate chips. Stir until melted. Spread on brownies. Consistency will be thin, but frosting sets up quickly on brownies.

Sheila O'Shea (Mrs. John)

CHOCOLATE-MARSHMALLOW FROSTING

2 Cups

1⅓ cups sugar
6 T. margarine
6 T. milk
90 to 100 miniature
  marshmallows
½ - ¾ cup chocolate chips

Bring sugar, margarine and milk to slow boil. After it starts to boil, time 1½ minutes. Remove from heat. Add marshmallows and chocolate chips. Stir until melted. Use on brownies or cake.

Margie Voss (Mrs. Fritz)

CREAM ICING FOR ANGEL FOOD CAKE

2 Cups

Makes a terrific birthday cake ! - Men love this dessert.

1 cup sugar
4 egg yolks (beaten)
1 cup whipping cream,
  unwhipped
½ tsp. vanilla
Pinch salt

Combine all ingredients and place in double boiler or teflon sauce pan. Place on medium heat and stir constantly until mixture coats the spoon heavily. Remove from heat. Put wax paper over top of pan. When cool, spread over angel food cake on top and sides.

Lynn Goebel (Mrs. George)

249

COOKIES
AND
CANDIES

HOLLY SPRIGS

1 cup butter
½ cup powdered sugar, sifted
1½ cups all purpose flour, sifted
1 tsp. vanilla
½ cup ground almonds
1 cup red raspberry preserves
Red and green frosting tubes

Cream butter and powdered sugar until well blended in a large bowl; stir in flour, vanilla and nuts. If dough is too soft, chill slightly. Roll dough, a level teaspoon at a time into balls between palms of hands. Place 2" apart on greased cookie sheet. Lightly grease the bottom of a small juice glass; dip in powdered sugar, press over each ball to flatten to about 1" round. Bake in moderate oven (350°) until golden around edges. Remove carefully to wire racks with spatula. Cool. Spread bottoms or half of cookies with raspberry preserves, top sandwich style with remaining cookies, flat side down. Decorate the top with 3 green frosting leaves and a few dots of red frosting to resemble holly sprigs.

These are time consuming but well worth the effort. One or two attractively garnishes a large tray of holiday cookies or compliments cranberry sherbet for a holiday dessert.

Heather Gosma (Mrs. John S.)

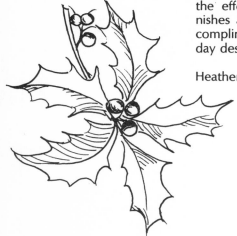

BUTTER COOKIES

1 cup butter
1 cup vegetable shortening
1¼ cups sugar
1 egg beaten
4 cups flour
1½ tsp. almond extract (or ½ vanilla and ½ almond)

Cream butter, shortening, and sugar together. Add egg, blend well. Add flour and flavorings. Roll in balls. Flatten with fork and sprinkle with sugar or colored sugar. Bake at 350° until light brown, 8-10 minutes.

Diann Moore (Mrs. Robert)

BUTTER PECAN CRESCENTS

3-4 Dozen

1 cup butter, room
   temperature
½ cup powdered sugar
2 cups all-purpose flour,
   sifted
¼ tsp. salt
2 tsp. vanilla
1 cup chopped pecans
Powdered sugar

Cream softened butter well with powdered sugar. Add sifted flour and salt, then vanilla and nuts. Shape into small balls or crescents. Bake at 350° for 10-12 minutes. Roll in powdered sugar while still warm, then roll again in powdered sugar when cool.

Doris Brown (Mrs. Tom)

ALMOND SPRITZ

5-6 Dozen

1 lb. butter
2 cups sugar
2 eggs
¾ cup almonds, finely
   ground
2 tsp. almond extract
5¼ cups flour

Cream butter, sugar and eggs. Add remaining ingredients and blend thoroughly. Chill. Put into cookie press with star point and "squiggle" on to cookie sheets in S shape. Bake at 325° until shine is gone. DO NOT BROWN. WATCH CAREFULLY.

Mary Hass (Mrs. Arthur)

PEPPARKAKAR   5 Dozen

"Swedish pressed cookie"

½ lb. butter
1 T. dark corn syrup or
   sorghum
1½ cup sugar
1 egg
1 tsp. soda
2 tsp. cinnamon
2 tsp. ginger
1 scant tsp. cloves
2½ cups flour, sifted

Cream butter, syrup and sugar until fluffy. Beat in egg. Sift dry ingredients together and stir into creamed mixture. Place into cookie press. Use bar attachment and squeeze into long ribbon strips. Place 4-5 strips on cookie sheet. Bake at 350° for 7 minutes. Cut into 2" pieces while hot with a spatula. Remove when cool.

This Swedish favorite is baked by the hundreds and served at the International Cafe at the Folk Festival each year in Bettendorf, Iowa.

Kay Runge (Mrs. Peter)

PEPPAR KAKAR   3-4 Dozen

"Swedish Cut-Out Cookie". A favorite for Christmas and other Holidays.

1 cup shortening
1½ cups sugar
1 egg
3 T. molasses
1½ tsp. water, sour milk
   or cream
3¼ cups flour, or more
2 tsp. soda
1½ tsp. cinnamon
1½ tsp. ginger
1 tsp. ground cloves

Cream shortening and sugar. Add egg, molasses and water and beat well. Sift together dry ingredients, blend into creamed mixture. Chill 2 hours or over night. Roll out thinly on lightly floured surface and cut in desired shapes with cutters, or divide dough into two long rolls, chill, then slice with knife. Sprinkle with plain or colored sugar. Bake on greased cookie sheet, at 350° for 10-12 minutes.

Mary Cleaveland (Mrs. Harry)

SVENSKA PINNER'S SWEDISH "ICE BOX" COOKIES

¾ lb. margarine
1 cup sugar
1 egg yolk
1 tsp. vanilla
3¼ cups flour
1 egg white (slightly beaten)
Nutmeats

6 Dozen

Mix margarine and sugar, add egg yolk and vanilla. Stir in flour until mixed. Shape into rolls, wrap in wax paper and refrigerate. When chilled, slice thinly, brush with slightly beaten egg white and top with scattering of chopped nutmeats. Bake on cookie sheet at 350° for 8-10 minutes.

Rolls can be kept refrigerated or frozen and baked as wanted.

Jeanette Carpentier (Mrs. Arthur)

SWEDISH COCONUT COOKIES

½ cup (1 stick) margarine
½ cup vegetable shortening (white)
1 cup sugar
1½ cups flour
½ tsp. soda
½ tsp. baking powder
½ cup coconut
Vanilla to taste

5-6 Dozen

Cream margarine, shortening and sugar until smooth. Then add dry ingredients and finally vanilla. Form into balls ¾" in diameter. Press down with a cup or pitcher that has a cut glass pattern on bottom. Dip cup in granulated sugar each time before pressing. Bake at 350° for 10-17 minutes.

Miriam Weeks (Mrs. Parker)

CINNAMON DIAMONDS

4-5 Dozen

A German shortbread recipe received from an elderly friend.

½ lb. butter or margarine
1 cup sugar
2 cups flour
1½ tsp. cinnamon
1 egg yolk, beaten
1 egg white, lightly beaten

Cream butter and sugar. Add flour, cinnamon and egg yolk and mix well. Pat out very thin on buttered cookie sheet. Brush lightly, with egg white over top. Mark off in diamond shape about 1¼" in size, putting pressure on each diamond. Marking off diamonds is tedious but the result is delicious. (It is easier to mark off in squares using a yard stick resting on the cookie sheet side as a guide.) Bake in slow oven (300°) about 45 minutes. Cut while hot as they harden quickly.

Miriam Weeks (Mrs. Parker)

KOURABREDES

100 Cookies

1 pkg. (10 oz.) almonds, chopped
1 tsp. butter
2 lbs. sweet butter, softened to room temperature
2 cups margarine or vegetable shortening (white)
Juice of 1½ oranges
3 egg yolks
1 cup Mastika or Cognac
1 box (2 lbs.) cake flour
2 cups powdered sugar

Place almonds in 1 tsp. butter and toast slightly. Set aside. Cream butter and shortening for 45 minutes. Add juice and beat 10 minutes more. Add egg yolks and beat 10 minutes more. Add liqueur and beat 10 minutes more. Fold in cake flour and almonds and blend well. Flour hands and shape dough into balls. Bake at 325° for 20 minutes. Roll in powdered sugar while warm.

Shan Corelis (Mrs. John)

SMORBAKELSER

3 Dozen

A very special "short" cookie.

1 cup butter
1⅔ cups flour
¼ cup ice water
1 egg white
¼ cup sugar

In a bowl, mix butter and flour with electric beater. When mixed, add water slowly. When it holds together, remove dough and form into two balls. Work with one, wrap the other in plastic and refrigerate. Roll out once on floured dough cloth. Roll into a roll and refrigerate for 10 minutes or more. Roll out again on cloth. Roll it up and roll out again. Then flatten dough into long strips 3" wide and ½" thick. Brush with egg white and sprinkle liberally with sugar. Cut into ¾" wide strips with pastry rolling cutter. Make two slits in top of strip and bend into crescents. Place on cookie sheet that has been rinsed with cold water and place in freezer. Heat oven to 400°. Bake for 10 minutes; lower to 350°; bake until light brown - about 5-7 minutes more, or 15 minutes in all. (Dough may be frozen or kept in refrigerator several days.)

Elsa Arp (Mrs. Henry)

MRS. DAVIS' GINGERBREAD COOKIES

Mrs. Davis' pre-school classes have enjoyed making these gingerbread boys through the years.

¼ cup shortening
½ cup (1 stick) butter
¾ cup sugar
¼ cup white syrup
½ cup light molasses
2 tsp. vinegar
1 egg
4½ cups flour
1 tsp. salt
¾ tsp. soda
1½ tsp. cinnamon
½ tsp. nutmeg
¼ tsp. ginger
1 tsp. vanilla

12 Large Cookies

Mix dry ingredients with moist. Add slightly more flour if necessary so dough isn't sticky. Construct in sections (like working with clay). Lay on dull side of foil and then put on cookie sheet. Bake at 350° for 12 minutes. Decorate with raisins. This is a fun project to do with children. Dough is easy to handle.

Kathy Reimers (Mrs. John)

257

FILLED BUTTER COOKIES

Cut out cookies that are special treats - use imaginative shapes.

⁷/₈ lb. of butter
  (no substitution)
1 cup granulated sugar
1 egg, room temperature
1 tsp. vanilla
4 cups flour
¼ tsp. baking powder
¹/₈ tsp. salt
Cherry jam

6 Dozen Single Cookies or 3 Dozen Filled Cookies

Soften butter. Cream together butter and sugar. Add egg and vanilla and mix well. Sift flour and mix dry ingredients together, add slowly to butter mixture, mixing well. Chill cookie dough ½ hour. Working with small amounts of dough, roll out on floured surface 1/16" thick. Use decorative cookie cutters, cutting two alike for each cookie. Place bottom pieces on ungreased cookie sheet. Place a teaspoon of chopped cherry jam (or favorite jam filling) on each cookie. Cover with top cookie. Press edges together with tines of a fork. Bake at 375° for 10 minutes; or until delicately browned. Frost with favorite butter or cream cheese frosting.

Takes an afternoon to cut out, bake and frost.

Mary Cebuhar (Mrs. Michael)

HEDGEHOG COOKIES   4-6 Dozen

2 cups shelled walnuts
1 cup dates
1½ cups coconut
1 cup brown sugar, firmly
  packed
2 eggs, unbeaten
Extra coconut

Preheat oven to 350°. Grind walnuts and dates in food chopper. Mix in 1½ cups coconut and remaining ingredients thoroughly. Scoop a spoonful of the mixture and shape into a roll about the size of a link sausage. Roll each hedgehog in coconut. Place on greased cookie sheet and bake about 10-12 minutes at 350°. (You can also roll hedgehogs in ground nuts and decorate with green or red candied cherries.)

Shan Corelis (Mrs. John)

CRISP OATMEAL COOKIES

5 Dozen

A crisp delicious tea cookie.

1 cup shortening or
   margarine
1 cup white sugar
½ cup brown sugar
1 egg, beaten
1½ cups flour
1 tsp. soda
1 tsp. cinnamon
¼ tsp. salt
1½ cups quick rolled oats
¾ cup finely chopped
   walnuts
1 tsp. vanilla

Cream shortening with sugars. Add egg. Stir in dry ingredients. Add vanilla. Chill. Roll into a ball. Press flat with buttered glass dipped in sugar. Bake at 350° for 10 minutes.

Mollie Montgomery (Mrs. Thomas)

OLD FASHIONED OATMEAL COOKIES

9 Dozen

A soft and chewy family favorite.

1 cup shortening
¾ cup brown sugar
¾ cup granulated sugar
2 eggs
1½ cups buttermilk
2¼ cups flour
1 tsp. baking powder
1 tsp. soda
½ tsp. salt
1 tsp. cinnamon
2 cups rolled oats
1 cup raisins
½ cup chopped nuts

Cream shortening and sugars. Beat in eggs. Stir in buttermilk. Sift together dry ingredients and add to creamed mixture. Stir in rolled oats, raisins and nuts. Drop by spoonfuls. Bake at 400° on ungreased cookie sheet until golden brown. Cool.

Kristyn Mahler (Mrs. Michael)

EVERYBODY HELP HEALTH NUGGETS

2-3 Dozen

Let the children make them - - no bake, healthful, instant eat!

2 cups seedless rainsins
1⅓ cups wheat germ
½ cup chopped walnuts
   (up to 1 cup if desired)
8 graham cracker squares,
   crushed coarsely
1½ cups peanut butter
4 T. honey
Extra chopped nuts or
   coconut

Help the children measure out all ingredients into mixing bowl; then just let them mix and squeeze and blend the ingredients until everything is thoroughly mixed and holds together. They can then roll the "dough" into small balls, roll them in the additional chopped nuts or in coconut. Some may be left plain. Best to chill any that are not eaten immediately.

Harriet Harmelink (Mrs. Roger)

GRANDMA JEAN'S NO-BAKE CHOCOLATE COOKIES

2 cups sugar
½ cup cocoa or 3 squares
   chocolate
½ cup milk
½ cup (1 stick) butter
1 tsp. vanilla
3 cups quick oats
½ cup nuts

4 Dozen

Boil together sugar, chocolate, milk and butter for 5 minutes or less. Add vanilla and while still hot, add oats and nuts. Drop with spoon on waxed paper immediately. DO NOT BAKE. Refrigerate those not devoured.

Nancy Thompson (Mrs. Robert)

MOLASSES ICE BOX COOKIES

6-8 Dozen

This is a large recipe - - I use it at Christmas time.

1 cup sugar
1 cup butter
1 cup lard or
   vegetable shortening
Pinch salt
1 cup dark molasses
1 tsp. baking soda,
   dissolved in a little
   hot water
½ tsp. cinnamon
½ tsp. nutmeg
½ tsp. ginger
½ lb. chopped almonds
4 cups flour, (approx.)

Cream together sugar, butter, shortening and salt. Add molasses, soda, cinnamon, nutmeg, ginger and almonds and blend well. Add flour to make a very stiff dough - - you may need a little more than 4 cups. Refrigerate. Roll in loaves any desired size. Keep refrigerated or can be frozen. When ready to bake slice very thin and bake in 350° oven until lightly browned.

Nan Power (Mrs. Gordon)

CHOCOLATE KISS COOKIES   4 Dozen

This is one grandma's favorite cookie jar stuffer.

½ cup shortening
½ cup peanut butter
½ cup white sugar
½ cup brown sugar
1 egg
2 T. milk
1 tsp. vanilla
1¾ cup flour
1 tsp. baking soda
½ tsp. salt
¼ cup white sugar to coat balls
2 pkgs. (3 oz. each) chocolate candy kisses

Cream together the first seven ingredients. Mix flour, soda and salt and add to the creamed mixture. Mix well. With rounded teaspoonfuls, shape into balls. Roll in the sugar to coat balls. Bake on an ungreased cookie sheet at 375° for 8 minutes. Press a candy kiss into the center of each cookie. Return to oven and bake for 2-3 minutes. Be careful not to overbake.

Emma Sissel (Mrs. Forrest)

LOIS HULL'S GUMDROP COOKIES   6 Dozen 2" Cookies

A colorful holiday cookie.

1 cup brown sugar
1 cup white sugar
1 cup shortening
2 eggs
2½ cups flour
½ tsp. baking soda
1 tsp. salt
1 tsp. baking powder
1 cup gumdrops (sliced)
1 cup quick cooking oatmeal
1 cup coconut

Cream sugars and shortening. Add eggs. Sift dry ingredients and add to creamed mixture. Add gumdrops, coconut and oatmeal. Mix well. Drop on ungreased baking sheet and bake at 350° for 12 minutes.

Mary Kae Waytenick (Mrs. Paul)

261

RANGER COOKIES

1 cup margarine, softened
1 cup white sugar
1 cup brown sugar
2 eggs
1 tsp. soda
½ tsp. salt
½ tsp. baking powder
2 cups flour
1 tsp. vanilla
2 cups quick oatmeal
2 cups Rice Krispies
1 - 2 cups of chocolate chips or butterscotch chips
½ cup coconut
½ cup chopped pecans (optional)

Cream margarine together with the sugar. Add eggs and beat well. Add and blend flour, soda, salt, baking powder and vanilla. By hand, stir in the remaining ingredients. Shape into 1" balls or drop by spoonfuls onto cookie sheet. Flatten balls with a fork. Bake at 350° for 10 minutes. Allow 2" between cookies, as they spread. Remove from cookie sheet before completely cooled.

Clara Hein (Mrs. Aaron)

OLD-FASHIONED SUGAR COOKIES

3-4 Dozen

½ cup sugar
½ cup powdered sugar
½ cup margarine
1 egg
½ cup oil
2½ cups flour
½ tsp. soda
½ tsp. cream of tartar
½ tsp. salt
½ tsp. nutmeg
1 tsp. vanilla

Cream sugars and margarine until light and fluffy. Beat in egg and oil. Sift dry ingredients, add to creamed mixture. Add vanilla and blend well. Chill dough until it can be handled, about 1 hour. Form into balls 1½" in diameter, and flatten with the bottom of a glass, dipped in sugar. Bake at 375° until light brown on edges, 8-10 minutes. Cool on wire racks.

Virginia Payton (Mrs. Edward)

COCONUT CHEWS

4 Dozen

CRUST:
¾ cup margarine
¾ cup powdered sugar
1½ cups flour

FILLING:
2 eggs, beaten
1 cup brown sugar, packed
2 T. flour
½ tsp. baking powder
½ tsp. salt
½ tsp. vanilla
½ cup pecans, chopped
½ cup flaked coconut

FROSTING:
1½ cups powdered sugar
2 T. butter
5 tsp. orange juice
¾ tsp. almond extract

For crust: mix shortening and powdered sugar well. Blend in flour. Press in ungreased 9×13" pan. Bake at 350° for 12-15 minutes.

For filling: Combine all ingredients listed and spread over crust. Bake at 350° for 20 minutes more. Cool bars.

For frosting: Combine ingredients and frost cooled bars.

Jane Maehr (Mrs. David)

SPECIAL K BARS

4 Dozen

A wonderful, fast, no bake bar cookie.

1 cup white corn syrup
1 cup white sugar
1 cup chunk peanut butter
6 cups Special K cereal
9 oz. chocolate chips
9 oz. butterscotch chips

Dissolve corn syrup and white sugar over low heat. Do not boil. Remove from heat and add peanut butter and Special K. Stir and spread into a greased 9×13" pan. Combine and melt the chocolate and butterscotch chips. Spread chocolate mixture on top of cereal mixture. Cool and cut into bars.

Sheila O'Shea (Mrs. John)

CHOCOLATE-NUT BARS

3 Dozen

A favorite for football game tailgate parties.

1 cup cake flour, sifted
½ tsp. baking powder
¼ tsp. salt
¹/₈ tsp. baking soda
⅓ cup butter
1 cup brown sugar, packed
1 egg, slightly beaten
1 tsp. vanilla
1 cup semi-sweet
   chocolate chips
1 cup walnuts, finely
   chopped

Sift flour once then measure; add baking powder, soda and salt; then sift again; set aside. Cream butter; add sugar gradually until light and fluffy; add egg and vanilla, mix well. Add flour mixture, mix well. Stir in chocolate chips and nuts. Pour into greased 11×7" pan. Bake at 350° for 25-30 minutes. When cool, cut into small squares.

Karen Brooke (Mrs. Charles)

CARAMEL BARS

2-3 Dozen

These are very rich and delicious!

1 cup flour
½ tsp. soda
¼ tsp. salt
¾ cup margarine
1 cup brown sugar
1 cup oatmeal
1 pkg. (14 oz.) caramels
5 T. milk
1 pkg. (6 oz.) chocolate
   chips
½ cup nuts, chopped

Sift together flour, soda and salt. Set aside. Cream the margarine and sugar. Add the flour mixture and oatmeal, mix well. Take half of the dough and pat into a 9x13" pan and bake at 350° for 10 minutes. Meanwhile, melt the caramels and milk over very low heat. Remove pan from oven and sprinkle chocolate chips over crust. Allow them to melt, spread them and then sprinkle with nuts. Spread caramel mixture over chocolate layer and top with remaining dough. (Dough is stiff and must be broken apart to spread over caramel mixture.) Return to oven and bake for 15 minutes more. DO NOT OVER BAKE. Caramel is soft at first, but sets up when bars are thoroughly cooled.

Vicki Reschly (Mrs. Chris)

LEMON BAR COOKIES

2-3 Dozen

Even though these bars are made with yellow cake mix and vanilla flavoring, people still think they taste like the original lemon bars.

½ cup (1 stick) butter, melted
1 egg, slightly beaten
1 box (18.5 oz.) lemon or yellow cake mix
1 tsp. vanilla or lemon extract
1 pkg. (8 oz.) cream cheese
2 eggs
1 box (1 lb.) powdered sugar (reserve 1/4 cup)

With a pastry blender cut together the butter, egg and cake mix until it resembles the texture of pie dough. Pat into a 9×13" pan. Combine the vanilla, cream cheese, eggs and sugar until creamy. Pour over crust mixture. Bake at 325° for 45-60 minutes. When cool, sprinkle with 1/4 cup powdered sugar.

Miriam Thor (Mrs. John)

CHEESE CAKE BARS

25 Bars

1 cup flour
⅓ cup butter
⅓ cup brown sugar
½ cup walnuts, chopped
1 pkg. (8 oz.) cream cheese, softened
¼ cup sugar
1 egg
2 T. milk
2 T. lemon juice
½ tsp. vanilla

Combine flour, butter and brown sugar. Blend until fine with a fork and add walnuts. Save 1 cup for topping and press the rest in an 8×8" pan. Bake at 350° for 12-15 minutes. Mix together softened cream cheese, sugar, egg, milk, lemon juice and vanilla. Pour onto baked crust and sprinkle with remaining 1 cup of crust mixture. Bake at 350° for 25-30 minutes more. Refrigerate. Can be frozen.

Annabelle DeCock (Mrs. Dale)

DIVINE CHOCOLATE NUT COOKIES

32 Bars

1½ cups unsalted nuts
1 cup butter
½ cup brown sugar, packed
½ cup white sugar
1 egg yolk
1 tsp. vanilla
1¾ cups flour, sifted
10 oz. favorite chocolate candy bar

Roast nuts in foil-lined pan for 10 minutes. Set aside. Stir together butter, sugars, egg yolk, vanilla and flour. Press into 9×13" pan, bake at 350° for 20 minutes. While hot spread chocolate over cookie crust, pressing down with a knife. When melted sprinkle toasted nuts on top. Cut while still warm.

Lois Leach (Mrs. James A.)

BUTTERSCOTCH BROWNIES

1 Dozen

½ cup flour
½ tsp. salt
1 tsp. baking powder
¼ cup butter
1 cup brown sugar
1 egg
1 tsp. vanilla
½ cup chopped nuts

Sift together first 3 ingredients. Melt butter and add brown sugar, egg, vanilla and nuts. Combine with dry ingredients. Spread into a buttered shallow pan. Bake at 350° for 30 minutes.

Charlotte Durkee

DOUBLE CHOCOLATE BROWNIES

16 Bars

2 squares (1 oz. each)
   chocolate
⅓ cup butter or margarine
1 cup sugar
2 eggs
1 tsp. vanilla
⅔ cup flour
½ tsp. baking powder
¼ tsp. salt
½ cup semi-sweet
   chocolate chips
¾ cup tiny marshmallows

Melt chocolate and shortening. Add sugar. Add eggs one at a time and beat well. Add vanilla, flour, baking powder, sale and finally chocolate chips and marshmallows. Pour into greased 9x9" pan. Bake at 350° for 25 minutes. Cool. Cut in squares.

Dorothy White (Mrs. F.B.)

EASY, RICH, CHEWY BROWNIES

16 Bars

⅓ cup butter
1 cup sugar
2 T. water
6 oz. chocolate chips
1 tsp. vanilla extract
1 tsp. almond extract
2 eggs, beaten
½ tsp. salt
½ tsp. baking powder
1 cup flour
½ cup walnuts, chopped
   (optional)

In a medium sized heavy saucepan, melt butter. Add sugar and water. Bring to a boil. Cook 1 minute stirring constantly. Remove from heat. Add chips and extracts and beat until chips are melted. Cool slightly. Add well beaten eggs and blend well. Add dry ingredients and nuts. Pour into a well greased 9x9" pan. Bake at 350° for 25 minutes. (These cut best when very cool, or partially frozen.)

Rose Ann Hass (Mrs. James)

266

MARY AL'S BROWNIES

18-24 Bars

"A light chocolate flavored Brownie"

½ cup (1 stick) butter
1 cup sugar
2 eggs
½ cup flour
3 tsp. (heaping) cocoa
⅓ cup milk
¼ tsp. salt
1 tsp. vanilla
½ cup pecans, chopped

Cream butter and sugar. Add eggs. Mix. Combine flour and cocoa. Alternately add flour-cocoa mixture and milk. Add salt and vanilla. By hand, add pecans. Spread in 9×13" buttered pan. Bake at 325° for 20-30 minutes. (For cake-like consistency, do not over cook.) After brownies are baked and slightly cooled, frost with favorite chocolate frosting.

Mary Ann Linden (Mrs. James S.)

OLD FASHIONED BROWNIES

24 Bars

½ cup (1 stick) margarine
1 cup white sugar
4 eggs
1 can (16 oz.) chocolate
　syrup
¼ tsp. salt
1 cup flour
½ tsp. baking powder
¾ cup nut meats, chopped
1 tsp. vanilla

Cream margarine and sugar. Add eggs one at a time. Add remaining ingredients. Bake in a greased 10×14" cookie pan at 350° for 25-30 minutes.

Sheila O'Shea (Mrs. John)

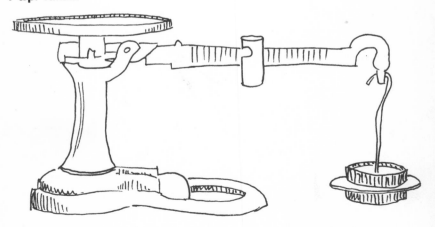

PEANUT CLUSTERS

14 Dozen

1 pkg. (2 lbs.) almond
   bark
18 oz. chocolate chips
2 squares of semi-sweet
   chocolate
2 lbs. salted Spanish
   peanuts

In a double boiler, melt almond bark and chocolates together. Add peanuts. Drop by spoonfuls on waxed paper. Cool.

Diann Moore (Mrs. Robert)

PEANUT BRITTLE

About 2 lbs.

1½ cups white sugar
½ cup light corn syrup
⅔ cup water
½ lb. raw Spanish peanuts
   (1½ cups)
2 T. butter (not margarine)
1 tsp. soda
1 tsp. vanilla

Cook sugar, syrup, water and peanuts until mixture reaches 295° on a candy thermometer. (Approximately 12 minutes) Stir occasionally to make certain that peanuts are coated and that mixture does not burn. Remove from heat. Add butter. Add soda which has been dissolved in vanilla. Blend thoroughly. Pour onto greased porcelain table top or a greased cookie sheet. As soon as edges begin to set pull until thin, using a buttered spatula under the candy and a buttered fork on top of candy. Be careful, mixture is very hot. When cool, break into pieces.

Mildred Clover (Mrs. Everett)

ENGLISH TOFFEE

2 Dozen

1 cup butter
1 cup sugar
3 T. water
1 - 2 tsp. vanilla
1 bar (8 oz.) chocolate
¼ - ¾ cup chopped nuts

Heat butter, sugar and water in heavy pot to hard crack stage. (Take off stove at 300° because it will continue to cook.) Add vanilla. Pour onto cookie sheet for thin toffee, or 9×9″ pan for thick toffee. Break up chocolate bar and put on top. When chocolate melts, spread with spatula. Sprinkle on nuts. Put in refrigerator to set. (Do not touch mixture because it is extemely hot.)

Jan Crow (Mrs. David)
Bonnie Moeller (Mrs. Gerald)

SPICED PECANS
8 Ounces Pecans

8 oz. large pecan halves
1 egg white
1 tsp. cold water
½ cup sugar
¼ tsp. salt
½ tsp. cinnamon

Beat egg white and water until frothy. Add pecans a few at a time and coat well. Mix sugar, salt and cinnamon in bowl. Add nuts and mix until well covered. Bake on a buttered jellyroll pan at 225° for an hour, stirring every 15 minutes.

Rose Ann Hass (Mrs. James)

INSTANT CHOCOLATE NUT CLUSTERS
1-2½ Dozen

2 cups semi-sweet
  chocolate pieces
1 T. butter
1½ cups chopped walnuts

Melt 2 cups of semi-sweet chocolate pieces with butter. Add 1½ cups chopped walnuts and drop mounds of the mixture on waxed paper. Refrigerate until firm. Store in refrigerator.

Mari Krause (Mrs. Ray L., Jr.)

PRALINES
15 3" Pralines

2 cups sugar
1 cup milk
8 large marshmallows
2 T. butter
½ tsp. vanilla
1 - 2 cups pecan halves

Combine first three ingredients in heavy 4 quart saucepan. Cook over medium heat to 234° (soft ball stage), stirring constantly. Remove from heat, stir in butter and vanilla. Beat until creamy. Add pecans. Beat just until mixture begins to thicken. Quickly drop mixture by tablespoons onto lightly buttered waxed paper. Cool. (Mixture hardens very fast.) Store in airtight container.

Mary Hass (Mrs. Arthur)

OLD-FASHIONED CARAMELS

6 Dozen ½" Cubes

Soft and chewy like a Holloway sucker.

1 cup sugar
¾ cup light corn syrup
½ cup butter
1 cup half and half cream
½ tsp. vanilla

Bring first 3 ingredients and ½ cup cream to a boil. Add the remaining ½ cup cream and cook over medium heat to firm ball stage (247°). Remove from heat, stir in vanilla. Pour into well buttered 9x9" pan. Score when cool; cut with scissors into bite sized pieces and wrap separately in plastic wrap. Can be frozen.

Marie Lindsay

MOLDED MINTS

2-3 Dozen

2 oz. cream cheese, softened
¼ tsp. almond or vanilla, extract, or any flavoring
1⅓ cups powdered sugar
Food coloring

Mash cream cheese. Add flavoring and food coloring. Then mix in powdered sugar, a little at a time. Knead until like pie dough. Roll into balls about the size of marbles. Place on one side, a small amount of granulated sugar. Press down in mold. Place on waxed paper. Allow to air dry overnight and then place in a tightly closed container and refrigerate. Can be frozen.

Anne C. Goebel

BON BONS

4-5 Dozen

2 lbs. powdered sugar
¼ lb. butter, softened
¼ tsp. almond or vanilla extract
Dash of salt
1 pkg. (14 oz.) coconut
1 can (13 oz.) sweetened condensed milk
2 pkgs. (6 oz. each) pecan halves

Combine powdered sugar, butter, vanilla, salt, coconut and milk and blend well. Roll mixture into balls, putting a nut half in the middle of each ball.

For topping: Melt chocolate chips and paraffin over hot water. Dip balls into topping. Refrigerate for two hours.

Diann Moore (Mrs. Robert)

TOPPING:
1 pkg. (12 oz.) chocolate chips
⅓ bar of paraffin

ADAPTABLE FUDGE   16-20 Pieces

An excellent fudge - - never turns to sugar!

2 cups sugar
½ cup (1 stick) butter or
   margarine
½ cup milk
¼ cup white corn syrup
2 T. cocoa
¼ tsp. salt
1 tsp. vanilla
½ cup nuts, chopped
   (optional)

Combine first 6 ingredients in a 1½ quart saucepan. Bring to a boil, stirring constantly. Cook to 233° on a candy thermometer, or for 7 minutes after mixture has reached a rolling boil. Remove from heat, add vanilla and beat until it begins to thicken and loses its gloss. Add nuts. Drop by teaspoons onto waxed paper or pour into buttered pan and score when cool.

Variations: For white fudge, omit cocoa. Candied fruit may be added. For penuchi, substitute brown sugar for white and omit cocoa. Cook to 234°F.

Olivette Werling (Mrs. R.R.)

FUDGE   8 Dozen Generous Pieces

2 lbs. sugar (4 cups)
1 cup milk
1 tsp. vanilla
1 cup butter
25 large marshmallows
13 oz. milk chocolate bar
   (1-8 oz. and small
   individual bars)
13 oz. semi-sweet
   chocolate chips
2 oz. unsweetened
   chocolate
1 cup chopped nuts

Mix sugar, milk, vanilla and butter. Bring to a boil and boil for 2 minutes. Turn off heat. Add marshmallows and stir until melted. Add chocolates one at a time. Stir until melted. Add nuts. Pour into greased 10×13" pan. Chill overnight to set well. May be warmed slightly to cut easily.

Jan Crow (Mrs. David)

RESTAURANTS

APPLETIME TEA ROOM
Geneseo, Illinois

Known for their lovely Luncheons and Style Shows.

CHEDDAR-SPINACH QUICHE   6 Servings

1 pkg. (10 oz.) frozen,
   chopped spinach
2 cups cheddar cheese,
   shredded
2 T. flour
1 cup milk
2 eggs, beaten
3 slices bacon, fried crisply
½ tsp. salt
Dash pepper
1 9" unbaked pie shell

Cook spinach and drain well on paper towel. Toss cheddar cheese with flour. Add spinach, milk, eggs, bacon and seasonings. Mix well. Pour into pastry shell. Bake at 350° for 1 hour. Garnish with additional bacon if desired.

CALICO CORNERS

Bettendorf, Iowa

A cozy Tea Room serving lunch daily, with a gift store for browsing.

CHEESY CORN CHOWDER   8-10 Servings

1 can (16 oz.) mixed
   vegetables
⅓ cup butter
¼ cup onion, chopped
1 tsp. dry mustard
¼ cup flour
¾ tsp. salt
2 cans (15 oz. each)
   creamed corn
Dash celery salt
2 cups milk
2 tsp. boullion
3½ cups (14 oz.) processed
   cheese, cubed
¼ tsp. Worchestershire
   sauce

Drain liquid from vegetables, reserve, add enough water to equal 2 cups.

In large saucepan cook onion in butter until tender; stir in flour, mustard and salt; gradually stir in reserved liquid, milk and boullion, heat to boiling. Boil and stir 1 minute. Stir in remaining ingredients, heat again to boiling.

275

THE CAPTAIN'S TABLE

Moline, Illinois

Dine on the Mississippi.

SEAFOOD CREPES

6 Servings

Featured Friday Luncheon Special.

BASIC CREPES:
   3 eggs
   ⅛ tsp. salt
   1 tsp. sugar
1½ cups flour
1½ cups milk
   2 T. butter, melted

FILLING:
   1 cup fresh mushrooms,
      sliced
   ¼ cup onion, finely
      chopped
   ¼ cup butter
   ⅓ cup all purpose flour
   ¼ tsp. salt
1½ cups milk
   1 can (7½ oz.) crab meat,
      drained, flaked and
      cartilage removed
   1 can (4½ oz.) shrimp
   ½ cup plus 3 T. white wine

For crepes: In medium mixing bowl, combine eggs, salt and sugar. Gradually add flour alternately with milk, beating with electric mixer or whisk until smooth. Beat in melted butter. Leave at room temperature 1 hour. Cook on upside-down crepe griddle or in traditional pan.

For filling: In saucepan cook mushrooms and onion in butter. Blend flour and salt. Add milk. Cook and stir until thickened and bubbly. Stir in crab and shrimp. Add white wine.

Fill cooked crepes with seafood mixture; fold over. Serve immediately.

276

THE CELLAR

Geneseo, Illinois

Lovely atmosphere and fine main courses are this charming restaurant's specialties.

The Cellar's Famous
CHARCOAL BROILED SHRIMP   6 Servings

BARBECUE SAUCE:
13 oz. Open Pit Barbecue
   sauce
 2 oz. melted butter
¾ tsp. liquid smoke

SHRIMP:
 3 lbs. large raw shrimp,
   peeled and deveined
Continental Coffee
   Company's All Purpose
   Seasoning (a combina-
   tion of paprika, salt
   and MSG) to taste

Drawn butter
2 lemon halves

For sauce: Mix all ingredients well.

Start charcoal fire and heat until coals are white. Place raw shrimp on skewers. Season lightly with All Purpose Seasoning. Place on flat grill about 6-8 inches above charcoal. Broil about 3 minutes on each side. Baste with barbeque sauce and keep turning and basting for another 6 minutes or until done. Remove from skewer. Serve with drawn butter and lemon halves.

DAVENPORT CLUB

Davenport, Iowa

At the close of World War II, a group of businessmen started this social club.

CHEDDAR CHEESE SOUP   8 Servings

1 onion, finely chopped
2 carrots, finely chopped
1 cup celery, finely
    chopped
Butter
¾ cup flour
2½ qts. boiling water
8 chicken bouillon cubes
12 oz. sharp cheddar
    cheese, shredded
½ tsp. liquid smoke
1 pt. half and half
Salt
Pepper

Saute onions, celery and carrots in butter until done. Add flour to make Roux. Add bouillon cubes to boiling water, then add Roux to stock using a whisk until smooth. Add cheddar cheese, liquid smoke and half and half, season to taste.

THE DAVENPORT COUNTRY CLUB

Pleasant Valley, Iowa

The club was organized in 1924. "With the intentions of a golf course and desiring an attractive place on the bluffs over the Mississippi River, the organizers purchased from Joseph R. Lane, a country gentleman, his dairy farm".

BACON WRAPPED PINEAPPLE

2½-3 Dozen

This is a favorite of the club members.

1 lb. bacon
1 can (20 oz.) pineapple rings
2 cups brown sugar, packed
Toothpicks

Cut each pineapple ring into fourths. Cut strips of bacon in half. Wrap around pineapple pieces. Secure with a toothpick. Place on cookie sheet, sprinkle with brown sugar. Bake at 350° for 20-25 minutes or until bacon is done.

279

THE DOCK

Davenport, Iowa

Continental Restaurant Systems, Inc.
Davenport, Iowa
Specialties of Fish in an Elegant Atmosphere.

ANCIENT MARINER (Baked Red Snapper)

6 Servings

1 gallon milk
1½ T. salt
¾ T. pure ground pepper
6 (10-12 oz. each) Gulf Red Snapper filets

Butter
2 lemon wedges
Paprika

Place milk in tub deep enough to cover all filets. Add salt and pepper to milk and stir well. Place thawed snapper filets in marinade with skin side up. Marinate for 18 hours.

Lightly brush a platter with melted butter. Place snapper filet skin side down on buttered platter. Squeeze 2 lemon wedges over fish. Brush melted butter lightly over top of fish. Sprinkle paprika lightly over entire snapper filet. Place plate in 350° oven and bake 15-20 minutes, depending on thickness. To check if snapper is completely done, insert knife into the middle. If it slides in and out without dragging, the fish is done.

Serve with drawn butter.

THE DRAWBRIDGE

Davenport, Iowa & Moline, Illinois

Dine in an authentic replica of an English castle.

CANADIAN CHEESE SOUP   12-15 Servings

½ lb. bacon
1 cup onions, minced
½ cup carrots, minced
½ cup celery, minced
12 cups chicken broth
6 T. butter, melted
1½ cups flour
2 cups cream with pinch
  of baking soda
1 lb. American cheese,
  shredded
½ tsp. liquid smoke
1 tsp. MSG
¼ tsp. Worchestershire
  sauce
¹/₈ tsp. white pepper
Salt to taste

Saute bacon and drain off fat; hold bacon. Saute onions, carrots and celery in 6 T. of melted butter until they are soft. Add flour and stir well. Add hot chicken broth and cook three minutes. Crumble bacon and add. Blend in shredded American cheese. Add hot cream and soda. Take off fire and season with liquid smoke, seasonings and Worchestershire sauce.

Note: Do not heat over 160°.

HAROLD'S
Moline, Illinois

Gracious dining on the Rock River.

HAROLD'S STEAK AND QUAIL

Quail
Steak
Butter
Sherry, dry
1 recipe Wild Rice Dressing

Cook quail in butter in skillet until brown. Remove from heat, pour sherry and flame. Place quail in individual casseroles over wild rice dressing. Pour butter and sherry from skillet over each. Cover and bake in 350° oven for 45 minutes or until tender. Just before quail is done, broil steaks to desired degree of doneness. Serve one quail and one steak per person.

WILD RICE DRESSING

Uncle Ben's Wild Rice
1 tsp. onion, chopped
1 cup celery, chopped
½ lb. fresh mushrooms, sliced
⅓ cup butter
Ground sage to taste

Cook rice according to package directions. Saute onion and celery in butter. Stir in sliced mushrooms and ground sage, add to rice and stir well to mix.

J K FRIZBEE'S

Davenport, Iowa

Elegant gourmet dining in a relaxed atmosphere.

STEAK MARSALA

4 Servings

4 (10 oz.) top sirloin,
   butterflied
¼ cup butter
1 cup mushrooms, sliced
1 medium onion, sliced
   and quartered
Flour
Salt
Pepper
Sweet Marsala Wine

Note: Tenderloin may be
   used instead of
   top sirloin

In a large skillet, saute steaks in butter, turning just once. Add enough Marsala Wine to cover steaks. Simmer 1 minute turn steaks, simmer an additional minute. Remove to a warm platter (steaks should be slightly pink in the middle so do not overcook.)

Add mushrooms, onions and additional ¼ cup Marsala Wine. Simmer over high heat until onions are transparent and sauce is reduced to half. Pour over steaks. Serve with potato, rice or buttered pasta.

SHRIMP VERA CRUZ

20 jumbo shrimp,
   butterflied
1 cup butter
2 fresh limes
2 garlic cloves, minced
Dry white wine
Parsley, chopped or dried

Note: If jumbo shrimp are
   not available use smaller
   shrimp and serve 6 to a
   serving.

Clean shrimp by removing the legs and slicing through the meat lengthwise from the leg side just to the shell. DO NOT CUT THROUGH THE SHELL. Hold the shrimp lengthwise with both hands and bend the shell backwards so that the meat is exposed and butterflied but the shell is still on. The shell should crack slightly and the digestive track is exposed. Wash and remove track.

Melt butter in large skillet with minced garlic. Place shrimp meat side down in the skillet and saute for 2 minutes over medium heat. Add enough wine just to cover the shrimp and the juice of 1 lime. (Add the squeezed limes to the pan.) Simmer for an additional 2 minutes. Turn shrimp meat side up, sprinkle lightly with parsley and place under broiler until shrimp are done. Serve with shells on, over a bed of saffron rice and with fresh lime wedges and drawn butter.

HIDDEN HILLS INN
I-80 & Middle Road · Bettendorf, Iowa

Enjoy Brunch or Lunch. Also a gallery of Country Handiwork, furniture and antiques for browsing and shopping.

INDIVIDUAL CHICKEN CASSEROLES   6 Servings

2 pkgs. (10 oz.) frozen
  broccoli spears, coarsely
  chopped
3 cups chicken, sliced
½ cup mayonnaise
1 can (10¾ oz.) cream of
  chicken soup
1 tsp. lemon juice
1 cup sharp cheddar
  cheese, grated
2 cups soft bread crumbs
1 T. butter, melted

Place broccoli and chicken in bottom of six (6) individual ramkins. Mix soup, mayonnaise and juice and spread over chicken and broccoli. Coat bread crumbs with melted butter. Toss with cheese and sprinkle over ingredients. Bake covered at 350° for 25 minutes or until bubbly.

O'MELIAS
Rock Island, Illinois

An informal supper club especially known for their fine salad bar.

1,000 ISLAND DRESSING   6 Cups

4 cups mayonnaise
½ cup sour cream
½ cup plus 2 T. relish, drained
1 cup plus 3 T. chili sauce
1 egg, hard boiled, diced
Dash Worcestershire

In mixer add mayonnaise, sour cream, and pickle relish. Mix on low: add chili sauce and Worcestershire; add egg when ready to serve.

ROCK ISLAND ARSENAL GOLF CLUB

Rock Island Arsenal
Rock Island, Illinois

Established prior to 1900, the Rock Island Arsenal Golf Club is famous throughout the area for its fine cuisine.

CHEESE STRATA

25 Servings

24 slices of bread
3¾ lbs. cheddar cheese, grated
3 T. brown sugar
¾ tsp. paprika
3 onions, minced
1½ tsp. pepper
18 eggs, slightly beaten
7½ cups milk
1½ tsp. dry mustard
1½ tsp. Worchestershire

Decrust bread and cube. Butter 6 quart casserole. Combine eggs, milk, brown sugar, paprika, onion, mustard, salt, pepper and Worchestershire. Alternate in layers: bread, then cheese and egg mixture. Cover and refrigerate overnight. Set in water in cold oven (not preheated) 300° for 2 hours.

287

HOT SPICED FRUITS

1 can (20 oz.) pineapple
  chunks
1 jar (20 oz.) kumquats,
  preserved
¼ cup vinegar
¼ cup brown sugar,
  packed
1 tsp. cloves, whole
2 cinnamon sticks, 3" long
1 can (20 oz.) peeled
  apricot halves,
  drained
2 cans (20 oz. each) purple
  plums, drained

Drain pineapple and kumquats. Combine syrup with vinegar, brown sugar and spices. Bring to a boil; reduce heat; simmer 10 minutes. Add pineapple chunks, kumquats, drained apricots and purple plums. Heat. Serve as an accompaniment to ham, other meats or poultry.

CHERRY ANGEL SQUARES

1 angel food cake, (10")
1 can (20 oz.) cherry pie
  filling
1 pkg. (4½ oz.) instant
  vanilla pudding
1 cup sour cream

Tear angel food cake into chunks; put half in a 9×13" lightly buttered pan. Spread cherry pie filling over. Put rest of cake over filling. Prepare vanilla pudding as package directs, fold in sour cream and stir until smooth. Pour over cake. Refrigerate.

SHORT HILLS COUNTRY CLUB

East Moline, Illinois

**Traditional Golf Club, also offering tennis and swimming.
Known for their fine prime rib.**

SHORT HILLS PRIME RIB   35-40 Servings

18 - 20 lb. choice prime rib
½ gal. water
2 oz. beef base, prepared
Touch garlic powder
1¼ cups Worchestershire

Place prime rib in roast pan with bone side down. Put in pre-heated 325° oven for 3½ hours or until end of prime rib is firm to touch.

To prepare au jus: Remove meat from pan and pour out grease. Add one half gallon water, prepared beef base, garlic powder, and Worchestershire sauce to roast pan. Return pan to oven and bring to boil, cook until water has absorbed all drippings from pan.

SHORT HILLS VEE SALAD

6 Servings

1 large head lettuce
1 can (16 oz.) mandarin
  oranges, drained
1 cup bacon, crumbled or
  bacon bits
½ cup sliced almonds,
  toasted

Tear or cut up lettuce; add oranges and toss. Combine bacon and almonds and top lettuce mixture.

Dressing: Use a Parisian type dressing such as sweet vinegar and oil. See page 70.

LETTUCE SALAD WITH FAMOUS SHORT HILLS DRESSING

6 Servings

1 large head lettuce
6 pieces Melba toast or
  1 cup salad croutons
4 cups real mayonnaise
1 cup deep red French
  dressing (Melani 1890)
3 T. (heaping) parmesan or
  romano cheese, grated
½ tsp. anchovy paste
Touch of garlic powder

Tear up lettuce. Break pieces of Melba toast or add croutons over lettuce. Add 1 cup Short Hills Dressing.

Dressing: Mix well.

THE RED OAK
Bishop Hill, Illinois

Authentic home cooking in an old store.

The Red Oak's
CHOCOLATE BUTTERMILK CAKE

2 cups sugar
2 cups flour
2 T. cocoa
1 tsp. baking soda
1 cup water
1½ sticks margarine
½ cup buttermilk
2 eggs
1 tsp. vanilla

ICING:
3 cups sifted powdered
   sugar
2 T. cocoa
¼ cup butter, melted
¼ cup milk
1 tsp. vanilla
½ cup walnuts, chopped

In large mixer bowl, combine sugar, flour, cocoa and soda. In small pan combine margarine and water; bring to a boil stirring to melt margarine. Add to dry ingredients; beat until smooth. Add buttermilk, eggs and vanilla. Beat 2 minutes at medium speed. Pour into jelly roll pan. Bake at 350° for 20-25 minutes. Cool.

For icing: Combine sugar and cocoa; stir in butter, milk and vanilla and beat until smooth, add nuts. Spread on cooled cake.

291

WAIKIKI RESTAURANT
Davenport, Iowa

Fine Cantonese cooking with exotic beverages.

CHICKEN YATKA MEIN SOUP   3 Servings

3 oz. egg noodles, extra
  fine
4 cups chicken broth
1 chicken breast, thinly
  sliced
6 - 10 peapod pieces
1 handful Bok Choy, cut
  in 1" pieces
1 tsp. MSG
½ tsp. sesame seed oil
1 bundle green onions,
  chopped
2 tsp. soy sauce

Add noodles to boiling water and boil for
10-15 minutes. Rinse in cold water. Add
the vegetables and meat to the broth, boil
5 minutes. Add noodles and simmer 2-3
minutes. Add spices and sprinkle green
onion on top.

METRIC CONVERSIONS

LIQUID MEASURE
1 teaspoon = 1/6 ounce = 5 milliters
1 tablespoon = 1/2 ounce = 15 milliters
1/4 cup = 2 ounces = 60 milliters
1/3 cup = 2 2/3 ounces = 80 milliters
1/2 cup = 4 ounces = 120 milliters
1 cup = 8 ounces = 240 milliters
2 cups = 1 pint = 16 ounces = 473 milliters
4 cups = 1 quart = 32 ounces = 946 milliters
To convert OUNCES to MILLITERS: Multiply OUNCES by 30.
To convert MILLITERS to OUNCES: Multiply MILLITERS by 0.034.

WEIGHT
1/6 ounce = 5 grams
1/3 ounce = 10 grams
1/2 ounce = 15 grams
1 ounce = 30 grams
1 3/4 ounces = 50 grams
3 1/2 ounces = 100 grams
4 ounces = 1/4 pound = 114 grams
4 3/8 ounces = 125 grams
8 ounces = 1/2 pound = 227 grams
9 ounces = 250 grams
16 ounces = 1 pound = 454 grams
1.1 pounds = 500 grams
2.2 pounds = 1000 grams
To convert OUNCES to GRAMS: Multiply OUNCES by 28.
To convert GRAMS to OUNCES: Multiply GRAMS by 0.035.

TEMPERATURE

°C		°F
0	Freezing	32
60	Beef, lamb (rare)	140
65	Beef (medium)	149
70	Ham, lamb (medium)	149
75	Beef, lamb (well done)	167
80	Veal, pork	176
85	Poultry	185
100	Boiling	212
150	Slow oven	300
180	Moderate oven	350
205	Hot oven	400

To convert FAHRENHEIT to CELSIUS: Subtract 32, multiply by 5, divide by 9.
To convert CELSIUS to FAHRENHEIT: Multiply by 9, divide by 5, add 32.

INDEX

294

296

305

ARTIST'S RECIPES

RESTAURANT RECIPES

STANDING OVATIONS
Junior Board of the Tri-City Symphony
P. O. Box 67 - 404 Main Street
Davenport, Iowa 52805

Please send me: _____
copies of STANDING OVATIONS @ $9.50 $ _____

Plus $1.50 postage per book _____ $ _____

☐ Check if you wish gift wrap at $.50 per book $ _____

(Make check for $11.00 ea. payable to the Junior Board of the Tri-City Symphony)

TOTAL ENCLOSED $ _____

All proceeds from the sale of this cookbook support the educational projects of the Junior Board of the Tri-City Symphony Orchestra Association.

Name _____
Street _____
City _____ State _____ Zip _____

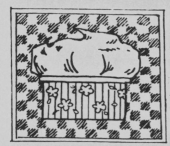

STANDING OVATIONS
Junior Board of the Tri-City Symphony
P. O. Box 67 - 404 Main Street
Davenport, Iowa 52805

Please send me: _____
copies of STANDING OVATIONS @ $9.50 $ _____

Plus $1.50 postage per book _____ $ _____

☐ Check if you wish gift wrap at $.50 per book $ _____

(Make check for $11.00 ea. payable to the Junior Board of the Tri-City Symphony)

TOTAL ENCLOSED $ _____

All proceeds from the sale of this cookbook support the educational projects of the Junior Board of the Tri-City Symphony Orchestra Association.

Name _____
Street _____
City _____ State _____ Zip _____

STANDING OVATIONS
Junior Board of the Tri-City Symphony
P. O. Box 67 - 404 Main Street
Davenport, Iowa 52805

Please send me: _____
copies of STANDING OVATIONS @ $9.50 $ _____

Plus $1.50 postage per book _____ $ _____

☐ Check if you wish gift wrap at $.50 per book $ _____

(Make check for $11.00 ea. payable to the Junior Board of the Tri-City Symphony)

TOTAL ENCLOSED $ _____

All proceeds from the sale of this cookbook support the educational projects of the Junior Board of the Tri-City Symphony Orchestra Association.

Name _____
Street _____
City _____ State _____ Zip _____

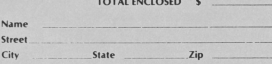

Names and address of book stores, gift shops, etc. in your area
would be appreciated.

_____

_____

_____

_____

_____

_____

Names and address of book stores, gift shops, etc. in your area
would be appreciated.

_____

_____

_____

_____

_____

_____

Names and address of book stores, gift shops, etc. in your area
would be appreciated.

_____

_____

_____

_____

_____

_____

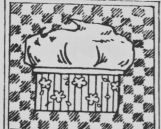

STANDING OVATIONS
Junior Board of the Tri-City Symphony
P. O. Box 67 - 404 Main Street
Davenport, Iowa 52805

Please send me: _____
copies of STANDING OVATIONS @ $9.50 $ _____

Plus $1.50 postage per book _____ $ _____

☐ Check if you wish gift wrap at $.50 per book $ _____

(Make check for $11.00 ea. payable to the Junior Board of the Tri-City Symphony)

All proceeds from the sale of this cookbook support the educational projects of the Junior Board of the Tri-City Symphony Orchestra Association.

TOTAL ENCLOSED $ _____

Name _____

Street _____

City _____ State _____ Zip _____

STANDING OVATIONS
Junior Board of the Tri-City Symphony
P. O. Box 67 - 404 Main Street
Davenport, Iowa 52805

Please send me: _____
copies of STANDING OVATIONS @ $9.50 $ _____

Plus $1.50 postage per book _____ $ _____

☐ Check if you wish gift wrap at $.50 per book $ _____

(Make check for $11.00 ea. payable to the Junior Board of the Tri-City Symphony)

All proceeds from the sale of this cookbook support the educational projects of the Junior Board of the Tri-City Symphony Orchestra Association.

TOTAL ENCLOSED $ _____

Name _____

Street _____

City _____ State _____ Zip _____

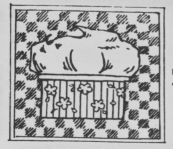

STANDING OVATIONS
Junior Board of the Tri-City Symphony
P. O. Box 67 - 404 Main Street
Davenport, Iowa 52805

Please send me: _____
copies of STANDING OVATIONS @ $9.50 $ _____

Plus $1.50 postage per book _____ $ _____

☐ Check if you wish gift wrap at $.50 per book $ _____

(Make check for $11.00 ea. payable to the Junior Board of the Tri-City Symphony)

All proceeds from the sale of this cookbook support the educational projects of the Junior Board of the Tri-City Symphony Orchestra Association.

TOTAL ENCLOSED $ _____

Name _____

Street _____

City _____ State _____ Zip _____

Names and address of book stores, gift shops, etc. in your are
would be appreciated.

_____

_____

_____

_____

_____

_____

Names and address of book stores, gift shops, etc. in your ar
would be appreciated.

_____

_____

_____

_____

_____

_____

Names and address of book stores, gift shops, etc. in your a
would be appreciated.

_____

_____

_____

_____

_____

_____